WORK ORIENTATION AND JOB PERFORMANCE

SUNY Series in Educational Leadership
Daniel Duke, Editor

Work Orientation and Job Performance

THE CULTURAL BASIS OF TEACHING REWARDS AND INCENTIVES

Douglas E. Mitchell
Flora Ida Ortiz
Tedi K. Mitchell

STATE UNIVERSITY OF NEW YORK PRESS

Research reported herein was performed pursuant to a grant from the National Institute of Education, U.S. Department of Education (NIE-G-80-0154). Points of view or opinions stated, however, do not necessarily represent official NIE position or policy.

The author gratefully acknowledges permission to reprint material from the following sources: *Work and Motivation* by Victor Vroom © 1964 by John Wiley & Sons. "Incentive systems: A theory of organizations" by Peter B. Clark and J.Q. Wilson in *Administrative Science Quarterly*, Volume 6, 1961.

Published by
State University of New York Press, Albany

© 1987   State University of New York

For information, address State University of New York
Press, State University Plaza, Albany, N.Y., 12246

Library of Congress Cataloging in Publication Data

Mitchell, Douglas E.
  Work orientation and job performance.

  (SUNY series in educational leadership)
  Bibliography: p.
  Includes index.
  1. Teaching — Case studies. 2. Achievement motivation — Case studies.
3. Incentive (Psychology) — Case studies. 4. Performance — Case studies.
5. Education — United States — Evaluation — Case studies. I. Ortiz,
Flora Ida. II. Mitchell, Tedi K. III. Title. IV. Series.
LB1027.M5415   1987   371.1'44   87-1905
ISBN 0-88706-567-8
ISBN 0-88706-568-6 (pbk.)

10 9 8 7 6 5 4 3 2 1

Contents

Foreword

This is a remarkable book, reporting a noteworthy program of research. It courageously combines in a single investigation two bodies of work traditionally pursued independently. In so doing, it moves the field of educational research ahead and promises new insights for educational policy makers.

The secret of research, we have always been told, is selective blindness. You can't study everything so you must discipline yourself to study only something in particular. In fact, what we call *disciplines* are legitimizing mechanisms for ignoring what you cannot study. What you have chosen to ignore is dismissed by muttering the magical incantation "all other things being equal." In this manner, educational researchers have performed studies of effective schools in which teachers and their lessons remain invisible. They have also conducted studies of teaching effectiveness in which the schools themselves are out of sight. It may be acceptable to be selectively blind, if you appreciate precisely how what you have chosen *not* to examine limits the generalizability of your findings. What scholars have achieved in studies of effective teachers and schools is to be mindlessly insensitive to the ways in which the design features of their research necessarily set limits to the policy implications of those inquiries.

Mitchell, Ortiz and Mitchell, however, are not satisfied with conducting the usual more limited study. They set out to conduct research in which data would be gathered from several levels of the system simultaneously: the lesson, the organization and management of the classroom, the character of leadership style of the principal, and the organizational culture of the school. They manage to describe in exquisite detail the manner in which teachers conduct their classrooms and they characterize the differences among those teachers in a provocative and meaningful way.

We are introduced to four kinds of teachers: helpers, coaches, instructors and master teachers. These differences grow out of careful description informed by well-crafted theory regarding the motivations of teachers and the goals they seek. The analysis of rewards and incentives for teaching lies at the heart of this monograph. "Incentives involve the motivation to 'do' something, not just to 'get' something for having done it. Thus incentives involve contemplating or imagining the *process* of performing a task not just anticipating its outcome or consequences." To understand the structure of incentives in teaching, therefore, we need to comprehend the motives teachers bring to teaching. The authors, in their most important distinction, discriminate between two primary motives: lesson teaching and school keeping. Each of these types of motivation draws its incentives from a different aspect of the teacher's activity. Whether the lesson's flow or the school's program is the source for incentives will determine where the teacher's attention and effort will be directed and how.

Just as there are four kinds of teachers, there are also four kinds of principals: administrators, supervisors, leaders and managers. The authors emphasize the importance of the principal learning to perform flexibly across these roles. I had to wonder why a similar observation regarding the desirability of such flexible switching was not offered with respect to teachers, who might also profit from the "code-switching" of moving between lesson teaching and school keeping. In fact, in my own research, there is ample evidence (as M, O & M must have also found) of precisely such movement. Flexible shifting between lesson teaching and school keeping can occur in teachers, as can switching from an emphasis on child development goals to a highlighting of achievement goals.

The monograph is a fine example of the use of case studies grounded in careful coding and analysis while richly informed by theory. Case studies provide the fine detail needed to understand, not only what occurs in classrooms and schools, but how it occurs and why. Case studies preserve both motives and context, which are often lost in the more traditional sociological studies of schooling. Motive and context, however, are the twin foci of this investigation. To understand why teachers teach, one must grasp their incentives; to understand incentives, one must probe the cultural context in which the technical activities of teaching and learning find their meanings.

The authors correctly observe that they have sacrificed generalizability in these studies of fifteen teachers in five schools. But their richly detailed and analyzed case studies of teaching and administering provide the occasion for the debunking of myth and the generation of theory, exceedingly crucial roles for the social sciences in education. The myth of a simple reward system for improving instruction is dealt yet another nail in its already well-hammered coffin. Practical implications for policy are offered. And an alternative theory of teaching incentives begins to emerge.

The authors frequently imbed their theoretical analysis within the four-fold analytic tables that have become Doug Mitchell's trademark. Some readers may become skeptical of how neatly the world seems to parse into two-by-two tables for these investigators. I find such analyses enormously valuable. We so typically think in terms of simple distinctions or a single continuum of values. Mitchell's work forces us to recognize that these continua must interact and intersect. He insists that we examine the consequences of examining several dimensions of a problem simultaneously, instead of our typical habit of treating one dimension at a time, as if the others had conveniently ceased functioning for the duration of our analysis.

I applaud Doug Mitchell, Flora Ortiz and Tedi Mitchell for writing a book from which I learned and about which I reflected. I long for the days when a National Institute of Education (or its current incarnation as the Office of Educational Research and Improvement) had sufficient funds to support important studies like this one through its grants competitions. I hope my colleagues in the world of school improvement and teaching reform will read this book and consider its lessons. Most important, I hope that the worlds of teaching and of school administration, now so divided by struggles over the functions of teachers and the perogatives of principals in school leadership, will grasp the important lesson of this research. Teaching and administration cannot be contemplated separately. Policies for one group cannot be promulgated in ignorance of the interests, functions and roles of the other group. A coherent policy for the improvement of schools must take account of the real character of teacher incentives and the sensitive interplay of teacher and principal in creating the effective culture of the school.

Lee S. Shulman

Acknowledgments

True understanding is more a gift than an accomplishment. We could never have succeeded in either collecting the data for this book or interpreting its meaning without the gracious and insightful assistance of many friends and colleagues. We want to begin by thanking the fifteen elementary schoolteachers who provided the real-life data on which our analysis is based. They willingly opened their classrooms to observation and tolerated our endless questioning of their motives and actions. We were impressed by their openness and their quiet confidence that what we were doing would be of value to others. Having promised them anonymity, we will not report their names, but they each have a special place in our memory. They are the ordinary, unsung heroes of the American school system. It is their hard work and that of their counterparts in thousands of school districts across the land that give real meaning to the concept of educational opportunity for the nation's children.

We are also indebted to the five principals who introduced us to these teachers and the other busy administrators in this southern California school district who exposed themselves to tiresome interviews and careful scrutiny.

Our intellectual debts are widespread. We cannot thank by name all those who have contributed to our analysis, but we want to single out a few whose contributions have been especially large. Professor Laurence Iannaccone played an important role in shaping our early thinking about the differences among teacher work orientations. He helped crystalize our thinking about the difference between achievement production and child nurture incentives in the schools. William G. Spady also contributed to our early thinking by taking a deep interest in the differences in work orientation among the principals in the study. Helpful insights were also provided by several critics and discussants of early papers presented at American Educational Research Association meetings while the research was in progress. We especially wish to mention David Berliner, Louis Smith, Ronald Blood, and Frederick Mulhauser.

A number of colleagues across the country have taken our ideas so far as to incorporate them into ongoing work. We are delighted that the work has been seen as useful by researchers at Michigan State University's Institute for Research on Teaching, and are especially intrigued by the work of Robert Kottkamp, Eugene Provenzo, and Marilyn Cohn, who have undertaken statistical testing of the basic typology of teacher orientations described in Chapter III. And we learned much from Charles Kerchner's early instructional use of the theory of incentives developed in Chapter II.

Our acknowledgments would not be complete without explicit thanks to the National Institute of Education (now the Office of Educational Research and Improvement) staff, who recognized the importance of our work, supported it with hard cash, and patiently worked through technical reports with clarifying questions and insights. Three staffers were especially helpful: Michael Cohen, who encouraged initial funding of the project, and Virginia Koehler and Jay Stratoudakis, who saw it through to completion.

CHAPTER I

Teacher Incentives and School Performance

Beginning with the 1983 publication of the report by the National Commission on Excellence's *A Nation at Risk*, a virtual firestorm of policy reforms swept across the school systems of this country. An editorial in the *Los Angeles Times* captured the mood, declaring, "Suddenly Education is a Hot Issue". Within less than two years, nearly every state in the union had adopted substantial new policies. Most of these emphasized raising program requirements and standards and requiring stricter accountability for students and staff. The most frequent policy initiatives included increased promotion and graduation standards, longer school days, merit pay and career ladder programs for teachers, instructional materials improvements, and academic prerequisites for participation in sports or other extracurricular activities (U.S. Dept. of Education, *The National Responds*, May, 1984).

As is so often the case, however, intensity of commitment could not guarantee either the wisdom of particular policies or success in their implementation. While support for school improvement remains strong, basic questions are being raised about how best to pursue this fundamental goal. It is one thing to raise standards and demand accountability; it is quite another to design a school system capable of sustaining the high performance needed to reach those objectives. The national commitment to education reform has produced political conflict and professional agony because it involves "two conflicting beliefs: that it is critical for the nation's economic survival that our education system be strengthened and improved [and] that educational institutions are simply not capable of delivering the critical improvements."

A scant three years after the release of *A Nation at Risk*, attention shifted dramatically — from specifying standards and elaborating program requirements to finding ways of insuring that teachers and administrators develop the capacity and the will to implement those new program mandates. Accountability for implementing reforms raised questions about whether educators have either the training or the motivation needed to sustain school performance improvement.

For many public policy makers, the solution to this problem seems simple and direct: link all teacher salary increases to improved teaching performance. Pay teachers, that is, in direct proportion to their contribution to effective schooling for the nation's children. Isn't that the American Way — to pay workers according to the value of their work?

On the surface this solution seems logical enough. After all, many observers have long argued that the failure of past investments in education is the result of putting too much money into the wrong things — worthless hardware, needless program development, or irrelevant paper pushing — while neglecting support for better teaching.

But teacher salaries are not easily linked to teacher performance on the job. Many teachers share the following bitter complaint:

> I've just about had all I can take of the "it's all the teachers' fault" articles that are currently rampant...so-called experts recommend paying extra to those who have merit. This is wrong. It simply means the administrators will pay those who assist them with their overload duties...Let's not promote favoritism, let's not further divide faculties, we must work together and improve together equally. Besides, who decides who has merit? (Savage, 1983.)

Politically, the issue of merit pay has proven quite explosive. In San Marino, California, a twenty-five-year-old merit pay plan was scuttled virtually overnight by public disclosure of which teachers were being given merit pay and which were not. The published list of "meritorious" teachers was so at odds with the judgments of teachers and community members that the school board had no choice but to dump the program. A senior administrator in the district further highlighted the dilemma by reporting that there was little agreement among administrators regarding which teachers deserved the merit pay bonuses (Savage, 1983, p. 17).

The San Marino case is not particularly unique. Most merit pay plans have been abandoned within a few years of their adoption. Or, as one study of long-standing merit pay programs demonstrates, they have been modified to such an extent that they are either trivial in size or largely disconnected from classroom teaching performance (Murnane and Cohen, 1984).

Can salary money ensure high performance in the schools? The issue is complex, but generally the answer is, no, it cannot. First, entry into the teaching profession cannot be interpreted as driven primarily by salary considerations. As (1983, p. 3) notes, "Starting teacher salaries are one-third to one-half less than starting construc tion workers and automobile assembly-line workers" (see also Peterson and Peterson, 1984). Young people for whom salary is the primary consideration in career choice are not likely to see teaching as particularly attractive. This does not mean, of course, that salary has no effect. Losses in real income for beginning teachers have been cited by many school districts as a major contributor to teacher recruitment difficulties. At the very least, however, we must recognize that teachers are motivated largely by nonmonitary rewards.

Second, whatever value salary levels may have in affecting the willingness of young people to enter the teaching profession, securing high performance once they have taken a teaching job is a very different matter. In shaping job performance, salary money appears to have more symbolic than economic value. In their study of long-standing merit pay systems, Murnane and Cohen (1984) note that teachers frequently view merit pay increases as public recognition of strong performance — rather than as a motivating force for the performance itself. Low teacher salaries may be more a symbol of low esteem than economic incentives for reduced performance. The primary message may be that teachers are not valued by society — and their salaries, particularly, show it.

The issue is job performance, however, not economics. As columnist Lester Thurow (1983, p. 3) puts it, "One of the universal American problems is quality control ... The "no standards" society is a low standards society and it all starts back in our refusal to set national quality control standards in education." Nevertheless, he insists, although good teachers need to be rewarded, to do so with merit pay is to violate everything that we have been learning about motivating workers to do a high-quality job. Reporting on his own teaching experience in two universities, he says, "Good teaching occurred in the department with good teaching because there was a very strong social ethos that good teaching was your first responsibility and would be rewarded with peer respect" (1983, p. 3). The merit pay issue is provocatively summarized by the research director for the California Commission on the Teaching Profession (Sykes, 1983, p. 1), who says, "It is good politics and lousy education policy...There is absolutely no evidence in all the research I've seen that monetary incentives have improved performance among teachers."

Well, if we can't buy effective teaching, how can we get it? Some people have given up hope and become cynical, believing that we simply cannot do anything to ensure high-quality schooling for the nation's children. More recently, however, a "second wave" of school reform proposals has tackled the job performance issue directly by concentrating on changing teacher recruitment, training, and job structure (see, for example, the Carnegie Task Force report, 1986; the Holmes Group report, 1986; and the California Commission on the Teaching Profession, 1985).

Three competing strategies for job performance improvement are found in these second-wave reform proposals. The first is to *repopulate* the teaching work force by motivating more able young people to enter the profession and by manipulating compensation and working conditions in ways that encourage poor performers to leave more rapidly. In addition to close supervision and more directive management, teacher education and certification reforms are proposed as important ingredients in this repopulation strategy. The second strategy is to *retrain* the existing work force by creating programs and requirements for professional staff development. This strategy is not new, but has been revitalized by policies aimed at linking salaries to new staff training and performance requirements. The third strategy is to *restructure* teaching work roles through staff differentiation, creating lead or mentor teachers, or creating a career ladder to give high-performing teachers more autonomy and control over the work of their less adequate colleagues.

While these second-wave reform strategies focus appropriately on the issue of job performance in the school, they are in serious danger of becoming just one more round of dramatic but ineffectual educational reform. Research on critical factors influencing school program quality and individual teacher effectiveness has made substantial strides in recent years, but the lessons of that research are too often misunderstood or ignored. We need to take a close look at the fundamental findings of recent research on school effectiveness and to link those findings to a careful analysis of the nature of the teaching process itself.

That linkage is the subject of this book. Through a comprehensive review of research on work motivation and an intensive study of fifteen elementary schoolteachers, we explore the job performance incentives available to all teachers. We examine the foundations of their motivation to effectively perform complex and difficult tasks under uncertain and sometimes strained conditions. Our study also examines how administrators are able to influence the teacher incentive system in order to make public schools more effective.

EFFECTIVE SCHOOLS AND TEACHERS

Three basic themes in the literature on school program and teacher effectiveness lay the foundations for the research reported in this book. First, a group of research studies generally referred to as the "school effectiveness" literature has clearly demonstrated that (a) it is impossible to predict the effectiveness of a school or program on the basis of quantitative measures of the resources or "inputs" provided to it, and (b) substantial explanatory power is developed if process, climate, or "ethos" measures are used (see, for example, Coleman, 1966; Averch, 1975; Purkey and Smith, 1982; Brookover et al., 1978; Edmonds, 1979 and 1982; Madaus et al., 1979; Good, 1983; and Rutter, et al., 1979). In brief, this literature shows that the effectiveness of schools depends more on the style or manner in which programs are executed rather than on the quality of the various raw materials they are given to work with.

A corollary to this general observation is that educational effectiveness depends upon the development of appropriate work motivations among teachers, students, and administrators. The motivations must involve an overall commitment to general program goals and a sense of responsibility for the means used to achieve those goals. It is not sufficient for educators to be driven by a desire for higher wages or more comfortable working conditions.

A different body of literature, generally called "teacher effectiveness" research, provides a second theme. This literature sheds some light on the most important characteristics of high-performing teachers (see, for example, 1973; Bennett, 1976; Brophy, 1983; Brophy and Evertson, 1976; Centra and Potter, 1978; Ebmeir and Good, 1979; Fey, 1969; Flanders, 1965, 1970; Good, 1983; Good, Biddle, and Brophy, 1975; Ornstein, 1982; Rosenshine and Furst, 1973; Schulman and Sykes, 1983; Shavelson, 1983; Soar, 1972; and

Tikunoff, Berliner and Rist, 1975). This research work, focusing on individual teacher (rather than school) effectiveness, indicates that teachers who use indirect methods (for example, questioning rather than lecturing) are more effective than those whose styles are more direct (Flanders, 1965). (It should be noted that in this literature references to the term *direct instruction* have a rather different connotation than in the school effectiveness research. School effectiveness researchers have lauded the importance of what they call "direct instruction," but they mean to contrast this method with "seat work," "small group" teaching, and other techniques which deprive students of immediate teacher attention. In teacher effectiveness studies, both "direct" and "indirect" instructional techniques presume the direct involvement of the teacher. The more effective "indirect" methods refer to the difference between eliciting student participation rather than presenting materials directly to them.)

Classroom management skills are also important to effective teaching (Brophy and Evertson, 1976). Rosenshine and Furst (1973) summarize the characteristics of effectively managed instruction as including clarity, variability in teaching methods and curricular content, enthusiasm, a task-oriented approach or a businesslike tone, and an indirect approach.

In a review of conditions and strategies for effective laboratory work, Lunetta and Hofstein (1981) suggest that the most important variables are teacher attitude and behavior, the content and nature of laboratory activities, instructional goals, social process (learning environment) variables, and teacher management of activities (timing, grouping, space utilization, and materials preparation). These authors indicate that certain student characteristics also play a major role in determining how effective a lesson will be (notably intellectual or conceptual sophistication, skill acquisition in reading and mathematics, and level of interest in the science itself). In this connection, Reif and others (1979) have written a useful paper on how to teach thinking skills and appreciation of physics in the laboratory. They confirm the importance of considering a teacher's impact on the development of student skills and interests as well as a teacher's success in presenting scientific information or concepts when assessing teacher effectiveness.

Natriello and Dornbush (1983) highlight the fact that student-teacher interactions are a two-way affair. They indicate that teacher behavior is affected more strongly by immediate student actions than it is by gross demographic characteristics of the student population. This point only underscores the obvious, that the system is interactive and that it is impossible to assess teacher effectiveness without understanding how teachers generate student responses or react to student initiatives in the classroom.

The third important theme found in this research concerns the appropriate methods for studying teacher effectiveness (see, for example, Simon and Boyer, 1967 and 1970; Bennett, 1976; Rosenshine and Furst, 1973; and Good, Biddle, and Brophy, 1975, chapter 4). This literature highlights the complexity of teacher work behavior analysis and underscores the importance of methodological care and sophistication. Hook and Rosenshine (1979) argue that teachers are not fully aware, at least at the verbal level, of the behaviors which they manifest while teaching. Accordingly, a full understanding of teacher motivation and incentive systems requires observing their work — not just listening to what they say about their goals or their work activities.

THE PLAN OF THIS BOOK

In form, this book is a report of our study of teachers, principals, and central office administrators in a moderately large, urban, unified school district in southern California. This first chapter describes the study and provides an overview of teacher motivations and incentives. Chapter II explores the problems of work motivation, rewards, and incentives in depth, and presents the theoretical framework which underlies our data collection and analysis. Chapters III through VI present and analyze our observation and interview data.

In Chapter VII we address the questions related to the relationship between teaching incentives and teacher effectiveness by presenting a broad overview of the data and their implications for theory and practice. And in Chapter VIII we examine the public policy implications of our study, identifying ten policy guidelines which should guide policy makers and school administrators in their efforts to improve teacher work performance.

DATA SOURCES AND RESEARCH METHODS

The district we studied has fifty-one school sites. There are substantial numbers of ethnic minority students (both black and Hispanic) within the district, and it is under a court-ordered desegregation program. The program involves the creation of several "magnet" programs in schools throughout the district with voluntary transfers used to help establish an ethnic balance across school sites.

In consultation with the district superintendent, who had been employed by the district for four years at the start of this study, it was agreed to concentrate our research on the elementary schools of the district. At a meeting of elementary principals held in September 1980, the proposed research project was described and volunteers were sought for participation in the study. Seven principals volunteered. After preliminary interviews, four of the seven were selected as participants. Subsequently, an assistant superintendent was asked to help recruit a fifth principal with personal background and school site characteristics not adequately represented in the initial group of volunteers. The addition of this fifth principal completed the sample described below.

The five schools in the final sample differed across the following important organizational and demographic dimensions.

A. Attendance areas
   1 suburban, middle-class school
   1 multiethnic, inner-city school
   1 predominantly Hispanic low-income school
   2 predominantly black schools, one drawing from a visibly lower income area than the other
B. Principals
   1 experienced (14 years) white male principal
   1 experienced (5 years) white female principal
   1 experienced (4 years) Hispanic male principal
   1 second-year black female principal
   1 second-year white female principal
C. School enrollments
   Enrollments ranged from 239 to 510, and staff size ranged from 10 to 22 teachers.
D. Program complexity
   A broad range of special programs and specialist staff roles were found in the schools. One school had no federally funded programs, while others had various combinations of desegregation, bilingual, (Elementary, Secondary Educational Act) Title 1, or California School Improvement Programs.

One central concern in the design and execution of this study was the analysis of how the overall character and effectiveness of teachers' task performance are influenced by the various rewards and incentives encountered during the course of their work. Since there are no widely accepted measures of effective teacher task performance, we relied upon school principals to assist in developing a sample with optimal variance on this crucial dimension. Each principal was asked to identify one "relatively strong" and one "relatively weak" teacher for participation in the study. Each was also asked to assist in identifying a third teacher with characteristics that would help to balance the sample with regard to the sex, experience, ethnicity, or grade level represented in the sample. Throughout this report, we use the terms *weak* and *strong* to denote these principals' judgments. One teacher is a special case. Although not initially identified as a "weak teacher," this teacher (labeled "Mrs. M [a helper]" in the text) is grouped with the weaker teachers because her principal felt it necessary to have her transferred to a new teaching assignment during the study year because of her perceived inability to handle her assigned special learning handicapped class.

When actually observing the teachers, our research staff naturally found that some were much more successful than others in getting students to respond to lessons and to comply with teacher directives. The teachers judged to be more successful are called "effective" in the body of this report (see especially Chapter V). As detailed in Chapters IV and V, there is a substantial (though not perfect) correlation between principals' judgments of strength or weakness and our observations of effectiveness.

The 15 teachers finally selected for study included the following:

12 female and 3 male teachers
10 majority and 5 minority teachers
11 tenured and 4 untenured teachers (that is, with less than three years' experience)
All grade levels from K to 6th
Two special education teachers
Two dual-role, vice-principal/teachers
One resource teacher

Two problems were encountered in the selection of a sample. One teacher, initially identified as a strong teacher by her cooperating principal, declined to participate (largely on the basis of her involvement in the teacher union, which was at that time engaged in tense labor negotiations). This teacher tried unsuccessfully to persuade all teachers in her building to refuse to participate. She was replaced, and the sample was completed without her participation. A second teacher originally identified as a weaker teacher by his principal initially agreed to participate and then withdrew after a preliminary interview. He was replaced by a stronger first grade teacher.

In addition to the teachers and the five principals, the following district personnel were interviewed or observed in the course of the study: the district superintendent, the associate superintendent and three assistant superintendents, and five coordinators and directors who work directly with the teachers and principals in the sample.

Interviews and observations of all participants were "open-ended" in character. Where feasible, tape recorders were used to preserve the data in their original form. Observations and interviews with teachers focused on the following:

1. How the teachers feel about their work and how they orient themselves to its task requirements and opportunities.
2. How classroom social life is structured — how control is developed and maintained.
3. How teachers conceptualize, structure, and teach the "lessons" for which they are responsible.
4. What relationships exist between teachers and principals, between teachers and other administrators, and between principals and other administrators.

All of the participants were formally interviewed at least twice. All of the teachers and principals and most of the other participants were observed for the equivalent of one or more full working days. Teachers were observed in their classrooms, on the playground, during coffee breaks, at lunch, and conversing informally with other staff. They were observed participating in such events as parent-teacher conferences, staff meetings, small group in-service sessions, cluster in-service sessions, and district-wide in-service and district committee meetings. Some participants were observed during after-school social gatherings and parties. One teacher was observed as she conducted an in-service meeting for parents interested in providing classroom assistance.

Principals were observed working in their offices, "making the rounds" of school buildings and playgrounds, and participating in meetings with students, teaching staff, parents, and other principals. The meetings included the regular monthly meeting of all elementary principals in the district, a meeting of principals and vice-principals serving schools that were receiving various compensatory education funds, and small group principals' meetings. Principals were also observed participating in district committee meetings, a district parent-advisory committee meeting, and in-service sessions.

Central office staff were observed as they met with others in the district office, with principals, and with teachers; as they conducted in-service programs for classroom aides, teachers, and principals; as they met with community members at district advisory meetings; as they honored community volunteers; as they evaluated a teacher's classroom performance; as they mediated school site personnel problems; as they interviewed prospective personnel; as they prepared district, state, and federal reports; and so on. One staff member was observed conducting an after-school session, held in response to a spontaneous request from several kindergarten teachers, in which she demonstrated how to integrate social studies into the kindergarten curriculum.

Interview and observation data were transcribed and subjected to content analysis, along with documents such as lesson plans, seating charts, principal memoranda, etc., gathered in the course of the study. The transcribed observation and interview data produced approximately 2,000 pages of typed protocols. As elaborated in the body of this report, the central categories for analyzing the data include (1) the unique characteristics of the rewards and incentives systems available to classroom teachers, (2) the structure of the lessons taught by teachers, (3) teachers' strategies of classroom management or social control, and (4) the fundamental assumptions about the nature and structure of teaching work implicit within the work orientations of teachers, principals, and administrative staff members.

A PRELIMINARY PERSPECTIVE ON TEACHING INCENTIVES

When this research project was first proposed, it was assumed (wrongly, we discovered) that the dominant conceptualization of rewards and incentives presented in recent literature on this topic would adequately guide data collection and analysis. Within this literature, the notion of a reward overshadows that of an incentive. In fact, comprehensive reviews of organizational behavior by such leading scholars as James March, Wayne Hoy, and Cecil Miskel have tended to drop all discussion of incentives in recent years, after giving substantial space to an examination of the meaning of this concept in earlier writings (compare March and Simon, 1958, with March and Olsen, 1976; and contrast Hoy and Miskel, 1978, with their revised volume in 1982). The phrase *rewards and incentives* is typically used as if it were a single, hyphenated, conglomerate term. In other words, an incentive is generally conceptualized as merely an anticipation, or "preremembrance" (Winter, 1966) of a reward which is expected to follow the performance of some task or engagement in a particular activity. It is recognized, of course, that sometimes such expectations are erroneous and that therefore the anticipated rewards are not actually received. The important point, however, is that incentives are typically viewed as rewards that are expected.

This conception of rewards and incentives treats worker wage payments (or perhaps the food pellets used to condition rats and pigeons) as the archetype for all rewards. It assumes that the primary motivations of all social behavior are rooted in the ability of individuals to contemplate the *consequences* of alternative possible actions. The choice of any particular action, this theory assumes, is governed by a combination of anticipated physical and cost constraints on the one hand, and reward values on the other. The strength of an incentive (or disincentive) can, at least theoretically, be calculated by subtracting the costs of an action from the value of the rewards which are contingent upon that action. Probability theory is sometimes incorporated into this analysis to accommodate the fact that the flow of rewards is often imperfectly linked to the performance of an action and that actors may not know exactly what consequences will follow from specific actions. Thus incentives are sometimes thought to be "discounted" (Axelrod, 1981) by the probability that they will not actually be received once the required actions have been taken.

As described in some detail in Chapter II, there are serious theoretical flaws in this conception of the relationship between rewards, incentives, and work behavior. Moreover, as our data amply confirm, this theoretical formulation encounters severe problems whenever it is used to interpret real-world data. The problem is that both the costs and the benefits of any given action depend upon individual beliefs and attitudes — beliefs rooted in cultural values rather than in objective realities. Thus, in contrast with the highly contrived experimental social settings often used to generate research data, actions taken in real social settings involve both cost factors and reward values that are exceedingly difficult to identify. And it is doubly difficult to reduce those costs and rewards, once identified, to a common metric for comparison. Even wage payments, which at first appear to have a simple dollars-and-cents metric, are difficult to compare because individuals vary greatly in their desire for wealth and in the way they balance cash payments against fringe benefits or employment security. The problems associated with making comparisons among wage rates are trivial, however, when compared to the difficulties encountered in trying to construct a similar metric for such nonwage rewards as commodious working conditions, social prestige, or opportunities for upward mobility. And these difficulties are compounded still further when analysts recognize the *subjective* perceptions regarding cost and reward values — not objective relationships between action and reward — actually control behavior. (see Weick, 1966, for a discussion of how experiences that one person counts as work inputs may be viewed by others as outcomes.)

Despite these complexities, however, a substantial body of research on rewards and incentives (for educators as well as noneducators) has developed over the last two decades. This literature has focused primarily on problems related to identifying, describing, and evaluating the effects of various objective (extrinsic) and subjective (intrinsic) rewards. (See Broedling, 1977.) With regard to teachers, this line of research has, in fact, made some substantial progress. It can now be said with considerable confidence that students provide the most potent subjective rewards to teachers (see Lortie, 1975; Miskel, 1974; Spuck, 1974; Miskel et al., 1980; Sergiovanni, 1967; Thompson, 1979; and ERIC 1980 and 1981 a & b). Specifically, teachers experience their work as most rewarding when they can attribute to themselves responsibility for improving the *achievement* level of their students. Second to improved student achievement is when students respond with *warmth*, enthusiasm, and appreciation for teacher efforts.

Compared with these student-controlled rewards, those distributed by parents, school administrators, or educational policy makers are rather weak. Of course, when salary differentials are so great that high school science and math teachers are able to double or triple their incomes by leaving the teaching profession altogether, substantial changes in teacher behavior can be expected, but the modest salary adjustments that are available under typical teacher employment arrangements appear to have a very limited effect on work performance. And, as noted above, the use of so-called merit pay programs aimed at rewarding cooperative and diligent teachers with higher pay or especially commodious working conditions and other perquisites are about as weak as gross salary and fringe benefit adjustments in offsetting the powerful effects of student achievement (or nonachievement) and student warmth (or noncooperation). Moreover, administrative complexities have led to the abandonment of merit pay schemes within a few years after adoption in many school districts (Educational Research Service, 1979).

We know that teachers prefer high-achieving students and that they are willing to move from school to school or even from district to district in order to work with those high achievers (Becker, 1952). The available evidence also suggests that if teachers feel that student achievement is not possible they will accept student warmth and cooperativeness as a "second best" but tolerable reward for their efforts. It is fairly safe to say, however, that if student relationships are tense and achievement is either lacking or largely attributable to nonteaching factors, teachers will find their work emotionally and physically draining in a way that neither administrators nor policy makers can easily overcome by providing alternative rewards.

Our research was originally intended to produce a fresh, broad-ranging, and detailed examination of teachers' subjective appreciation of the particular rewards received during the course of their teaching work activities. We had hoped to give substantial guidance to administrators and policy makers by examining how school principals and other key administrators control the flow of rewards to teachers. We had expected to find that several potent rewards are at the disposal of administrators and that various mechanisms serve to link these rewards to effective teacher job performance. In other words, we had hoped to contribute to the improvement of teaching in public elementary schools by showing how potent rewards can become more effective by being more appropriately linked to high-quality teaching.

As the body of this report documents, however, our data indicate that a whole new way of looking at work incentives is required if we are to substantially improve teacher work performance. It is not helpful, we discovered, to attempt to (a) draw a sharp distinction between work activities and rewards received, or (b) to focus attention on administrative control over specific material or objective rewards. To our surprise, the data served primarily to challenge the prevailing conception of rewards and incentives rather than to either identify new rewards or to describe new mechanisms for linking rewards to job performance. The most important finding in our data is that *incentives* for teachers are not best conceptualized as anticipated future rewards or as a simple cost/benefit calculation of the ratio of subjective values associated with expected rewards to the work effort required to obtain them. As we elaborate more fully in later chapters, we found that it is impossible to interpret the most important variations in teacher work efforts on the basis of either simple variations in their subjective appreciation of particular rewards (most teachers seem to have the same degree of sensitivity to student achievement and warmth) or basic differences in the degree of which those rewards are actually received within their work (there are, of course, great variations in the rewards received, but they do not seem to drive work effort directly). We found, instead, that there is a certain "indirectness" in the way teachers incorporate available rewards into both their imagination and their enactment of work responsibilities. We found that teachers are rewarded most effectively by student achievement and student cooperation quite apart from whether they self-consciously direct their teaching activities toward either of those rewarding outcomes.

As we watched and talked with teachers, we gradually realized that their incentive system is deeply embedded in school and classroom cultural values. It does not rest on a straightforward pursuit of identifiable rewards. In fact, reward values are not generally the primary or immediate objective of thought when teachers contemplate and plan for their work. We came to recognize that interpreting incentive systems requires that we grapple with a new perspective on teacher work experiences. To oversimplify, we came to realize that although rewards are "gotten" — and getting them is what is anticipated when a teacher (or anyone else) contemplates a task in terms of the rewards to be reaped — incentives moderate behavior in a rather different way. Incentives involve the motivation to "do" something, not just to "get" something for having done it. Thus incentives involve contemplating or imagining the process of performing a task, not just anticipating its outcome or consequences.

Perhaps an illustration will make this distinction clearer. A member of the Dallas Cowboys football team was interviewed on national television following a shutout victory over Tampa Bay in a 1981 NFL playoff game. He explained the team's performance on the field that day by referring to the bonuses paid for playing in postseason games and by saying that his teammates were "playing for the money" that afternoon. This phrase, "playing for the money," reflects, of course, the dominant notion of rewards and incentives described above. The Dallas Cowboys, we were being told, were playing that day in order to "get" the financial rewards which would accompany winning that particular game. Note, however, that this remark was offered as an explanation for an especially impressive victory on that particular day. By implication, we are also being told that professional football players (who frequently receive for a single game more than a classroom teacher earns in a year) do not ordinarily play "for the money." They usually play in order to win, to display their skills, or for other reasons that relate to the process of playing the game rather than the rewards to be received after it is over. Though high financial rewards can motivate short-term behavior in a single game, the difference between the rewards which are "gotten" and the game playing which must be "pursued" is vitally important. Football players, like teachers or anyone else, can only work for specific rewards (even very large ones) for a brief period without losing the motivation to excel. A football season, like a school semester, is too long for the contemplation or anticipation of monetary or other rewards to effectively control behavior.

Incentives—reasons for engaging in the process of one's work — must be present or a job quickly becomes burdensome and uninteresting. it may be easy to "work for the money" on special occasions, when the money is more of a prize than a salary. Ordinarily, however, the link between work activity and financial compensation is either too remote or too routine to serve as the immediate stimulus for action.

It is equally important to note that, even when impressive rewards are intimately linked to successful performance of a particular task, workers will only have an incentive to perform that task if they can vividly imagine themselves as successfully engaged in the execution of the activities required for success. Few of those who watched the Dallas Cowboys win that game had a strong incentive to participate in the process — not because they would not have enjoyed the rewards, but because they could vividly imagine for themselves only the "agony of defeat" rather than the "thrill of victory."

Incentives, in other words, are destroyed if we cannot concretely imagine ourselves performing the activities needed for success. It is not, as is too often assumed, poor rewards or some uncertainty about actually receiving them which weakens most incentives. Nor is it just a question of whether one believes that the chances of success in performing a task are high enough to balance the effort required. Incentives involve *imaginatively rehearsing* the performance of a task and finding meaning and pleasure in the rehearsal as well as in the performance itself.

Incentives as motivators for "doing something" are uniquely related to thinking of our activities as work. The activities which we think of as "play" or as "gambling" are responses to very different motivations. Gambling, for example, is distinguished from working by the fact that the gambler does not differentiate between the rewards to be gained and the incentives for participating in the action. Gambling, that is to say, differs from working in the same way that the pursuing rewards differs from responding to incentives. By relying on chance processes unrelated to one's skill or diligence, gambling breaks the linkage between personal effort and the outcomes of that effort. When external chance factors rather than personal effort control the outcomes of an activity, the participants are free to focus entirely on the rewards to be reaped and thus respond entirely to a calculation of the relationship between the costs of participation, the probability of success, and the value of the rewards to be garnered through winning. Too frequently, incentive theories confuse this calculus of rewards with real incentives. Our data reveal that teachers respond more to the incentive to do something than to any rewards which will subsequently be received. And it is recognition of this fact which makes sense of the ways in which elementary school teachers respond to their work responsibilities.

The data collected for this study can only be understood if interpreted by means of what we will call a "cultural theory of incentives." From a cultural perspective, incentives are any anticipated and valued goals, social relationships, or personal rewards (either material or psychic) that provide effective stimulii or reasons for engaging in particular work activities. And, as our analysis of principals' work activities will clarify, cultural incentives are managed by *interpretation*, not by manipulation. The principals we observed, like managers in the well-run companies studied by Peters and Waterman (1982), manage by "walking around" — by making their values known and their presence felt throughout the school and its classrooms. But we are getting ahead of our story. Before examining the incentives of our fifteen teachers and the influence of their principals, we need to look more closely at the relationships between work motivations and the availability of rewards and incentives.

CHAPTER II

Work Motivation, Rewards, and Incentive Systems: A Review of Prior Research

The research literature devoted to interpreting various aspects of the motivation and control of work behavior is vast and complex. Lawler (1970) reported that more than five thousand studies of employee attitudes and motives had been published before 1970. Depending on how broadly the issues are defined, several hundred to a few thousand additional studies have been published between 1970 and the present. It is virtually impossible for any individual scholar to adequately catalogue, much less analyze and interpret, the divergent concepts, conflicting findings, and diffuse theoretical frameworks found in this literature.

Over the last two decades, dozens of review essays have been written aimed at summarizing and evaluating various empirical and theoretical dimensions within the literature. Some reviewers tackle the broad fundamental concepts of "work-motivations" (see, for example, Herzberg, Mausner, and Snyderman, 1959; Atkinson, 1964; Vroom, 1964; Deci, 1975; Korman, Greenhaus and Badin, 1977; Hoy and Miskel, 1978; Thompson, 1979; Sergiovanni and Carver, 1980; and Broedling, 1977), "incentives" (see, for example, Clark and Wilson, 1961; Coleman, 1969; Miller and Swick, 1976; or Pincus, 1974), and "rewards" (see, for example, Miller and Hamblin, 1963; Cherrington, Reitz and Scott, 1973; Spuck, 1974; Slavin, 1977,

1980; or Whiddon, 1978). Others confine their attention to narrower and more specialized concepts, such as "attribution" (Kukla, 1972), "efficacy" (Fuller et al., 1982), "equity" (Pritchard, 1969; or Goodman and Friedman, 1971), "expectancy" (Peters, 1977; or Miskel, DeFrain, and Wilcox, 1980), or "self-esteem" (Tharenou, 1979).

Despite the extensiveness of the literature and the frequency with which various aspects of it have been reviewed, however, a number of serious theoretical and empirical problems remain unsolved. Empirical studies, for example, continue to support all of the possible relationships between worker satisfaction and job performance. Herzberg (1966) and his colleagues are the leading supporters of the view that worker satisfaction leads to improved performance. Vroom (1964) reviewed correlational studies on the subject and concluded that there is a consistent, though weak, support for this position. Porter and Lawler (1965) and Dawis, England, and Lafquist (n.d.), by contrast, interpret their data to mean that the causal linkage is in the other direction — worker satisfaction is a result rather than a cause of high work performance. March and Simon (1958) support this view theoretically when they argue that "motivation to produce stems from a present or anticipated state of discontent and a perception of a direct connection between individual production and a new state of satisfaction" (p. 158).

Cherrington, Reitz, and Scott (1973) offer the view that job performance and worker satisfaction are independently stimulated by reward systems. Vroom (1964) embraces this view, arguing that satisfaction and performance each depend upon different organizational characteristics, with no apparent causal link between them. Greene (1973) analyzes this problem in some detail and offers evidence which, while supporting the view that satisfaction, performance, and reward systems interact with each other, explains only a small fraction of the variance in these variables.

Although weaknesses in research design and data analysis are fairly widespread in the literature, the widely divergent findings related to these basic variables spring more from theoretical problems than from any data collection or design problems. The conceptual frameworks employed by various scholars diverge so sharply that it is often difficult to tell how their findings can even be compared, much less whether they offer corroborating or conflicting evidence. Important theoretical discontinuities occur at two quite different levels. First, similar terms are differently defined by various scholars, rendering comparison of their methods and findings very difficult. At a deeper level, we find that scholars have relied on at least six different and largely incompatible psychological theories of human motivation in formulating concepts and designing research, frequently without explicitly identifying which theory they are using.

To compound the situation, theoretical problems at one level interact with those at the other, creating further difficulties in assessing the validity, reliability, and significance of research findings. Scholars who begin with different psychological assumptions, naturally, define their terms differently. All too often, however, research findings are presented without a clearly formulated psychology of motivation, thus creating substantial confusion about the basis on which definitions of key terms have been constructed.

A theory of motivation, while necessary, is not all that is required to generate an adequate theoretical framework for interpreting work behavior. Work, at least for teachers, takes place primarily within organizations and social groups. In order to explain how work behavior is influenced or controlled, it is necessary to interpret relationships between the psychological bases of individual motivation and the social and organizational factors which establish the context within which individual workers are motivated (or not motivated) to action.

Because most of the research on work motivation has been undertaken by psychologists, it has been rather weak in conceptualizing these social and organizational context factors. In the remainder of this chapter, therefore, we will concentrate on developing a conceptual framework capable of linking organizational and social contextual factors with the motivation of workers. To do so, we first examine the concepts of work motivation, reward, and incentive. Once these terms have been reviewed, we turn to an examination of the six alternative psychological theories underlying the development of these concepts, and trace the links between these psychological frameworks and the ideas of motivation, incentive, and reward.

MOTIVATION, REWARDS, AND INCENTIVES

Even a superficial reading of major scholarly works on the control of work behavior quickly reveals that various scholars define the terms *reward, incentive,* and *motivation* in very different ways. Deci (1975) and Lortie (1975), for example, each develop a taxonomy of the rewards which are believed to motivate workers. Each of these researchers enumerates three fundamental reward categories, and each includes "extrinsic" and "intrinsic" rewards among their basic types. (See Broedling, 1977, for a discussion on the distinction between them). However, Deci (1975, p. 121) labels his third type of reward "affective," while Lortie (1975, p. 101) uses the term *ancillary* to describe his third category (see also Lortie, 1969). A close reading of Deci's "affective" rewards category indicates that it is completely included in Lortie's "intrinsic" category; that is, Lortie defines "intrinsic" or "psychic" rewards to include both the "feelings of competence and self-determination" which Deci calls "intrinsic" and the "affective responses to stimulus inputs" which Deci calls "affective rewards." In Lortie's words, intrinsic rewards include all "subjective valuations made in the course of work engagement" (p. 101).

In separating "ancillary" rewards from intrinsic and extrinsic ones, however, Lortie creates a category which Deci does not recognize. In fact, various elements in the reward group which Lortie (p. 101) calls "ancillary" (that is, "objective characteristics of the work which may be perceived as rewards by some") fall into all three of Deci's basic types.

If we accept, for the moment at least, that both Deci and Lortie have made important and useful distinctions among reward types and that each has found a conceptual scheme which is helpful in interpreting real-world data, further progress in the analysis of rewards will require the development of a new theoretical framework — one which accounts for the similarities as well as the differences between these two taxonomic schemes.

Distinguishing Incentives from Rewards

Problems related to the definition of rewards are compounded by widespread confusion over the relationship between rewards and incentives. In a frequently cited article on organizational incentive systems, Clark and Wilson (1961) argue that there are three basic types of incentives: material, solidary, and purposive. In describing these incentive systems, however, they explicitly refer to material and solidary incentives as "rewards." They define material incentives as "tangible rewards: that is, rewards that have a monetary value or can easily be translated into ones that have" (p. 134). And when describing solidary incentives, they say the following:

> Solidary rewards are basically intangible; that is the reward has no monetary value and cannot easily be translated into one that has. These inducements vary widely. They derive in the main from the act of associating and include such rewards as socializing, congeniality,

the sense of group membership and identification, the status resulting from membership, fun and conviviality, the maintenance of
social distinctions, and so on. (pp. 134-135)

Interestingly, Clark and Wilson never use the term *reward*
when discussing purposive incentives. They say, rather, that
"purposive, like solidary, incentives are intangible, but they derive
in the main from the stated ends of the association rather than the
simple act of associating" (p. 135). They elaborate:

> The end system is deeply implicated in the incentive system of the
> association. The members are brought together to seek some change
> in the status quo, not simply to enjoy one another's presence ... pur-
> posive inducements must be carefully distinguished from solidary
> ones. If organizational purposes constitute the primary incentive,
> then low prestige, unpleasant working conditions, and other material
> and solidary disadvantages will be outweighed — in the mind of the
> contributor — by the "good" ends which the organization may even-
> tually achieve. (p. 136)

Incentives, in this formulation, are actually rewards, or at
least operate like rewards, in order to "satisfy the variety of
motives that help to maintain participation in the enterprise" (p. 136).
As Clark and Wilson put it, "All viable organizations must provide
tangible or intangible incentives in exchange for contributions of
individual activity to the organization" (p. 130). Moreover, "classification of incentive systems makes it possible to distinguish
analytically significant types of organizations," and "the incentive
system is altered (largely by the organization's executive) in
response to changes in the apparent motives of contributors, or
potential contributors, to the organization" (p. 130).

Thus, Clark and Wilson draw into a single conceptual framework the notions of incentive, reward, and motivation. Their view
is generally supported by Hoy and Miskel (1978), who argue as
follows:

> Incentives are defined as the organizational counterpart to indivi-
> dual motivation, that is, a worker receives incentives from the
> employing organization in return for being a productive member.
> Incentives, then, are the rewards or punishments given in exchange
> for an individual's contribution to the organization. (p. 116)

Taken from this perspective, incentives appear to be a special
class of rewards — those that are offered or exchanged for specific
work behavior. In Creighton's phrase (1974, p. 16), an incentive is
"not just a reward but an anticipated reward." But defining
incentives in this way creates a conundrum. How is the class of

rewards called "incentives" related to taxonomies of reward types delineated by Deci (extrinsic, intrinsic, and affective) or by Lortie (extrinsic, intrinsic, and ancillary)? The Clark and Wilson incentive types obviously contain some elements of each of the reward types identified by Deci and Lortie. Just as obviously, these classification systems are wholly incompatible with each other. The Clark and Wilson concepts cut across rather than extend the reward categories identified by the other two scholars. Thus, although they define incentives as rewards, they cannot mean that incentives are an additional and distinct category of rewards. To the contrary, the various types of incentives identified by Clark and Wilson are distinguished by variations in the social and organizational contexts through which they are mediated — not on the basis of differences in the essential character of the rewards offered or exchanged.

The conceptual problem here — one which plagues much of the literature on this topic — springs from the fact that the statement *Incentives are rewards* has two possible meanings. On the one hand, it could be taken to mean that incentives are a special class of rewards wholly distinct from all other reward categories — albeit, a class which itself may have subclasses. On the other hand, this statement can mean that an incentive is a particular attribute or characteristic of a reward — an attribute which, under certain conditions, could be possessed by any reward. In the first case, incentives will show up as one category (or set of categories) in a taxonomy of rewards. In the second, the term *incentive* does not refer to the rewards at all, but to the circumstances or conditions under which the rewards take on the attributes which give them an incentive value. Although much of the literature (including the Clark and Wilson essay) is insensitive to this distinction, only the second meaning of the assertion that incentives are rewards can provide an adequate basis for linking analysis of incentives to the study of rewards. Treating incentives as a separate class of rewards would lead to the absurd view that some rewards never serve as behavioral incentives.

What, then, are the conditions or circumstances under which rewards take on an incentive value? The Latin root from which the word *incentive* is derived sheds some light on this question. *Incentive*, Webster's dictionary tells us, is a transliteration of the old Latin word *incentus*, which means literally "to set the tune." Thus, while the term *reward* focuses on the pleasures or satisfactions gained from an activity or experience, the word *incentive* refers to the fact that contemplating access to those satisfactions leads people to modify their behavior in order to secure rewards and avoid punishments. In essence, all rewards have both a *reward value* and an *incentive value*. The reward value refers to the type and amount of pleasure or satisfaction that is produced. The incentive value refers to the nature and extent to which the reward "sets the tune" for one's behavior. Incentives, therefore, are always contemplated (or in Creighton's, 1974, terms, "anticipated"). Other rewards may come as surprises or happy accidents, but it is only meaningful to speak of incentives when the recipients have contemplated their arrival.

There is an important corollary to the fact that incentives are contemplated. In order to contemplate the flow of rewards, one must understand (or at least imagine) both the character of the particular experiences which one would find rewarding (that is, understand one's own motive), and the mechanisms which control the distribution of those rewards (thus turning them into incentives). Thus, in addition to the objective characteristics of the rewards available in the workplace, the incentive system available to a worker depends upon two basic factors. First, the incentive value of any particular reward depends upon the set of motivations with which each worker enters the workplace. Changes in motivation will lead workers to alter their interest in, and sensitivity to, various types of rewards. Second, since the capacity of any work organization to control the flow of various rewards is always limited, the incentive system will be shaped by the specific mechanisms for controlling reward distribution and the ability of the work organization to bring that system of control to the attention of the workers.

It was Chester Barnard (1938, p. 141) who first noted the possibility for improving the incentive value of an organizational reward system by either altering a worker's "state of mind" or by improving the capacity of the work organization to offer rewards which are already recognized as "worthwhile." As he put it in his classic formulation:

> An organization can secure the efforts necessary to its existence...
> either by the objective inducements it provides or by changing states
> of mind. It seems to me improbable that any organization can exist as
> a practical matter which does not employ both methods in combina-
> tion. In some organizations the emphasis is on the offering of
> objective incentives — this is true of most industrial organizations.
> In others the preponderance is on the state of mind — this is true of
> most patriotic and religious organizations. We shall call the process
> of offering objective incentives "the method of incentives"; and the
> process of changing subjective attitudes "the method of persuasion."

Barnard's distinction between altering objective reward systems and altering the workers' state of mind will be taken up later in our discussion of the psychological frameworks underlying the various theories of work motivation. The important point here is that incentives represent a "methodological" use of rewards — an effort by social groups and organizations to encourage or induce specific behaviors. Thus the concept of an incentive is, theoretically speaking, "orthogonal" to that of a reward: the relationships between incentives and rewards can be graphically represented as the two intersecting dimensions in a chart, such as in Figure II-1. The same activities and experiences which, from one perspective, are seen as rewards (because they produce varying levels of self-fulfillment, personal pleasure, or satisfaction) can be seen, from another perspective, as incentives (because they "call the tune" for a person's behavior by being contingent upon participation in, or performance of, particular activities).

Along the reward dimension, Figure II-1 has been divided into only two columns (labeled "extrinsic" and "intrinsic"). As noted previously, there is virtually unanimous agreement among serious scholars that these two types of rewards are fundamentally different in character. None of the numerous other categories of rewards proposed in the literature have either the conceptual clarity or empirical reliability of these two. Some other proposed reward categories, like Deci's (1975) notion of affective rewards, are best seen as subtypes of the intrinsic and extrinsic categories. Others, like Lortie's (1969, 1975) ancillary rewards category, fail to distinguish clearly between the reward and incentive perspectives on these experiences.

Following Lawler's (1977) distinctions between individual, group, and organizationwide wage payment schemes, the incentive dimension of Figure II-1 has been divided into three rows. Although Lawler recognizes that the most important differences between incentive payment systems lie in whether payments are made to individuals, work groups, or organizational units, his analysis overemphasizes the distribution of extrinsic monetary incentives. The three rows in Figure II-1 are conceptually closer to Clark and Wilson's (1961) typology of incentives than to Lawler's. The Clark and Wilson categories, while more theoretically sophisticated than Lawler's, need to be renamed and to some extent redefined, however, in order to highlight their importance as mechanisms controlling reward distribution rather than the characteristics of the rewards being distributed. Clark and Wilson overemphasize differences in the rewards themselves and give too little attention to the distribution mechanisms. It is in this respect that Clark and

FIGURE II-I. CROSS-CLASSIFICATION OF REWARDS AND INCENTIVES

REWARD CATEGORIES
(SELF-FULFILLMENT, PLEASURE, OR SATISFACTION)

INCENTIVE SYSTEMS	INTRINSIC (PSYCHIC/SUBJECTIVE)	EXTRINSIC (PHYSICAL/OBJECTIVE)
INDIVIDUAL INCENTIVES (DIVISIBLE, PERSONAL DISTRIBUTION)	Deci's (1975) "Intrinsic & Affective" Lortie's (1975) "Intrinsic" or "Psychic" Coleman (1969) Broedling (1977)	Deci's (1975) "Extrinsic" Lortie's (1975) "Extrinsic" Clark & Wilson (1961) "Material" Lawler's (1977) "Individual Plans" Merit/Incentive Programs Yukl & Latham (1975) Yukl, Latham & Purcell (1976) Training (1979, 1980) Creighton (1974)
	←— Calder & Staw (1975) —→ ←— Kopelman (1976) —→ ←— Pinder (1976) —→ ←— Whiddon (1978) —→ ←— Daniel & Esser (1980) —→ ←— O'Reilly & Caldwell (1980) —→	
GROUP INCENTIVES (SOLIDARY, SOCIAL DISTRIBUTION)	←— Lortie's (1975) "Ancillary" —→ Clark & Wilson (1961) "Solidary" Ouchi (1981) Peters & Waterman (1982) Schein (1985)	Lawler's (1977) "Group Plans" Slavin (1977, 1980) London & Oldham (1977) Deutsch (1949a, 1949b)
	←— Miller & Hamblin (1963) —→ ←— Schwab & Cummings (1976) —→	
ORGANIZATIONAL INCENTIVES (PURPOSIVE, STRUCTURAL DISTRIBUTION)	Schein (1985) Clark & Wilson (1961) "Purposive" Peters & Waterman (1972) Ouchi (1981) Berman & McLaughlin (1976) Coleman (1969)	Lawler's (1977) "Organizationwide Plans" Tax Incentive Schemes Pincus (1974) Porter & Warner (1973) Carlson (1965)

Wilson, in their otherwise powerful analytic framework, are most misleading. The rewards which they associate with "solidary" incentives (such as conviviality, group membership, and maintenance of social distinctions), for example, are distinguished from those which they call "material" in a way which is much more important than simply whether or not they can be given a monetary value. As their overall name for this category of incentives suggests, these incentives are given, if at all, to *social groups* rather than to individuals. Solidary incentives are not infinitely divisible — they arise within groups (usually informal groups) and, when available, are given to all group members together.

Similarly, Clark and Wilson overemphasize the material character of the rewards in their first group, failing to see that the essential feature of this set of incentives is that they are infinitely divisible and are parceled out among individuals. In fact, Clark and Wilson completely overlook the various individual incentives which have been of most interest to Deci (1975) and his followers. The intrinsic rewards associated by Deci with feelings of "competence" and "self-determination" are quite beyond the assignment of monetary values. Nevertheless, these personal intangibles are individual rather than "solidary" or group-based rewards.

The problem is that Clark and Wilson have confounded the distinction between intrinsic and extrinsic rewards with the equally important distinction between individual and group incentives. By not appreciating the existence of individualized intrinsic rewards, and by not recognizing the possibility that groups are just as likely to receive collective and indivisible extrinsic rewards, these authors have inadvertently equated individualized incentive schemes with extrinsic rewards and group incentives with intrinsic ones.

Theoretical confusions like that found in Clark and Wilson have played an important role in supporting the development of highly competitive incentive systems in the typical American classroom. By concentrating on the use of objective, tangible, and material incentives for individuals while treating excitement, joy, and conviviality as group incentives, this theoretical framework invites educators to believe that individual learning is stimulated largely by extrinsic and, if possible, material rewards while the fun parts of schooling are relegated to socialization in extracurricular activities or on the playground. Conversely, it leads to a belief that, when behavior is inappropriate, a whole group of students can be threatened with the withdrawal of intrinsic solidary supports while individuals are given extrinsic sanctions. Provocative work on cooperative learning undertaken by Slavin and others (Slavin,

1977, 1980) contrasts sharply with this prevalent view. This work is based on the realization that easily measured, extrinsic classroom incentives can just as easily be restructured and given to groups who must cooperate in order to acquire them. Interestingly, cooperative learning incentive systems have been shown to substantially improve group solidary rewards.

In a similar view, within what they call the "purposive" incentive system, Clark and Wilson concentrate too much on the intrinsic character of these solidary rewards. While it is true that there are important rewards that can be acquired only by an entire organization at once (and are linked to the purposes which the organization is pursuing), it is not true that these purposive rewards are not tangible or material. It makes sense, for example, to talk about a "tax incentive" system for stimulating various kinds of industrial innovation or investment practices because the obviously material rewards associated with these special tax provisions are given to whole organizations and are given in order to induce them to change their purposes and their resulting business practices. Such tax incentives fit precisely the Clark and Wilson (1961, p. 135) conception of a purposive incentive because they "are suprapersonal (i.e., they will not benefit members directly and tangibly) and ... have nonmembers as their objects." To be sure, business organizations are unlikely to take advantage of the tax incentive system if there are no tangible benefits for individuals, but the benefits flow first to the corporate entity (in direct relation to the organization's willingness to alter its purposes) and are spent or distributed within the organization on the basis of the same sorts of processes which are already used to provide groups and individuals within the organization with other incentives for participating in, or producing for, the corporation.

Within the cells of Figure II-1 are shown references to a number of research studies and commentaries focusing on the various reward/incentive intersections. As the larger number of references in the first row of the figure suggests, researchers have focused heavily on the individual-level reward/incentive systems.

In sum, the conception of rewards and incentives developed here (and used throughout this report as the basis for analyzing data from elementary schoolteachers and principals) emphasizes the orientation of individual workers to the context and experiences of their work. Any anticipated and valued organizational goals, solidary interpersonal relationships, or personal rewards (whether intrinsic or extrinsic) that provide a stimulus or reason for engaging in particular work activities are considered teaching incentives and thus are given careful attention in analyzing factors influencing teacher work behavior.

The Work Motivation Literature

Motivation is the third basic concept in any analysis of work behavior stimulation and control. The research literature on motivation is broader and more complex than that dealing with either rewards or incentives. In large measure the complexities in this literature spring from divergence in the psychological frameworks used by various scholars. Behaviorists, need psychologists, and cognitivists rely on sharply divergent conceptions of human nature and have equally incompatible ideas about what sorts of human behavior can or should be explained. We will take up these important problems in the next section of this report in a discussion of the alternative psychological frameworks underlying various theories of work incentives, rewards, and motivations. At this point we want to examine the relationships between the concept of work motivation and the notions of rewards and incentives just described.

Vroom (1964, pp. 8-9) frames the problem of motivation in its most fundamental form:

> There are two somewhat different kinds of questions that are typically dealt with in discussions of motivation. One of these is the question of the arousal or energizing of the organism. Why is the organism active at all? . . . The second question involves the direction of behavior. What determines the form that activity will take?

He summarizes his own viewpoint as follows:

> We view the central problem of motivation as the explanation of choices made by organisms among different voluntary responses. Although some behaviors, specifically those that are not under voluntary control, are defined as unmotivated, these probably constitute a rather small proportion of the total behavior of adult human beings. It is reasonable to assume that most behavior exhibited by individuals on their jobs as well as their behavior in the "job market" is voluntary, and consequently motivated.

Landy and Trumbo (1976, p. 295) explicitly assert what Vroom here implies:

> Work motivation is only one instance of a more general process. While the conditions under which work is performed differ substantially from the conditions under which other behavior patterns occur, new theories are not needed to account for industrial behavior.

The work context only requires some different ways of measuring the components of existing motivational models.

When examining the use of rewards and incentives, motivational researchers have been primarily interested in how the behavior of individual workers is influenced by variations in the types or levels of the rewards they receive (see, for example, March and Simon, 1958; Vroom, 1964; Herzberg, 1966; House and Wagdon, 1967; Porter and Lawler, 1965; Dawis, England, and Lafquist, n.d.; Hinton, 1968; Sergiovanni, 1967; King, 1973; Schwab and Cummings, 1973; Cherrington, Reitz, and Scott, 1973; Spuck, 1974; O'Reilly, 1977; O'Reilly and Caldwell, 1980; and Terborg, Richardson, and Pritchard, 1980). Curiously, the single most prominent analytical distinction in this literature is that made between job "performance" and worker "satisfaction." It is curious that this distinction is so prominent because the concept of satisfaction has long been recognized as being theoretically weak (Drucker, 1954; Locke, 1969). Moreover, satisfaction is an *attitude* variable — one that is conceptually unrelated to the fundamental parameters presented in most motivation theories. Drucker (1954, p. 158), for example, views the concept of worker satisfaction as virtually useless. His sentiments are captured in the following passage:

What motivation is needed to obtain peak performance from the worker? The answer that is usually given today in American industry is "employee satisfaction." But this is an almost meaningless concept. Even if it meant something, "employee satisfaction" would still not be sufficient motivation to fulfill the needs of the enterprise.

A man may be satisfied with his job because he really finds fulfillment in it. He may also be satisfied because the job permits him to "get by." A man may be dissatisfied because he is genuinely discontented. But he may also be dissatisfied because he wants to do a better job, wants to improve his work and that of his group, wants to do bigger and better things. And this dissatisfaction is the most valuable attitude any company can possess in its employees, and the most real expression of pride in job and work, and of responsibility. Yet, we have no way of telling satisfaction that is fulfillment from satisfaction that is just apathy, dissatisfaction that is discontent from dissatisfaction that is the desire to do a better job.

Fifteen years later, Locke (1969, pp. 309, 310) reported that the number of scholarly articles on job satisfaction had reached approximately four thousand. Yet, he asserts, "despite this proliferation of studies, our understanding of the *causes* of job satisfaction has not advanced at a pace commensurate with research efforts." Moreover, "judging from the size of the research literature, this lack of progress is not due to an absence of interest in the subject of job attitudes."

After exploring the issue in some depth, Locke (1969, p. 316) makes the following conclusion:

> Job satisfaction is the pleasurable emotional state resulting from the appraisal of one's job as achieving or facilitating the achievement of one's job values ... *job satisfaction and dissatisfaction are a function of the perceived relationship between what one wants from one's job and what one perceives it as offering or entailing.*

This conception identifies satisfaction with experiencing one's work as rewarding — not with either "energizing the organism" or determining what "form that activity will take," the basic categories in Vroom's theory of motivation.

In contrast with satisfaction, job performance is directly related to the level of energy and the specific form of action characterizing a worker's behavior. To the extent that motivation raises a worker's energy and shapes appropriate behavioral patterns, it plays a key role in determining overall job performance. Thus, job performance can properly be said to represent an operational measure of worker motivation. (On the basis of this rationale, Kopelman, 1976, operationally defined work motivation as the number of hours worked, technical and professional reading time, and the level of effort expended on the job.) In the absence of changes in the characteristics of a job or the capabilities of a worker, expanded or improved work performance depends on increased energy or more focused work efforts — key elements in the definition of motivation.

Spuck (1974, p. 21), following Katz and Kahn (1966), elaborated the concept of work motivation to include

> three major classifications of behavior required for organizational functioning and effectiveness: joining and staying in the system (recruitment, absenteeism, and turnover), dependable behavior/role performance in the system (meeting or exceeding quantitative and qualitative standards of performance), and innovative and spontaneous behavior/performance beyond role requirements (creativity, self-training, creating favorable climate, protecting the system, and cooperation).

Lawler (1977, pp. 168-172), in a similar effort to delineate the major dimensions of motivation, identifies four specific features of work behavior which express a worker's level of motivation: (1) joining the work organization, (that is, seeking and taking a job), (2) coming to work regularly and on time, (3) performing

assigned tasks effectively, and (4) accepting the structural arrangements and authority system of the work organization.

Virtually all efforts to specify the basic components of work
motivation concur in making some distinction between the motivation to *participate* in a task work group or organization and the
motivation to *perform* effectively required tasks. Spuck's first
concern — motivation to join and stay in the system — reflects an
interest in participation motivation, as do the first, second, and
fourth components of Lawler's framework. The level of participation or intensity of engagement in one's work is also at the center of
attention in Kopelman's (1976) operational indicators of motivation. However, as Spuck (1974, p. 21) points out, "motivational
patterns essential in the recruitment and retention of organization
members are not necessarily the same ones which lead to increased
productivity."

What is the relationship between this conception of motivation
and the concepts of incentives and rewards discussed previously?
Clearly the relationship is intimate. Motivation is always an
important consideration when researchers undertake to investigate
either rewards or incentives. Similarly, when scholars tackle
questions of work motivation, they invariably come to discussing
incentives and rewards. The reason, of course, is that these three
concepts each refer to a unique aspect of the same work experiences.
When viewed from the perspective of motivation theory, we are
interested in whether these experiences stimulate and direct
worker's actions. Incentive theory analyzes whether they are
anticipated and thus are the basis of participation in, or performance of, work activities. And reward theory seeks to interpret
whether they produce feelings of self-fulfillment, pleasure, or
satisfaction. Thus, as suggested in Figure II-2, motivation theory
represents a third dimension in the reward/incentive picture
presented in Figure II-1.

As indicated in Figure II-2, the juxtaposition of motivation,
reward, and incentive concepts creates a total of twelve unique
combinations of responses to the following three basic questions:
(1) Are workers motivated primarily to participate or to perform?
(2) Are available rewards primarily intrinsic or extrinsic? (3) Are
incentives offered primarily to individuals, to groups, or to
organizational units?

Spuck's (1974) attempt to examine the impact of rewards on
recruitment, absenteeism, and turnover among public high school
teachers illustrates how various types of reward structures may be
related to the different dimensions of this motivation-reward-
incentive framework. The "Material Inducements" (monetary re-

FIGURE II-2. RELATIONSHIPS BETWEEN WORK MOTIVATIONS, REWARDS, AND INCENTIVES.
(WITH SPUCK'S, 1974, REWARD SCALES)

Cell
2   Scale I. Material Inducements
9   Scale 2. Community Support
10   Scale 3. Physical Conditions
3   Scale 4. Pride of Workmanship

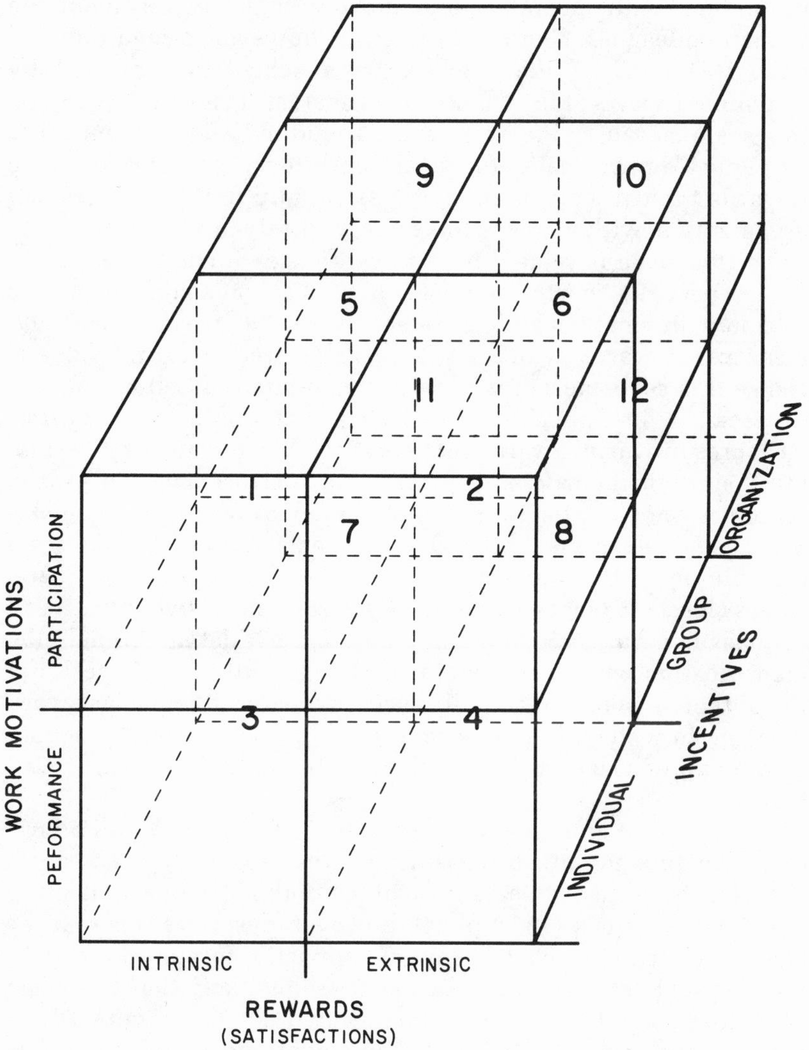

Cell
5   Scale 5. Peer Interaction
6   Scale 7. Policy Influence
8   Scale 8. Environmental
              Conditions

wards) which Spuck attempted to measure in the first of his eight reward structure scales are clearly extrinsic in character, are offered to individual teachers, and are contingent upon holding a teaching job (that is, upon participation) rather than upon any specific performance. Thus these rewards reflect the sorts of experiences associated with Cell 2 of Figure II-2. His second scale, "Support and Recognition of Community," represents an array of intrinsically meaningful experiences which are generally available (if at all) only to the entire school system faculty. To some extent, of course, the level of recognition and support experienced by individual faculty members deviates from that generally available to their colleagues. Generally speaking, however, recognition and support for all of the teachers in a school are affected by community views of the whole school system. Typically, therefore, this scale measures the experiences found in Cell 9 of Figure II-2.

Spuck's third scale, "Physical Conditions," assesses extrinsic rewards typically given more or less equally to the whole school organization, without being linked very closely to job performance. Thus this scale is related to the experiences found in Cell 10 of Figure II-2. His fourth scale, "Pride of Workmanship," is clearly intrinsic in character. It is also related to performance and measures rewards which are available directly to individuals. Hence this scale measures experiences related to Cell 3.

Scale 5 in Spuck's study, "Social Interaction with Peers," measures intrinsic rewards that are available to group members on the basis of their participation rather than performance. This scale, therefore, should reflect experiences in Cell 5 of our figure. Spuck's sixth scale, 'Agreement with District Goals and Policy," though a bit oblique to the conceptual framework being presented here, comes closest to what Clark and Wilson call "purposive incentives." It measures intrinsic rewards that are available through the identification with the school faculty because the faculty feel that the accepted goals are actually incorporated into important work being performed within the school. Thus this scale should probably be thought of as measuring experiences in Cell 11 as well as in Cell 9 of the figure.

Spuck's seventh scale, "Ability to Influence School Policy," could be thought of as measuring either extrinsic or intrinsic experiences. It also appears to combine both individual and group experiences. Spuck (1974, p. 24), however, describes this scale as closely related to teachers' sense of support from, and cooperation with, school administrators. Hence it seems likely that this scale measures something of the contents of Cell 6 in Figure II-2 — extrinsically rewarding policy accommodations provided to informal groups within the school that succeed in establishing sustained cooperative relationships. Scale 8, "Environmental Working Conditions" (shown in Cell 8 of Figure II-2), refers, according to Spuck (1974, p. 24), to the manner in which students and classes are assigned and to teachers' ability to teach in the manner they choose. This scale, like Scale 7, is difficult to relate directly to our framework. Spuck sees it as predominately concerned with group life within the school. It also appears to be related to teachers' task performance—not just to their enjoyment of peer relationships. Whether it should be viewed as primarily intrinsic (and thus in Cell 7) or extrinsic (thus in Cell 8) is not at all clear. It assesses experiences in Cell 8 if it is sensitive to actual changes in school operations. But Cell 7 is the target if changes in teacher feelings are the principal cause of variability in measurement.

Though Spuck's work tapped experiences in most of the different cells of Figure II-2, the measurements which he took did not systematically differentiate between the motivation, reward, and incentive perspectives on these experiences. It is not surprising therefore, that his data analysis was not able to provide a very satisfactory explanation of teacher recruitment, turnover, or absenteeism. His data does confirm the typical finding in this literature—that intrinsic rewards serve as the best incentives for teachers (see Lortie, 1975; Miskel, 1974; Spuck, 1974; Miskel, DeFrain and Wilcox, 1980; Sergiovanni, 1967; Thompson, 1979; and ERIC 1980, 1981 a and b). And his work does suggest that group and organizationwide incentive systems play a vital role in shaping teacher behavior. Beyond these very general statements, however, his work raises more questions than it answers about how teacher rewards serve as incentives or assist in motivating increased participation or performance within the schools.

The Dangers of Overreliance on Some Incentives

The available literature suggests that improved work motivation is not simply a matter of expanding the incentive value of all possible rewards. A number of scholars have indicated that overreliance on, or inappropriate use of, extrinsic rewards can seriously damage the capacity of workers to derive intrinsic satisfaction from their work, and can even reduce their willingness to perform needed tasks (see, for example, Deci, 1972, 1975; Herzberg, 1966; Kessleman, Wood, and Hagen, 1974; Larson, 1982; Martin, 1978; Miller and Hamblin, 1963; Notz, 1975; and Ouchi, 1981).

Figure II-3 identifies the types of rewards typically used to shape worker participation and task performance motives. In the third column of the figure are listed some possible results of overreliance on each of the different types of incentive systems. Overreliance on the various individual-level incentive systems, for example, can be expected to produce "irresponsible autonomy" among workers by inducing alienation from other worker or frustration among workers who are unable, by their own efforts, to produce results which are rewarded. Such outcomes are most likely in work environments where unclear or conflicting demands for participation and performance are present or where techniques needed for high productivity are not well understood. Many would say that these conditions are abundantly present in schools, and that it is therefore dangerous to rely heavily on individualistic incentive systems for teachers.

Group incentive systems can be expected to overcome individual alienation and frustration (see, for example, Slavin's, 1977 and 1980 analyses of how cooperative learning systems improve student engagement with both peers and subject matter). Overreliance on these incentives, however, can also assist in the development of authority systems which are perceived by managers to be subversive. Several studies of merit pay programs, for example, support the conclusion that work performance is improved by these programs only if workers have collectively participated in the development of the pay plans—but managers almost invariably view these worker-designed payment plans as threatening to their capacity to control the work organization (see Scheflen, Lawler, and Hackman, 1971; and Jenkins and Lawler, 1981).

Dehumanization is the most likely negative outcome of overreliance on organizational incentive systems. Use of the largely intrinsic organizational incentives described by Clark and Wilson (1961) as "purposive" can easily lead to chauvinistic prejudice or opportunistic insensitivity to persons outside the organization because workers narrowly focus their attention on the identity provided to them through membership in the organization. More extrinsic organizational incentives, such as profit making or high prestige for organization members, can induce parochialism or social irresponsibility if they become too central to the motivation system of organization members.

To summarize: work motivation, reward, and incentive are best conceptualized as three independent (orthogonal) perspectives on all of the experiences which stimulate and shape worker participation in, and performance of, the tasks and other role responsibilities which constitute workers' jobs. Motivation theory examines how these experiences energize and shape work behavior.

FIGURE II-3. WORK INCENTIVE SYSTEMS: TYPICAL REWARDS AND THE DANGERS OF OVERRELIANCE ON THEM

INCENTIVE SYSTEMS	TYPICAL REWARDS	DANGERS OF OVERUSE
INDIVIDUAL INCENTIVES		IRRESPONSIBLE AUTONOMY
FOR PARTICIPATION		ALIENATION
1. Intrinsic	(Interesting Work; Enjoyable Working Conditions)	Nonproductivity
2. Extrinsic	(Fixed Salary/Hourly wages)	Disengagement
FOR PERFORMANCE		FRUSTRATION
3. Intrinsic	(Efficacy; Accomplishment)	Noncooperation
4. Extrinsic	(Piecework; Merit Pay)	Faking
GROUP INCENTIVES		SUBVERSION OF AUTHORITY
FOR PARTICIPATION		CLIQUISHNESS
5. Intrinsic	(Solidarity; Esprit; Attractive Co-Workers)	Idle Socializing
6. Extrinsic	(Group Recognition)	Divisiveness
FOR PERFORMANCE		COMPETITIVENESS
7. Intrinsic	(Team Victories)	Conflict
8. Extrinsic	(Group Bonuses)	Rigidity
ORGANIZATION INCENTIVES		DEHUMANIZATION
FOR PARTICIPATION		CHAUVANISM
9. Intrinsic	(Shared Purposes)	Prejudice
10. Extrinsic	(Membership Prestige)	Parochialism
FOR PERFORMANCE		OPPORTUNISM
11. Intrinsic	(Symbolic Successes)	Insensitivity
12. Extrinsic	(Profit Making)	Irresponsibility

Reward theory analyzes whether workers find these experiences intrinsically fulfilling or extrinsically gratifying. Incentive theory looks at these experiences as intentionally offered in order to simulate worker contributions to the work organization. Incentive analysis inquires into whether the experiences are offered directly (and divisibly) to individual workers, to informal cooperating groups of workers, or to formal structural units or whole organizations.

SIX UNDERLYING PSYCHOLOGICAL THEORIES

While careful analysis reveals an overall integration of the concepts of work motivation, reward, and incentive, the opposite is true when we examine the basic psychological frameworks found within this literature. As described more fully below, there are six psychological theories to be found in this research literature. These six theoretical frameworks differ in such fundamental ways that a choice among them, rather than a synthesis of their basic elements, is required.

The various psychological theories used by incentive, reward, and motivation scholars are identified in the six cells of Figure II-4. The three rows of this figure separate behaviorist (for example, Watson, 1924; and Skinner, 1953, 1971), need-based (for example, Erikson, 1950; and Maslow, 1954), and cognitive psychologies (for example, Mead, 1934; Lewin, 1935; and Bandura, 1977b).

The two columns distinguish between what Lewin (1935) described as "historical" and "ahistorical" explanations of behavior. Vroom (1964, pp. 13-14) summarizes Lewin's viewpoint:

> Lewin (1935) distinguished between historical and ahistorical explanations of behavior. He pointed out that the former had its roots in Aristotelian thinking and the latter in Galilean thinking. From an ahistorical point of view behavior at a given time is viewed as depending only on events existing at that time. The problem is one of accounting for the actions of a person from a knowledge of the properties of his life space at the time the actions are occurring. From an historical standpoint, behavior is dependent on events occurring at an earlier time. The historical problem is to determine the way in which the behavior of a person at one point in time is affected by past situations he has experienced and the responses he had made to them. Freud's constant emphasis on the dependence of adult behavior on events which occurred in childhood and Hull's stress on reinforcement of previous responses provide us with good examples of historical explanations.

FIGURE II-4. PSYCHOLOGICAL THEORIES UNDERLYING ALTERNATIVE
CONCEPTIONS OF WORK MOTIVATIONS, REWARDS, AND INCENTIVES

	AHISTORICAL THEORIES (STATIC) FOCUS ON TRAITS	HISTORICAL THEORIES (DYNAMIC) FOCUS ON LEARNING
BEHAVIORIST PSYCHOLOGIES (WATSON, 1924 SKINNER, 1953)	Reinforcement or Rational Exchange (Taylor, 1911; Keller & Szilagyi, 1978)	Conditioning or Nonrational Exchange (Nord, 1969; Jablonski & Devries, 1972)
NEED PSYCHOLOGIES (MASLOW, 1954; ERIKSON, 1950)	Hierarchical or Genetic Needs Herzberg, et al., 1959)	Developmental or Evolutionary Needs (Argyris, 1957, 1973)
COGNITIVE PSYCHOLOGIES (MEAD, 1934; LEWIN, 1935)	Expectancy or Attribution (Vroom, 1964; Deci, 1975)	Cultural Orientation or Social Information Processing (Salancik & Pfeffer, 1978; Adams, 1963; Bandura, 1977b)

Ahistorical theories assume, in other words, that human
dispositions to act can be treated as if they were static and
unchanging over time. Such theories focus research attention on
the identification of individual traits or social circumstances that
account for differences in behavior. By contrast, historical theories
assert that inclinations to act are dynamic — changing over time.
Vroom's identification of change perspectives found in Freud and
Hull is accurate enough, but these historical theories emphasize
relatively slow, long-term changes in individuals. They give too

little attention to the frequent and fairly rapid changes in behavior which can occur in situations like political campaigns or the development of friendships. Research based on the dynamic, historical psychologies focuses attention on learning processes which change individual orientations and thus modify the energy levels or the purposes of specific actions.

Behaviorist Theories

B.F. Skinner (1953, 1971) is the most widely read and theoretically sophisticated of the behaviorist psychologists. His work is widely interpreted to mean that workers (like rats or pigeons) are induced to engage in work behavior through positive reinforcement of desired behavior and through explicit conditioning of work habits.

Static behaviorists emphasize the concept of reinforcement. They see human behavior as guided by a utilitarian "economy" of costs and benefits within which individuals balance the effort and costs of engagement in (or avoiding) a particular action against the rewards or benefits which would accrue from it. This theory assumes an essentially rational exchange model of action. It was epitomized in Taylor's (1911) Principles of Scientific Management. Taylor and his followers saw work as wholly instrumental in character; rewards are assumed to come in the form of monetary payments or social recognition completely controlled by agencies outside the individual worker. Research work based on this theory concentrates on ascertaining whether changes in the size, type, frequency, or mode of delivering reinforcements changes the performance (or, less frequently, the participation) of workers in assigned tasks. The three dominant themes in this research have been (1) the contingency relationship between rewards and measurable task performance, (2) the schedule on which rewards are supplied to workers (especially the difference between continuous and variable ratio schedules), and (3) comparisons between attitudinal and performance-level changes stimulated by various reward contingencies. For examples of this kind of research, see Georgopoulos, Mahoney, and Jones, 1957; or Keller and Szilagyi, 1978).

The appeal of static behaviorism lies in the simplicity with which it links rewards to behavior. By denying the importance (and sometimes even the existence) of mental states, static behaviorists are able to dramatically simplify research designs and data analysis procedures. This simplicity has encouraged widespread use of this framework — especially in the study of so-called incentive- or performance-pay programs. Unfortunately, because it presupposes such a simple relationship between reward contingencies and worker actions, most of the experimental research grounded on this framework fails to examine important social and interpersonal side effects of the experiments themselves. Keller and Szilagyi (1978), to cite a typical example, elaborately designed a study of the effects of continuous versus variable reinforcement on the performance of two groups of fur trappers. They indicate that all participants knew that the payment programs were experimental and that they would last for only a brief period. Yet these researchers make no mention of the possibility that this knowledge — rather than the payments themselves — was responsible for work performance changes. Moreover, they fail to consider seriously the implications of statements by some respondents indicating that the experimental conditions had stimulated some behaviors (such as trappers infringing on one another's territories) which would almost certainly produce long-term organizational tensions.

Dynamic behaviorism elevates the concept of conditioning above that of reinforcement. The historical emphasis of this theory highlights the more nonrational aspects of relationships between reward distribution and worker behavior. Nord (1969) and Jablonsky and DeVries (1972) are representative of the most sophisticated applications of this theory of motivation to work behavior. Whereas static behaviorism assumes that both the actor and the distributor of rewards know what behavior is being rewarded and what experiences serve to reinforce that behavior, dynamic theorists such as these scholars presume that rewards can just as easily be used to encourage unintended (and perhaps even unconscious) behaviors among workers. Dynamic theory focuses attention on the potential for a perceptual gap between work behavior and reward experiences. Whereas static theorists generally assume that workers will "know" (even without their having cognitive processes) what activities they are being "paid" to do and that they will adjust their efforts in direct relation to the level, rate, or scheduling of those rewards, dynamic theorists see this relationship as much more problematic. Dynamic theory assumes that the link between behavior and reward is unconscious for both managers and workers. In this theory, workers are not necessarily aware of either the behaviors that trigger a flow of rewards or which aspects of their experience actually produce the pleasures which they desire.

Conditioning theory asserts that, although individuals can tell whether their reward levels are going up or down, they only "learn" at a subconscious level which experiences actually constitute the rewards being received and which behaviors serve to control the delivery of those rewards. Thus, while static theory says workers can be expected to work for their pay, dynamic theory only expects them to do whatever makes them feel better. From this perspective, then, behavior is to be "modified" by changing particular reward contingency patterns — not by changing contractual arrangements or other verbal agreements regarding reward distribution. More importantly, since habitual behaviors have been conditioned by previous reward patterns, new behaviors have to be sufficiently rewarded to overcome the tendency for individuals to rely on rewards associated with previous habits. Once "behavior modification" has been successful, however, this theory expects that the new habits can be sustained with relatively lower levels of reinforcement (MacMillan, 1973).

Need Psychologies

The work of Abraham Maslow (1954) serves as the psychological touchstone for a massive body of literature which assumes that workers have characteristic needs or dispositions which must be met in their work life if they are to experience satisfaction (rewards). Maslow's theory is of the "ahistorical" type. It hypothesizes that five fundamental needs (physiological, safety and security, belongingness, esteem, and self-actualization or fulfillment) are constantly active in every human being. A hierarchical ordering of these five needs — rather than the history of their development — is viewed as responsible for determining which needs will motivate any particular action. Erikson (1950) is a good example of an historical or developmental need psychologist. Erikson, like other developmentalists, asserts that needs evolve over time and that researchers must be sensitive to the particular developmental stage within which a person is operating before they can hope to accurately predict behavior.

Static or hierarchical need theory has been most successfully applied to work behavior by Herzberg and his colleagues (Herzberg, Mausner, and Snyderman, 1959). Herzberg's most important contribution to the study of work motivation was to distinguish between those experiences which give workers a sense of pleasure and fulfillment (which he calls "motivators") from those which produce aggressive unhappiness or dissatisfaction (which he calls "hygiene" factors). When interpreted in the context of Maslow's (1954) conceptualization of the hierarchy of human needs, Herzberg's work suggests that the hygienic factors involve lower needs (physical needs, safety, and possibly belongingness) while the motivators involve the higher-order needs of esteem and self-actualization. Herzberg's work has been replicated in a school setting by Sergiovanni (1967), who found the same split between satisfaction-producing and dissatisfaction-producing experiences for teachers. Herzberg has had his critics (see, for example, House and Wagdon, 1967) but, on balance, work following his conceptual framework leaves little doubt that work motivation is more complicated and less objectively structured than behaviorists would like to believe.

Developmental need theory has not been widely used in the study of work motivation. Among widely read theorists, Argyris (1957, 1973) has stood virtually alone in insisting that organizational contexts can and do play a major role in encouraging (or inhibiting) the development of mature adult need patterns among workers. This isolation is all the more surprising given the extent to which these developmental assumptions are natural partners to the widely recognized organizational theories of McGregor (1960) and Ouchi (1981).

Argyris, like Erikson (1950), argues that under the right circumstances individual needs will develop over time from dependency on short-term immediate gratification to an increasingly autonomous and self-expressive pattern. To the extent that this dynamic is operative, the attention of Herzberg and his followers has been too narrowly fixed on organizational and job characteristics rather than on human development problems within industry.

In a narrow framing of the developmental problem, Katz (1978) offers convincing evidence that workers change substantially in what they find important and rewarding about their jobs as they remain in the same job over an extended period of time. These changes, which sometimes occur in a matter of a year or two, seem to confirm Argyris' belief that time and circumstance render old needs and hence old reward patterns obsolete.

Cognitive Psychologies

G.H. Mead (1934) is probably the most widely read cognitive psychologist. He argued that motivation depends upon the development of socially anchored meaning systems, not just on the genetic or developmental characteristics of human beings. He, like Lewin (1935), Voeglin (1952), or Bandura (1977a, 1977b), offers a theory of human behavior which is inherently transactional in nature. The cognitivists see human action as dependent upon the emergence of the human capacity to "mind" — to perceive, interpret, and evaluate experience in relation to social and personal meaning systems.

Static, ahistorical cognitivism views are exemplified in the work of Vroom (1964) and Deci (1975). These theorists accept the notion that motivation depends upon the construction of personal meaning systems which orient individuals to the value of obtaining particular rewarding experiences and interpret for them the possibilities that such experiences can be gained through personal effort. These theorists, along with hundreds of others using their general conceptual frameworks, provide compelling evidence that differences in individual motivation are rooted in divergent interpretations of social and organizational circumstances — not just in the objective availability of rewards or the levels of unfulfilled needs.

The two most important concepts of static cognitivist theory are *expectancy* and *attribution*. Vroom (1964) gave expectancy a prominent place in this framework when he argued that rewards will only motivate behavior to the extent that individuals believe (a) that the delivery of rewards depends upon their own behavior (that effort is "instrumental" in producing outcomes), and (b) that the rewards have a significant "valence" or value for them personally. Both instrumentality and valence are, according to cognitivist theory, dependent upon how individuals perceive and interpret their work environment. Thus expectancy (the belief that valued rewards can be secured through personal efforts) intervenes between initial interest and ultimate action.

Attribution theory, originally formulated by Heider (1958), involves a slightly different formulation of cognitive psychology. Recognizing that individuals can attribute social outcomes to one or more of four fundamentally different causes (ability, effort, difficulty, or chance), attribution theorists argue that the motivating power of any particular action-reward contingency will depend upon individual beliefs about the causal linkages between actions and outcomes. Thus, attribution theory argues that this aspect of cognition will override many of the objective characteristics of any task or reward system within which workers are called upon to perform. Although attribution theory could just as easily be formulated in dynamic terms, it has generally been used within a static, ahistorical framework (see Kukla's, 1972, excellent review).

Dynamic cognitive psychologies are the most complex of all those found in the work behavior literature. In fact, these theories are so complex that none have yet been subjected to comprehensive empirical tests. The best formulations of this psychological framework are found among anthropologists (Geertz, 1973; Spradley and

McCurdy, 1972), phenomenologists (Merleau-Ponty, 1964; Husserl, 1962; Heidegger, 1972; Schutz, 1967), and pragmatists (James, 1890; Dewey, 1920; Pierce, 1963). Bandura (1977a, 1977b) and Salancik and Pfeffer (1978) offer versions closely tied to work motivation issues.

According to these theorists, every individual formulates a set of cognitive interpretations of self-in-world relationships. These cognitive constructs operate dynamically to shape the extent to which various experiences are perceived to be (a) interesting, valuable, or rewarding, (b) likely to occur, (c) linked to specific current, prior, or future actions, (d) important to development or preservation of one's self-concept, self-identity, or efficacy, or (e) controlled by effort, ability, difficulty, or chance factors. Using these interpretive constructs, individuals formulate dynamic, cognitive maps of their self-in-world relationships. These cognitive maps serve to guide expectations, values, and meanings regarding actual and potential events. These, in turn, create a system of commitments to, and typifications of, social processes which guide actions and reactions.

As we elaborate below, a cultural framework was used to interpret data collected during the research being reported here. Two other versions of the dynamic cognitive perspective deserve mention, however: equity theory and social-information-processing theory.

Equity theory, variants of which have been proposed by Adams (1963), Homans (1961), Jacques (1966) and Patchen (1962), asserts that individuals form cognitive judgments regarding the balance between their work efforts and their reward outcomes and that they compare those judgments with those of others. These theories assert that tension or "cognitive dissonance" (Festinger, 1957) occurs when there is an imbalance between effort and outcomes in either absolute or comparative terms. As Goodman and Friedman (1971) and Pritchard (1969) point out, there is strong evidence to support the conclusion that feelings of inequity have a powerful influence on individual work attitudes and behavior. As Weick (1966) notes, however, which experiences will count as inputs and which as the outcomes of work effort are subjectively defined by individual workers and cannot be measured in any objective or universal metric.

Social-information-processing theory has appeared in two different forms. The first, and most clearly relevant to work motivation theory, is that articulated by Salancik and Pfeffer (1978). Their work is based on a symbolic interactionist psychology of the type generated by Mead (1934), and asserts that individuals "process" information derived from their prior experiences, social commitments, and immediate feedback from their actions. The processing of this information produces the meanings which are attached to actions and leads to subsequent adjustments of attitude and action commensurate with those meanings. A second version of social-information-processing theory is offered by Herbert Simon (1979), whose analysis is based on an analogy between social behavior and information processing in a computer. Both of these theories assert that the meanings of individual actions are fluid and constantly being reinterpreted on the basis of events and experiences which are encountered during the course of ongoing social interaction. While social information-processing-theory appears to offer a comprehensive view of motivation and action, it is a view which has yet to be adequately tested with empirical data.

To summarize: in this all too brief review, we have identified six psychological theories within the literature on work motivations, rewards, and incentives. Behaviorist theories are the simplest (some would say "simplistic") and static behaviorism the simplest of all the theories. As we move from behaviorism through need theory to cognitivism, the theories become increasingly complex. The dynamic cognitivist theories associated with cultural anthropology and found in social-information-processing theory are the most complex of all. The simplicity of static behaviorist theory has made research on its fundamental propositions easy to design, but interpretation of results are particularly difficult. By contrast, dynamic cognitive theories, which are closest to the complexity of real human behavior, have thus far eluded effective empirical testing.

A phenomenological and cultural approach to data collection and analysis was used for the research being reported here. The approach used is phenomenological in that it assumes that all human perception and action are guided by the adoption of particular orientations toward experience — orientations that both limit the ability of individual actors to make sense out of their work experiences and that also provide the basis for their responses to them. It is cultural in that it assumes that the values and meanings associated with these orientations are developed and shared by social groups; they are not simply individual attitudes and beliefs. Thus incentives are shared among subcultural groups or communities whose behavior takes on a common pattern as a result of shared values and meanings.

We turn now to a brief description of the dynamic cognitive conception of work motivation, rewards, and incentives which provides the central concepts for data analysis and interpretation throughout the remainder of this report.

TOWARD A CULTURAL THEORY OF TEACHING INCENTIVES

The phenomenological and cultural theory developed in the course of this research draws upon the work of a number of social philosophers and cultural theorists. Most importantly, it recognizes that American pragmatism (James, 1890; Pierce, 1963; Dewey, 1920; Mead, 1934) and European phenomenology (Husserl, 1962; Heidegger, 1972; Merleau-Ponty, 1964; Schutz, 1967) agree that the perception and comprehension of both natural and social phenomena depend upon the prior existence of some kind of fundamental human interest in the relevance of those events for one's existence. This fundamental interest is variously described as rooted in the human need of, or capacity for, "problem solving" (Dewey and Pierce), "intentionality" (Merleau-Ponty), "judgment" (Husserl), or "appropriation" (Heidegger). Despite important differences in their core concepts, however, all of these theorists unequivocally agree that experience comes in a confusing, undifferentiated continuum of sensations which are essentially meaningless unless and until we bring these fundamental interests to bear upon it. It is in the context of this purposeful appropriation of experience that the perception of discrete persons, objects, and events becomes possible and the meaning of these distinctive perceptual units becomes interpretable.

In Merleau-Ponty's provocative phrase, our capacity to even recognize, much less interpret, the concrete elements of our experience depends on our capacity to organize those events into perceptual units which "count in our scheme of things." In other words, we must adopt a "point of view" or develop a "frame of reference" which focuses our attention on particular sensations and reinterprets the relevance of those sensations for us. Without such a schematic frame of reference for perception, our sensations of shape, sound, color, and texture become fleeting intrusions on our consciousness but fail to orient us to their meaning or to provide us with a basis on which we might respond to them.

Cultures represent the *shared* frames of reference or common points of view used by groups of people to give common meaning to their experiences. A culture is shared to the extent that individuals who are nominal members of a group are able to define common problems and bring common intentions, judgments, and interests to bear on the interpretation of experience and thus develop comparable systems of perceptual recognition and meaningful interpretation of jointly encountered persons, objects, and events. Spradley and McCurdy (1972, pp. 8-9) define culture as "the knowledge people use to generate and interpret social behavior." They point out that individuals must learn how to interpret the social meanings of their own behavior. Children in every society, as they put it,

> are taught to "see" the world in a particular way...Through a long process of socialization children learn to organize their perceptions, concepts and behavior. They acquire the knowledge that members of their society have found useful in coping with their life situation. They are taught, in short, a "tacit theory of the world" (Kay, 1970, p. 20). This theory is then used to organize their behavior, to anticipate the behavior of others and to make sense out of the world in which they live.

Geertz (1973) puts the same point more subtly when he argues that cultural anthropologists are engaged in interpreting what members of a cultural group "mean" or intend by what they say and do. Cultural meaning does not exist as a set of abstract or universal interpretations of behavior, but rather as a set of meanings concretely shared (more or less fully) by specific groups at particular times and places. Cultures, like languages, have unique syntactical and semantic structures — structures which are understood by ordering their component parts into a holistic system, not by testing the discrete elements of one culture against those of another.

Winter (1966), following the lead of Schutz (1967), argues that the meanings of both individual and group behavior necessarily rest on the nature of the enterprise or "project" in which a person or cultural group is engaged. As Winter (p. 131) puts it:

> The decisive criterion for the "meaning of action" is the project of the actor — the anticipated state of affairs in his own preremembrance or retrospective recovery of that project as elapsed; that is, meaning is "what is meant"...The apprehension of the project may be inadequate, but the project is the criterion of meaning.

He argues that this notion of an intentional project or enterprise is the basis for meaningfully interpreting behavior within all social groups:

> The common culture is, so to speak, the system of meaning of the societal processes — the project of that society in the most comprehensive sense...Actors participate in the common culture according

to their location in the society and the degree of responsibility which they assume; however, their particular projects are judged within the common culture according to the accepted understanding of how things are done and what is or is not done. We take it for granted that their projects reflect that common culture which we share. Hence social action and social relationships presuppose sharing common typifications and meanings with roughly similar systems of relevance. (pp. 130, 133)

Eric Voeglin (1952, p. 27) puts the point similarly:

Human society is not merely a fact, or an event in the external world to be studied by an observer like a natural phenomenon. Though it has externality as one of its important components, it is as a whole a little world, a cosmion, illuminated with meaning from within by the human beings who continuously create and bear it as the mode and condition of their self realization.

This conception of culture as simultaneously a collective project and a shared meaning system operates at each of the three levels (organization, group, and individual) through which experiences acquire incentive values.

A Cultural Perspective on School Organizations

Building, then, on the work of a number of cultural theorists — notably, Voeglin (1952), Winter (1966), Spradley and McCurdy (1972), and Geertz (1973) — we sought to develop a cultural perspective on schools and classrooms which would illuminate the meaning systems and incentives for action which control the work of teachers and principals. Although any attempt at a comprehensive theory is still premature, three points about the cultural analysis of schools are basic to interpreting teacher job performance.

First, the cultural perspective highlights the linkage between school organizations and the larger society. As cultural projects, public schools are driven by demands and expectations regarding educational outcomes which emanate from the society and are embodied in its legal, fiscal, and organizational structures. These societal projects play a significant role in creating teaching incentives. Not only do they fix the overall levels of community support, legal power, and fiscal resources provided to school systems, but they also provide the ideological symbols which generate a sense of purpose or direction and thus mobilize and guide educator work efforts.

Second, the need for a cultural project to inform the development of shared meanings and social norms within any social group underscores the fact that classrooms, which are themselves sub-cultural systems, require collective projects and systems of shared meanings for interpreting the behavior of all who participate within them.

Third, by accepting the cultural project or mission of the school as their own, teachers acquire the organization-level incentives which Clark and Wilson (1961) call "purposive." These incentives produce intrinsically rewarding experiences, such as the feeling that one is doing significant work or realizing worthwhile social goals. Because legal, moral, and fiscal support for education flows primarily to whole organizational units, teachers also acquire such extrinsic incentives as desirable physical working conditions and professional prestige through identification with institutional definitions of the meaning and mission of educating children.

The fact that schooling is part of a national culture or collective social project means that schools are "meant" to be something for, and to do something on behalf of, the larger society. What schools are meant to be or to do may be unclear, but knowing that they are intended for some societal purpose is a fundamental prerequisite for interpreting the actions of their participants. Whether we are thinking of teachers or of students, administrators, parents, or school board members, the motives and behaviors of all participants in the school becomes interpretable primarily in reference to some presumed conception of the proper business of schooling. Thus, we can expect that teachers with substantially different conceptions of the enterprise of schooling will also orient themselves in different ways to their work responsibilities and will, in effect, be engaged in quite different kinds of work.

When schools are viewed from a particular cultural perspective, teachers can be, and frequently are, classified as more or less responsible and as more or less competent in terms of how well they embody that cultural project within their work activities. Such classifications, however, obscure as much as they reveal about the teachers thus classified. Only when the teachers themselves have adopted the presumed cultural system within which they are being evaluated can appropriate judgements regarding their competence or dedication be made. Teachers with different cultural presuppositions may be performing, with skill and diligence, tasks which are not recognized or valued, and will probably fail to perform valued tasks because they do not see them as meaningful. See Clarke (1973) and McDowell (1973) for empirical studies showing that principals' evaluations of teachers are sharply affected by the principals' beliefs about proper schooling methods and goals. McDowell's study also suggests that teacher behavior is altered significantly by changes in belief about method or purpose.

To put this point in terms of teaching incentives, meaningful incentives for teaching are embodied in the cultural project or enterprise which is used to give schooling its significance in society. Among the teachers whom we studied, we found two fundamentally different perspectives on the societal mission of the schools constituting one basic element in what Goldthorpe et al. (1968) refer to as a "work orientation." Some teachers identify schooling primarily with "producing achievement," while others adopt the view that schools have as their primary purpose "nurturing development" among children. We will elaborate on the differences between these two views more fully when interpreting our data in Chapter 3. For the moment, suffice it to say that teachers whose dominant incentive is to produce achievement approach the process of teaching quite differently from those whose dominant commitment is to child development and nurturance. Among equally competent and dedicated teachers, ones who accept an achievement production definition of their cultural role attend to very different aspects of the behavior of their students and structure their own teaching activities quite differently from those who embrace a child development definition of schooling.

Classrooms as Subcultural Groups

In addition to highlighting alternative conceptions of the organizational mission of the school, a cultural analysis of motivation, rewards, and incentives underscores the importance of classrooms as primary social groups within the school. In the typical elementary school, classrooms serve as authentic subcultural groups — generating shared meanings and collective projects which establish social norms and expectations as well as the typifications needed to interpret the behavior of students and teachers.

At this level, teachers experience the intrinsic rewards associated with what Clark and Wilson (1961) call "solidary incentives." They will find the classroom group (and their fellow teachers) to be either a close, warm, primary group or a distant, cool, and alien subculture. In addition to the intrinsic rewards of close association, they can receive rewards of a more extrinsic sort mediated through this group-level subculture. This process occurs, for example, when close cooperation among group members enables them to secure public recognition or prestige, or perhaps gain a prize or bonus for their efforts.

Of course, not all group-level rewards are positive. Interpersonal tensions can spring up in groups where basic group solidarity is well established, thus destroying the rewards of close fellowship. And negative sanctions can be applied to a group by external forces, thus weakening the reward value of existing intrinsic identity rewards.

It is important to remember that neither children nor teachers bring the entire range of their cultural meanings into the school. Both recognize that the school is a place created for special purposes and in which they must learn to participate as members of an emergent group with a unique meaning system. Within each classroom, activities and events acquire an integrity and meaning which only experienced participants can fully grasp. That is why teachers must struggle anew each September to transform a relatively chaotic collection of disparate individual students into an authentic subcultural group. Until the subcultural frame of reference emerges and engages the attention of all members of the classroom group, events continue to be mystifying for the participants, instructions lack coherence and meaning, and requirements appear arbitrary and capricious.

In the same way that the organization-level analysis of schooling reveals divergent and sometimes contradictory interpretations of the larger cultural enterprise of education, classrooms can express different subcultural commitments and goals. See, for example, Clarke's 1973, description of the difference between "child centered" and "academically oriented" classroom orientations.

As elaborated in Chapter 3, among the fifteen teachers we observed, we found a strong tendency for some to embrace a conception of their classroom cultural mission as "keeping school," while others held "teaching lessons" to be central to their work responsibilities. In other words, some teachers were guided primarily by a desire to reproduce, within their classrooms, the basic organizational expectations for orderly classroom behavior, dutiful adherence to district curriculum policies and superordinate directions (that is, they had a group-level incentive to "keep school"), while others responded to the classroom as a place where activities are invented, where children are engaged and confronted with opportunities, or perhaps even demands, for social and intellectual learning (that is, they had a group-level incentive to "teach lessons").

Culture at the Individual Level

At the individual level, a cultural approach to interpreting motivation, rewards, and incentives draws attention to the importance of self-identity for all participants in a social system. Noncultural theories may conceptualize a teaching "labor market" as an objective fact and assume that teacher behavior can be accounted for on the basis of certain measurable characteristics of that market. Such theories presume that workers "sell" their labor for various salaries, fringe benefits, social prestige, co-worker relationships, commodious working conditions, or some other rewarding experiences. Cultural analysis reminds us, however, that being "in the labor market" is a state of mind — not simply an objective condition. One indicator of the extent to which the labor market behavior of teachers is guided by cultural semantics rather than objective realities is the amount of time and energy union organizers invest in trying to persuade teachers that they need union representation to protect and further their interests as laborers.

Work role and *career* are the central terms in a cultural analysis of teacher work motivation. As culturally given, teacher work roles are fairly ambiguous. This ambiguity is reflected in a fairly widespread belief that teachers are always inadequately trained to know how to do their jobs. It is also reflected in the oft-cited adage that teaching has no adequate "technology" which links specific activities to expected results (Dreeben, 1970). The cultural perspective, while bringing this role ambiguity into focus, does not require that we view it as a problem. Rather, cultural analysis seeks to understand how and why individual teachers respond to this ambiguity. Cultural analysis asks whether, and if so how, teachers are able to establish sufficiently explicit role definitions to be able to plan and perform specific tasks. More importantly, cultural analysis illuminates the ways in which different participants in the school acquire different work role definitions and what happens when these divergent conceptions are being simultaneously enacted. As described more fully in the next chapter, the fifteen teachers in our study displayed rather different work role definitions with commensurate differences in their work style and emphasis.

From a cultural perspective, careers represent the long-term project or enterprise aspect of individual motivation. Whereas work role definitions rest on a more immediate sense of meaning, personal careers are only perceived by individuals whose cultural meaning systems include longer-range goals or purposes. Cultural frameworks, which include a sense of career as well as immediate work role definitions, enable teachers (as well as other workers) to tolerate and perhaps even effectively perform tasks which would be less attractive or rewarding in the absence of this sense of career.

We found significant differences in the degree to which subjects in our study (both teachers and administrators) possessed a sense of their work as a career. There were also substantial differences in the sorts of careers being pursued by those whose career perspectives were easily recognized.

To summarize: a cultural perspective on teaching offers the richest and most comprehensive framework for interpreting incentives, rewards, and work motivations. Cultures consist of shared meanings (used to typify and evaluate everyday events and activities) and collective projects (which guide intentions, plans, and actions). Cultural analysis can be applied to teacher incentives at all three levels (organizational, group, and individual). Organizationally, the cultural perspective highlights differences in the incentive value of achievement production and child nurturance as the basic mission of the school. At the group level, cultural analysis draws attention to the difference between "keeping school" and "teaching lessons" as the primary incentive or purpose for classroom activities. And at the individual level, cultural analysis highlights the importance of differences in perceived work role and career definitions for teachers.

CHAPTER III

The Work Orientations and Incentive Systems of Fifteen Elementary Teachers

The last chapter concluded with the proposition that teacher incentives are best interpreted from a cultural perspective. Moreover, it was argued, such a cultural perspective illuminates the relationship between teachers' overall work orientations and their responsiveness to individual, group, and organization-level incentives for teaching. This chapter presents interview and observational data drawn from fifteen elementary schoolteachers. The focus of attention is on critical similarities and differences in these teachers' cultural orientations which separate them into four distinct groups.

The fifteen teachers in this study are described in Figure III-1. They are arranged into four groups according to their overall work orientations, as described in detail below. The first three teachers, Mrs. A [M], B [M], and C [M], are all experienced, Anglo, female teachers. (The bracketed letters designate whether the teacher is a master [M], an instructor [I], a coach [C], or a helper [H].) In addition to sharing a common perspective on the nature of teaching, each has a work assignment which includes administrative responsibility. Mrs. A [M] and Mrs. B [M] are teaching vice-principals, while Mrs. C [M] is a resource teacher with special responsibilities for assisting other teachers with mainstreamed special education students. Two of these teachers, Mrs. A [M] and Mrs. B [M], are assigned to the two predominately black inner-city schools in our sample. Mrs. C [M] is assigned to the larger, multiethnic urban school.

Mr. D [I], Mr. E [I], and Ms. F [I] constitute the second group in our sample. This group is much more heterogeneous in character than the first. Mr. D [I], a Hispanic teacher with several years of secondary school experience, moved voluntarily to the predominantly Hispanic elementary school in our sample in order to teach second graders. He explained his move as one which would enable him to work with younger children and be more effective because, as he put it, these are the years during which their basic attitudes and abilities are formed. Mr. E [I] and Ms. F [I] are young, nontenured, Anglo teachers. He works in one of the predominately black schools; she works as a special education teacher in the most suburbanized of the sample schools.

The third group of teachers, Mrs. G, H, I, and J [C], are also fairly heterogeneous. Two of them, Mrs. G [C] and Mrs. H [C], are very experienced teachers of younger children. They are both Anglos and work in the two predominantly black schools. Mrs. G [C]'s kindergarten is a special class created as part of the district's "magnet school" desegregation program. Thus, although she is located in a predominantly black school, the majority of her students are mentally gifted Anglo children. Mrs. I [C] is the only Asian-American in our sample. She works in the multiethnic urban school. Mrs. J [C] is a young Hispanic female working in the predominantly Hispanic school.

The fourth group is made up largely of veteran teachers. The exception is Mrs. M [H], a first-year special education teacher working in the suburban school. The four veterans in this group have in common the fact that they were identified by the cooperating principals as the "weak" teachers in our sample. Mrs. M [H], though not initially identified as weak, did have difficulty coping with her teaching assignment and was eventually transferred to a different school. Mr. K [H], who had been a principal for ten years, had just returned to classroom teaching duties. He had moved to California for health reasons and was reestablishing himself in this state.

The remainder of this chapter is divided into three sections. First, the teachers' orientations toward organization level, or "school mission," incentive systems are examined. Data are presented to show that six of the fifteen teachers in our sample (teachers A through F) believe that the primary cultural mission of schooling is the "production of achievement," while the other nine

FIGURE III-I. TEACHER CHARACTERISTICS, ASSIGNMENTS, AND OVERALL WORK ORIENTATIONS

WORK ORIENTATIONS

TEACHER	SEX	ETHNIC IDENTITY	YEARS EXPERIENCE	TEACHING ASSIGNMENT	SCHOOL TYPE	TO SCHOOL MISSION	TO GROUP PROCESS
Mrs. A	F	Anglo	10+	4-5/ Vice Principal	Black	Achievement	Keeping School
Mrs. B	F	Anglo	9	5-6/ Vice Principal	Black	Achievement	Keeping School
Mrs. C	F	Anglo	10	Resource Teacher	Urban	Achievement	Keeping School
Mr. D	M	Hispanic	8	2nd	Hispanic	Achievement	Teaching Lessons
Mr. E	M	Anglo	2	4-5	Black	Achievement	Teaching Lessons
Ms. F	F	Anglo	1	Special Ed.	Suburban	Achievement	Teaching Lessons
Mrs. G	F	Anglo	20	Kindergarten	Black	Nurture	Teaching Lessons
Mrs. H	F	Anglo	26	1st	Black	Nurture	Teaching Lessons
Mrs. I	F	Asian	6	5th	Urban	Nurture	Teaching Lessons
Mrs. J	F	Hispanic	1	1st	Hispanic	Nurture	Teaching Lessons
Mr. K	M	Black	20	6th	Suburban	Nurture	Keeping School
Mrs. L	F	Anglo	20+	2-3	Hispanic	Nurture	Keeping School
Mrs. M	F	Anglo	0	Learning Handicapped	Suburban	Nurture	Keeping School
Mrs. N	F	Anglo	20	2-3	Urban	Nurture	Keeping School
Mrs. O	F	Black	20	2-3	Black	Nurture	Keeping School

(Mrs. G. through Mrs. O) identify the "nurture of children" as their primary organizational purpose. Following this discussion, a section is devoted to data on the teachers' group-level, or "classroom life," incentive systems. As this section shows, eight of the fifteen teachers (A through C and K through O) view student group life primarily in terms of "keeping school," while the other seven teachers interpret these group processes primarily as a matter of "teaching lessons."

The implications of these organization and group-level incentive systems for individual teacher work orientations are explored in the third section. Data presented in that section indicate that the organization and group-level incentive systems interact to form four separate groups of teachers. The three teachers in Group 1 (A, B, and C [M]) aim at producing achievement by keeping school. Group 2, also made up of three teachers (D, E, and F [I]), seeks to produce achievement by teaching lessons. Group 3 (teachers G, H, I, and J [C]) relies on the teaching of lessons to enhance child nurture and development, while the fourth group (K, L, M, N, and O [H]) uses school-keeping strategies for this purpose. As indicated in this section, individual-level incentive systems are forged, teaching work roles are defined, and career perspectives are formulated as teachers bring their individual motivation and reward system into line with these organization and group-level incentive systems.

ORGANIZATIONAL INCENTIVES: ACHIEVEMENT PRODUCTION VERSUS CHILD NURTURE

How do teachers decide whether their work is contributing to the basic purposes of the school? Our teachers answered this question in many different ways, but two broad themes emerge from close scrutiny of their interview responses and their teaching behaviors. One theme is clearly expressed in the following remark, made by Mrs. A [M]:

> I really feel that if the child can learn inner discipline and learn to accept the fact that some things are not always fun — for example, reading for some children is not fun — but the only way it's ever going to be fun is to keep plugging at it. So, if they at least get the attitude that there are certain things that must be done despite the fact that we don't like it — then everything else will work.

At another point, she reiterates this perspective:

> The most important consideration is probably getting up to grade

level. Covering the material, not just covering it, but teaching it, really teaching it. I think it's always been. Maybe that's why I have always been considered a fairly good teacher, because I refuse to accept the fact that just because a child was placed in a turkey reading group, that the child can't learn more.

This teacher believes that schools exist to produce objective, measurable achievement gains among students. She feels that she is contributing to the mission of the school if her children are able to read easily and compute accurately using the materials prescribed for their age group in the district curriculum.

Mr. D [I] places less importance on such standardized measures of achievement as the district curriculum guides, but he still identifies achievement as the primary purpose of schooling.

The most important consideration in what I teach is getting the children to like learning. You would expect that math is maybe the main thing, or reading is the main thing, or whatever a teacher's preference. To me, however, it is just getting a kid to learn to like to learn. Because once you get them hooked on learning they go into everything on their own. And, of course, being a good reader and knowing elementary math, those are part of the tools you have to have in order to become a good learner. But that is basically it.

For Mr. D [I], if children like learning and show real progress in their studies, he feels that he is contributing to the school. He elaborates:

The most important thing that I teach is probably...the love of learning, or how to learn, or getting used to learning, things of that sort. Because, to say that anything, like behavior, is more important than attitude or attitude is more important than academics...it all goes together and I think it is just to get the kids to like to learn. And it sort of includes all those other things.

For a third teacher, Mr. E [I], achievement is not only the primary purpose of schooling; it also takes time to show itself.

It seems like in teaching a lot of your results, a lot of things that you see, you don't see until maybe four, five, six years down the road when you see a kid doing extremely well. For example, a kid making progress — especially a kid that had a lot of problems before and people had just given up on him...Some teachers just give up on kids, saying "Oh, you're just not going to learn anything," or "Oh, he is just at this level and he is not going to do any better." If I see him make progress then I feel proud of myself. I think I feel prouder of myself than I do of him.

Contrast the views of Mrs. A [M], Mr. D [I], and Mr. E [I] with the following remarks by three other teachers. A fifth-grade teacher, Mrs. I [C], says the following:

> I see my class as "young broncos" that need to be tamed. Like I'm taking them into a new world. I keep on telling them, "You are in the fifth grade now," because they like to play games in third and fourth, but I keep on telling them, fifth grade is like you are taking a step into a whole new world. And maturity, hormones, the whole thing is bubbling and I have to kind of grab them by the hand and lead them through this tunnel. And a lot of them don't even know they are going through it. But eventually they will know that they are going through it. So, I see them as like young broncos that have to be tamed and I really like the challenge.

For this teacher, child growth and development are at the center of the school's mission. Academic achievement is desirable, but she sees nurturing her children through their transformation into adolescence as the most critical function a teacher can perform. Mrs. G [C], a kindergarten teacher, offers a similar view of the school's central mission:

> The most important consideration in what I teach is what I am giving them. I want to be sure they are comfortable in school. I want them to be happy coming here. At this particular stage, you know, in kindergarten, if they get a lot of heavy academics it does not make that much difference because what they need to know is that school is a nice place to come to. A place where you can learn, but also a place that will welcome and make you feel like it's not drudgery. I do want them all to learn too. I want them to have their reading skills and I want them to get their math skills so we spend time on it, but I don't want any pressured situations for them at this stage. They don't need that. They have a lot of time to grow up and be pressured.

Mrs. L [H], a second-third-grade teacher, provides a third example of this commitment to child development rather than achievement:

> I make curricular decisions, usually, by where I feel the children need help. I try to help them. I don't try too much to impose a regimen. Of course, we have a certain regimen in the curriculum that is selected, etc. But I try to let them go where they are able. And I help them where I feel they need help. And they come and say they need help.

Mrs. L [H]'s views are much more passive than those of Mrs. I [C] and Mrs. G [C], betraying a substantially lower level of confidence on her part that she does anything that contributes greatly to the school's primary mission. Nevertheless, she conveys an unmistakable commitment to the preeminence of nurture and development goals rather than achievement production.

Of the fifteen teachers in our sample, a total of six share the achievement production orientation of Mrs. A [M], Mr. D [I], and Mr. E [I]. The other nine teachers share the child nurture views of Mrs. I [C], Mrs. G [I], and Mrs. L [H]. The six achievement producers share three beliefs which serve to support their view of the school's basic mission. First, they all feel strongly that teachers — not students — are responsible for initiating the learning process. Second, schooling is serious work — work which even at its best is not always fun for either students or their teachers. And third, teaching work is primarily instructional rather than evocative or educative in character; that is, they believe that they should aggressively present materials and learning experiences to the children, materials based on their eventual goal of improving student achievement, not just on students' current interests or abilities.

The nine teachers with child development orientations share the obverse of these beliefs. They each express the view that students bear the ultimate responsibility for initiating their own learning processes; that schools should appeal to the children's interest, curiosity, or sense of play; and that teaching works best if learning is evoked or "educed" from children rather than pressed upon them.

A good example of the achievement producers' acceptance of the responsibility for initiating actions is seen in the following excerpt from Mrs. B [M]'s interview:

> The important consideration in my teaching is to make sure that the students are grasping the concepts, whether it be math, reading, health, or whatever. And by getting feedback from them — whether it be body language, verbally, or written — I know whether or not I am doing my job, whatever subject it might be that we are working on.

She makes more explicit her belief that this responsibility is for the children's educational achievement:

> I think I am being responsible for their education. I cannot dwell too much on their problems at home. I can empathize and I can see to it that, perhaps, counseling or a certain agency that could maybe provide contingency funds — if there is no one in the house, or whatever. I can do those things, but when it comes time that they are in this classroom, then by gosh, at that time I must insist that we get on with the lessons, or I could be having therapy in here all day and I would not really be doing the kids a service as far as making sure that they have math skills and reading skills, so when they do get out on their own they won't be cheated and that they will be able to survive

and hopefully get off the welfare syndrome that's, maybe, been in their family for generations.

As revealed in this passage, her commitments are clearly instructional in character. She delivers specific math, reading, or other subject matter skills which she and the other achievement producers believe will enable the students to survive and prosper in later life.

The achievement producers' belief that schooling is work is captured in a remark by Mrs. B [M]:

> There's kind of a fine line where I can be loving and caring to my kids, but also be assertive — such as, "I'm sorry that happened, Susie, or Johnny, nevertheless, we have work to do today, now let's get on with it." I will not let their plight interfere with developing them as a person, as far as their academic work.

At first glance, Mrs. B [M]'s use of the term "development" in this remark might seem to mean that she has taken the child nurture view. Her parenthetical phrase, "as far as their academic work," was added, however, just to keep our interviewer from being confused. Mrs. B is unequivocally committed to the proposition that schools are academic achievement producers, not extensions of family life or social service agencies.

The achievement producers' belief in the teacher's responsibility for initiating the learning process, combined with an emphasis on the view that teaching and learning are serious work, was enunciated by Mr. E [I].

> Teaching is not very redeeming at the particular moment when you're doing it. I think it is something you have to stand back, look at, and say, "Well, you know we have done this, and I can see how far they have come." And, I think that with a combination class, because I have a couple of kids back from last year and see what they are like this year, that I can more or less compare the fifth grade with the fourth grade. And, I can see the big difference. I can see the big gap right there and I think, "I'm doing a pretty good job after all. You know, I did not do such a bad job." I think that is probably the most redeeming thing — making progress. That makes me feel really good.

In this view, *progress* — Mr. E [I]'s word for student achievement — springs directly from the willingness of teachers and students to get down to business. While serious, however, this business does not have to be tedious or boring. Mr. E [I] also said the following:

> I try to add a little bit to it. I try to be a little funny with the kids. I try to say things that the kids will think are funny. I'm reading a book right now, a book about the best Christmas pageant ever. The thing is

hilarious, just hilarious. It's about a very poor family, by the name of Herdmann. Right? And they have nasty dispositions and it is just a hoot. The book so far, what I have read, has just been a hoot, and the kids are getting a kick out of it and I'm getting a kick out of it. It is fun to read. It is not real drab material. I don't like the picture of the school marm sitting up there in the class saying "You're going to do this" or "You're going to do that." That would be drab.

Teachers with the child nurture orientation discuss these issues in very different terms. Mrs. I [C], for example, articulates the child nurture viewpoint when she says: "I'm not here just for myself. I'm here for them, and I need them as much as they need me. Without each other we really could not accomplish anything." She expands on this view:

> Yes, their accomplishments in, say tests or what have you, did make me happy, but I think it was more of this relationship that we had with each other because I was able to relate to them and they were able to relate to me. Like we were to do math or addition or multiplication, or whatever. So I guess what I am saying is the physical thing, it doesn't have to be touch, or it doesn't have to be $20 or a fur coat, it is just "Wow, thank you very much. I really enjoyed it." And, I find that this year the sixth graders who were in my class last year are coming back to see me at recess. "Do you need any help? How are you? Gee, the room looks much different from last year's." And that kind of thing. So I am going "Wow!" I am patting myself on the back and I am feeling fantastic. I feel really great.

Another nurturer, Mrs. L [H], highlights the tendency to see children as the initiators of action: "What I like is really a sense of the kids wanting to learn. I like it when children start to see what they can accomplish." Mrs. H, a first-grade teacher, is typical of this group in her emphasis on the importance of children finding school experiences both broadening and enjoyable.

> I think that children need to be involved in "doing," so that they are functioning well at both the right and left brain levels when they are seeing and doing. And, I think that, as much as possible, this kind of thing needs to be done well all the time. Sometimes it is very very difficult, but their response is in how well they learn, and whether or not they are happy with what they are doing. And yet, at the same time, maintaining good discipline in the classroom so that everybody is functioning and doing — and having a good time.

To summarize: six of our teachers expressed, in one way or another, a commitment to the proposition that the school's primary mission is the production of achievement — achievement that can be measured and therefore recognized by everyone. The other nine teachers give primary weight to the school's function as an agency of child nurture and development. For this group, children show growth and maturity in ways that are subtle and complex and that may not be easily measured.

GROUP-LEVEL INCENTIVES: KEEPING SCHOOL VERSUS TEACHING LESSONS

In addition to balancing the tension between achievement and nurture as the ultimate goals of education, every teacher in the sample displayed a clear preference for one of two basic strategies for organizing their classrooms. This second general work orientation parameter represents the group-level incentive system described in Chapter 2. In selecting an approach to classroom organization, teachers determine the type of cultural meaning system that will be developed among their students. They also define the nature of their own "solidary" or group participation incentives.

Some teachers see the development of programs, the proper placement of children within those programs, and the encouragement or insistence upon student compliance with the demands of those programs as the most basic elements in their teaching strategies. These teachers — let us call them the "school keepers" — believe that educational objectives, whether relating to achievement or nurturance, are best pursued by creating a classroom environment which surrounds students with opportunities and expectations that both respond to their current abilities and also move them toward long-term learning goals. For teachers holding this view, education consists of a set of "experiences" which children encounter, learn to cope with, and eventually master.

Eight of the fifteen teachers we studied (teachers A through C and K through O) held this perspective on classroom organization. As elaborated below, these teachers find their own group identity, if at all, primarily among the other adults in the school system rather than with the children.

The other seven teachers in our sample (D through J) focus their classroom strategies on the structure and conduct of lessons rather than the organization and implementation of programs. These teachers express the view that learning is more the result of "activities" than "experiences." In other words, they believe that students learn through high-quality engagement in particular lesson activities, and they take a special interest in stimulating and directing that engagement. For these teachers, solidary group incentives are focused inside the classroom, with the students.

The School-keeping strategy, as expressed by achievement-oriented teachers, is captured by Mrs. A [M]:

> The most important thing I teach is study skills, work skills, and responsibility. I think that a kid can learn. There are certain things that must be done, whether it is an enjoyable experience or not, then all other things will fall into place, whether it is reading, math, or whatever. I have personally enjoyed teaching math more than anything else. I think it is fun because I have always enjoyed math, although I have not been stupendously successful, I guess I have been above average. I love reading. I like to teach reading. But reading — there is not any instant success with reading.

This same orientation is embodied in some of her other remarks. After telling us that getting children "up to grade level" and "covering" or "teaching" curricular materials are the most important considerations in teaching, she says, "It's all in your expectations, but I expect them to work at grade level."

Mrs. B [M], who is not as clearly committed to this programmatic approach, nevertheless reports getting her greatest joy from turning around the "snottiest kid you can give me."

> I find it very rewarding to be working with students who are showing growth. Not only academically, but as far as their attitudes, their behavior. I really turn on to the snottiest kid you can give me to be able to help that child discover self-worth and the joys of reading and being able to work out a long division problem. Being able to feed back to me their multiplication tables. To see that growth and to see that joy within themselves, when they have mastered a task, or they are just about ready to and they can feel it.

As Mrs. B [M] sees it, the learning tasks — reading, working out long division, or whatever else might be expected of sixth graders — are given in the curriculum. Her job is to help the kids experience mastery over those tasks.

The school keepers, who take nurture rather than achievement as their primary goal, articulate this programmatic issue somewhat differently. Mrs. L [H], for example, sees it more as a matter of making her life as a second-third-grade teacher easier and ensuring that the whole educational system becomes more respectable.

> I think that if we had K-1 classes where children were put in a 1 to 10 ratio and then evolved — either tested, taught or screened — so that by the time they got to third grade they could test into the third grade. Then ... they would still vary in their abilities and speed of learning, so you would still have plenty of groups, but the point is, it would give them some feeling of "I've reached a landmark in my school. I've

made third grade." And then there would be better respect for the system.

Mrs. O, less concerned with the larger issue of school operations, sees program structure as an important framework for organizing her teaching efforts. She is particularly concerned with the importance of the clock and the schedule as devices for controlling the classroom activity system.

> I can determine what can get done in a class period by the actual time of the work schedule. Now some children, as we all know, are faster workers than others. Some can complete this writing lesson in, maybe, 10 minutes. And for some it will take 39 minutes. So, those that have not completed it, will have to go on with their reading. In their spare moments they have to come back and get their writing assignment completed.

A little later she elaborates as follows: "Those that I know could work a little faster, I encourage them to complete their work at a certain time. 'Look at the clock now. By the time that long hand gets to a certain number, I would like you to be through writing.' Some are slow workers, but I know they are picking up now."

The Lesson-teaching approach contrasts sharply with the school keeping strategy for classroom organization. Mr. D [I] articulates the starting point for the lesson teachers when he says, "I love learning and I really get interested in, and turned on, to the things that I am doing in class. I expand on it." He is so taken by the content of his lessons that he "discover[s] new things, right along with the kids." Mr. E [I] says he likes this year's fourth-fifth-grade class for the following reason: "We have discussions and a huge amount of the class takes part in the discussions. It's not the type of class that you are trying to wring answers out of them. They all have something to say. So, it is nice. It is a fun class. They are curious about things." He elaborates on how his lesson-teaching focus creates a tension between his own interests and those of the district program and curricular structure:

> A lot of curriculum decisions are already made for me by the district and by the state, and so it narrows things down a little bit. Certain things do have to be covered. But there are areas that I like teaching. I teach a unit on weather every year, and I like that. I teach a health unit on nutrition and I enjoy that. I enjoy teaching U.S. history because I enjoy the history of the United States. There are certain things that I just like to teach and then there are certain things that I am obligated to teach, like reading, math, and language. There are things that the state of California [mandates]...everybody, like kids, needs to learn this anyway. It is part of teaching, anyway, and it

has been since the beginning of time. But I do have certain areas that I really like teaching so I teach those areas because I have somewhat of a free hand in those areas. I am pretty well locked into the other areas. I have to meet certain objectives in other areas.

Obviously, Mr. E [I] finds opportunities to realize his primary interest, teaching lessons, within the relatively more distasteful and mundane process of keeping school. Miss F [I], a special education teacher working with seriously handicapped aphasic students, displays her interest in teaching lessons in her insistence that hers "is not a 'behind' class" but a "language class":

> During spelling drills, for example, I give a clue. "The opposite of tight is..." I use a language-oriented spelling test as one approach to the work. Earth, for example, is related to "a planet" and "dirt." That's the way I teach spelling. Trying to get as much language into it as I can. These children are stronger auditorily than visually. I'm hoping that by giving verbal inputs they might be more successful.

Among the child nurturers, the lesson-teaching rather than school-keeping focus is well articulated by Mrs. H:

> When I decide what to teach — first of all, I take into consideration the children and what level they are, which seems to be different every year. Then I usually try to determine a form of presentation and introduction — something to make the lesson or whatever exciting, something the children will be interested in and that also depends on the group. I do something a different way each year, depending on the type of child and what their interests are. We set this up, and then if I need extra material I go see where we can get that, whether it is audio visual, or I have to go buy something.

In the following remark, Mrs. G, a kindergarten teacher, exhibits some tension between the achievement and nurture goals, but there is no mistaking her commitment to taking possession of the teaching process when she says, "The most important thing I teach in the schedule is — I'm weighing that because, although I feel that reading is important, and math is important, I feel that learning to socialize and get along is even more important — so, I guess the social aspect is very important to me." And when asked about this "social aspect," she makes it clear that this is a lesson to be taught, not just a set of social experiences within the classroom. As she puts it, the social aspect "kind of falls where it falls." She continues: "Other than our social studies — where we discuss behavior, and 'How do we treat our friends?' — it's things that happen during the day, you know. 'How did so and so treat so and so? Do you think that was the right way? What can we do to change that?' "

In sum: eight of our fifteen teachers approach classroom organization programmatically and see their role as "keeping school," while the other seven concentrate on interacting with the children and see their role as "teaching lessons." The first group emphasizes the importance of children's abilities and teachers' expectations. The second group looks more at the students' engagement and teachers' preparation of specific learning activities.

INDIVIDUAL INCENTIVES: ROLE DEFINITIONS AND CAREER ORIENTATIONS

The fifteen teachers in our study fall into four distinct groups when organization-level, purposive incentives and group-level, solidary incentives are considered simultaneously. The four groups are depicted graphically in Figure III-2. The three teachers who combine achievement production with keeping school (teachers A, B, and C) are shown in the upper left cell of the figure. The three who rely more on teaching lessons to realize this goal (teachers D, E, and F) are in the lower left cell. The four who focus the lesson-teaching strategy on child nurture and development goals (teachers G, H, I, and J) are in the lower right cell, and the nurture-oriented teachers who rely on the school-keeping strategy (teachers K, L, M, N, and O) are in the upper right cell of the figure.

Critical elements in the purposive and solidary incentive systems are suggested along the margins of Figure III-2. As previously described, adopting an achievement production goal encourages teachers to concentrate on instructional processes, whereas nurture goals call for an evocative or educative approach to teaching. Similarly, achievement producers concentrate more on curricular content, while nurturers emphasize teaching relationships. Achievement producers see school as work; nurturers see it as an opportunity or an adventure.

As indicated along the left margin of the figure, school-keeping strategies emphasize grade-level performance within district curricular programs, while lesson teaching concentrates on the presentation of novel, potentially exciting materials and activities which the teacher is confident will produce specific learning outcomes for a particular class or group. Consequently, school keepers find children's *abilities* an important factor in thinking about and planning their teaching activities, while the lesson teachers see student *interest* as more important.

In the remainder of this chapter, we examine the work

FIGURE III-2. FOUR ALTERNATIVE TEACHING WORK ORIENTATIONS AND INCENTIVE SYSTEMS

PURPOSIVE ORGANIZATIONAL MISSION
INCENTIVE SYSTEMS

| | | PRODUCING ACHIEVEMENT | NURTURING CHILDREN |
		INSTRUCTION EMPHASIS, LEARNING AS WORK	EDUCATIVE EMPHASIS, LEARNING AS OPPORTUNITY
	KEEPING SCHOOL ABILITY-BASED EXPERIENCES PROGRAM-STRUCTURED ADULT-CENTERED	THE MASTER TEACHERS Teachers A, B, & C Becoming Academically Disciplined Success: Getting up to Grade Level Hardest: Reaching the Difficult Kids Distasteful: Lack of Administrative Support	THE HELPERS Teachers K, L, M, N, & O Learning to Cope With the Curriculum Success: Functioning as Students Hardest: Imposing an Order or Regimen Distasteful: Kid Who Hates Being There
SOLIDARY, GROUP PROCESS INCENTIVE SYSTEMS	TEACHING LESSONS ENGAGEMENT-BASED ACTIVITIES TASK-STRUCTURED CHILD-CENTERED	THE INSTRUCTORS Teachers D, E, & F Making Intellectual Progress Success: Kids Turn on to Learning Hardest: Pacing the Instruction Distasteful: Having to Discipline	THE COACHES Teachers G, H, I & J Exploring New Worlds Success: Kids Click With the Teachers Hardest: Emotional Energy Required Distasteful: School Organization Stuff

orientations and individual-level incentives shared by the members of each of the four subgroups in our sample. The bracketed letters designate the group to which each teacher belongs: either master [M], instructor [I], coach [C], or helper [H]. Each group shares a common set of cultural meanings regarding the following six basic elements in their work:

1. A common view about what teaching activities contribute most to student learning.
2. A common set of criteria for determining whether their teaching is being successful in realizing its fundamental goals.
3. A common viewpoint regarding what students need to do in order to be successful, and how successful students can be recognized.
4. A common sense of what the most difficult aspect of teaching is — difficult in the sense that teachers who can handle this task well are truly good teachers.
5. A common view regarding the most distasteful part of teaching — distasteful because it represents a perpetually unsolvable problem which constantly interferes with their work.
6. A common view regarding the central mystery of teaching — the marvelous thing which makes learning possible and which can be celebrated, but cannot be entirely predicted or controlled.

These shared cultural meanings shape the ways in which teachers develop an individual incentive system. They define the nature of the teaching work role and they tell teachers how to imagine their futures and pursue their careers. Members of each group who share these individual-level incentives think, talk, and act in similar ways within the school and classroom.

Group 1. The Master Teachers

The first group of teachers (A, B, and C) we have called the "master teachers." They have each been recognized by their superiors as strong contributors to the school system as well as effective classroom performers. These teachers have a deep commitment to the production of achievement — a commitment which they tend to articulate in terms of "bringing kids up to grade level." This achievement is their basic criterion for successful teaching. For these master teachers, "academic discipline" is the key to improved student learning. Mrs. A [M] expresses this goal well:

> I think that probably the nicest thing about teaching for me right now, is seeing a child who is kind of squirrelly, totally irresponsible, start building a sense of responsibility in terms of bringing home his homework, you know, seeing the level of concern raised in a child so that he or she really cares about getting that work finished, about

learning those times tables. I think, seeing them develop into responsible students is probably the most satisfying thing for me right now.

Later, she expands on this matter of effort and responsibility:

I expect them to work at grade level, or as close to it as they possibly can. And for the most part they do — because I want them to. And they work hard to catch up to it and I've always explained it to parents, that that's the way I feel, and they can accept that and they will push to make sure that the children get to it.

She concludes: "So if they at least get the attitude that there are certain things that must be done — it may be a fact of life that we don't like it, but then everything else will work. It's self-discipline."

Mrs. B [M] puts the goals in organizational terms:

Most of the students in this class are identified as being anywhere from one to three years below grade level in reading and/or math. The class is primarily made up of black students. We have two Mexican-American students and six Anglos and one Indian. And you might think, "Gee, why do you think about that so much?" Well, at our school we are very concerned with numbers because, as you may be aware, the district schools have been involved in a lawsuit for the past number of years.

She expands on this legal and organizational situation:

We are a comp. ed., Title I school and we are receiving special moneys from the state. We entered into an agreement where we have a school plan — anytime you receive money there are strings, and one of the strings happens to be that we have a school plan — and we have pretty much written our whole program, curriculum in all areas, staff development, etc. It's covered in the school plan, so I always address that. Also, I make sure that all of my kids have been exposed, at least exposed, to mastering the minimum proficiencies before they go on to the next grade.

For these teachers, students succeed by "getting with the program," by "buckling down," and by "plugging away" at their schoolwork. The greatest mystery for the master teachers is that when you really expect more from students, even handicapped or squirrelly ones, they will do more.

The hardest thing about teaching, as these master teachers see it, is "getting to" the difficult kids. Mrs. A [M], quoted above, talks about this process as seeing a kid who has been "kind of squirrelly" starting to become academically responsible for his homework. Mrs. B [M] describes it as taking the "snottiest kid" and helping him or her to discover "self-worth" through the "joys of reading."

For Mrs. C [M], the special education resource teacher in this group, the tough cases which she takes pride in handling tend to be other teachers rather than students. In the following comments, she is declaring her own sense of mastery as much as reporting on her staff colleagues: "I love the people I work with, as far as the staff members here. Even the staff member that is tactless or the member who gripes."

This attitude is an important part of her work: "My responsibility is to the principal — to support him in the smooth running of the school. I help teachers in ordering supplies. I put in the instructional program those things that are needed to carry out mandates...I am a go-between [between the principal and the teachers].

As master teachers, the members of this group take pride in successfully handling difficult interpersonal problems. But they find it distasteful, and ultimately intolerable, if they do not get support from their principals. Mrs. A [M] told us the following:

> Had I not gotten interested in working for a principal who really supported me and liked me, I probably would have become a very discontented, burned-out person because I was getting to that point rapidly. I had been teaching eight years, and I had worked for a number of principals, many of whom were totally nonsupportive simply because I don't think they had the skills to work with people and to stroke them once in a while and say, "This is a nice thing that you are doing." And I felt like it did not really matter what I did. I was still considered "average," and I was getting rapidly burned out. Now with my newest job I find that I do see some of the people I work with that just work so hard and some who have either become, or maybe they always were, kind of negative or burned-out acting, and I really wish they would do themselves and the kids a favor and go into something else. I really am a firm believer, if you don't like what you are doing, get out, because it's so unfair to yourself and the people that you work with — and this is true for any profession, whether it's teaching or perhaps you work as a sales person — you have to like what you do or you will not be effective. It's hard though, sometimes, to really look at yourself and search yourself as to "Should I continue?" I think sometimes people get into teaching not realizing all of the ramifications.

She reaffirms the view that this problem of working relationships is an ongoing one for some teachers:

> So many teachers now in comp. ed. schools are becoming more program managers, where they are directly working with and responsible for several staff members...instructional aides, maybe parent volunteers. I think that for some teachers this is very

threatening — teachers who perhaps have always worked by themselves. Now, the teachers that have been hired more recently, and who have worked with comp. ed. schools, they are used to it. But I think that for teachers who have worked for a number of years in a solo classroom — I think they're glad for the help, yet it's also a scary thing because, whether you're good or not, until you develop a trust with the people you work with, who are in the classroom, it can be an intimidating thing.

Group 2. The Instructors

The three teachers who combine a commitment to achievement with an emphasis on teaching lessons are called the "instructors." These three teachers believe that the most fundamental teaching responsibility is the development and execution of lessons. They tend to be the loners whom Mrs. B [M] describes as "solo" teachers. They view teaching as a technically sophisticated, skilled craft, and believe that students learn through active engagement in intellectually stimulating activities.

Mr. D [I] offers the typical instructor's description of the wonderful mystery of student learning:

> Watching a child make a discovery is satisfying. They didn't exactly understand something and the excited voice of "Oh, now I understand!" is one of the most satisfying things for me. And I always try to remind myself that I really don't have much to do with it. It is a realization that comes upon them sort of on its own. You provide them with the materials and you build up the right climate for it to happen, but the learning takes place in their own mind. But it is neat being there at the time that you see it happen.

Mr. E [I] describes the instructor's view of success in terms of student "progress," which he says makes him "feel really good." Miss F [I], working with aphasic students, illustrates this group's intense concern with the specifics of children's achievement progress: "I work with students by arranging my priorities. It takes a long time for these students to learn something. For example, N...has been working on the clock for three days. She finally seems to have gotten it." Miss F then reiterates the main point for these instructors when she confesses: "I dread regression. I hope they remember what we learned yesterday."

For these teachers students will be successful if they are given learning activities which accurately match their needs. Miss F [I] illustrates the technical vocabulary with which the instructors tend to discuss this issue:

For this class, auditory problems prevail for all children. Some have severe memory problems. I look for the deficient area and teach to that. All of these kids have memory problems. All have low vocabulary. All have receptive and expressive problems. The non-verbal things tend to be most successful. It is the language factor that is the problem. I make curricular decisions based on several steps. First, I make a diagnosis, then prognosis, for example auditory discrimination. Like one child will never be a reader. From there you need to determine what the realistic expectation can be. Aphasic kids are successful in math. However, because the child is successful in that you can't just teach that.

Mr. E [I] tells us that it is this inventiveness which makes teaching fun.

The most important thing I teach is a little bit beyond just the curriculum. I think it's teaching kids to like themselves. I have one girl in the class who is shy and I am trying to bring her out of her shell. I try to do this by teasing her, trying to make her laugh a little bit and things like that. That is what I enjoy about teaching — the one thing that really makes it fun for me. If I had to come in and just teach, that would be it. I don't think I could handle it. I would not do it any more, it would not be any fun.

Remember that this is the remark of a dedicated achievement producer. He is not talking about viewing child nurture as the primary mission of the school. Rather, he is highlighting the instructors' penchant to be inventive and creative in their strategies for engaging children in the lesson activities which they believe will lead to the goal of high achievement.

Mr. D [I] links technique to social relationships:

How do you get kids to like learning? I think that the only way we can do it is by being an example of it. If you want the kids to like learning you have to like learning yourself. You have to be enthusiastic about what you are doing. If you are going to present a math lesson, and you absolutely hate math, and you get up to the board you are going to start hating what you are doing, they are going to see it. And it is going to be that way with anything you are doing. And I know from personal experience that a lot of elementary schoolteachers prefer reading or the language arts areas over math areas. Unfortunately, a lot of children end up with a proreading bias by the time they leave elementary school and a rather antimath bias, and I think that is tragic. I think in that respect we should either be nonbiased toward either, or biased toward both. Just be enthusiastic about everything.

Thus, for the instructors, the important thing is to get the kids turned on to learning by getting them engaged in activities which are both emotionally and intellectually geared to their needs.

The hardest part of this process — the one which is mastered only by the best instructors — is learning how to pace instructional activities properly. Miss F [I], who uses a system of learning contracts to individualize instructional activities for her special education students, says the following: "You have to have goals. The contracts seem to show that is required. For example N . . . can handle this. It's because they know they have a plan to follow. My hardest thing is to establish how much they can do. I still don't know the exact pace for all of my students.

Mr. D [I] sees the problem as one which could be addressed by effective in-service training programs:

> What I want in an in-service is something that I can bring directly back to the classroom and use. I want, maybe, a teacher to perform a science experiment bilingually and equip me with all of the terminology and all the apparatus used in the experiment and have it printed out. We will watch the experiment, maybe, jot down some stuff on the papers, on handouts that he or she has brought with them, and we will be able to come back and do it. That is the kind of thing I need.

Among these teachers, Mr. E [I] expresses the most confidence about his ability to appropriately pace his teaching:

> I have mastered the daily requirements of the work, I think, just by repetition. Just repetition. You do it long enough, pretty soon it becomes automatic. I think that I could probably — especially in the basic subjects — go through the school year without ever writing a lesson plan and still teach the basic subjects. I've seen those books so many times I almost have them memorized. I can sit down — I know about what page every kid is on — it just becomes automatic after a while. After you have done it for a while it is just something you pick up intuitively.

The instructors all agree that a good teacher has to be able to handle curricular materials competently so as to creatively structure and appropriately pace their lessons.

The persistently distasteful aspect of teaching for the instructor group is discipline. Mr. E [I] speaks for all of them:

> I hate disciplining. I don't like to discipline. It makes me crazy. I hate being confronted by kids that are belligerent — and that has happened two or three times since I have been here at this particular school. Certain kids just have a lot of problems and are belligerent and I don't like dealing with that. I would just as soon not have to do the discipline part. I am paid to teach. That is what I want to do. I want to teach all the kids.

Group 3. The Coaches

The third group in our sample consists of the four teachers who combine the child nurture mission of schooling with a belief that teaching lessons is the best strategy for pursuing that goal. These teachers see themselves as responsible for evoking learning responses from the children and tend to feel that being "with the children" as they explore new worlds is their most important contribution to the learning process. These teachers want to make classroom life exciting, challenging, and stimulating for the children. We have labeled these teachers the "coaches" because they move back and forth between imposing rigorous demands for student engagement and offering them warmth, encouragement, and a guiding hand.

Mrs. J [C] speaks for the group in the following statements: "I love teaching. I find it very rewarding. I find it rewarding emotionally and academically. Emotionally, I am happy when the children's personalities are clicking with mine. And academically, by watching the children progress." Mrs. I [C], who sees her work alternately as "taming young broncos" and grabbing the kids by the hand to "lead them through this tunnel" into a new world, celebrates her success in making emotional contact with fifth graders in the following words:

> Before I had a fifth-grade class I was used to being in a preschool, and you know how they would always hug you and they would grab you and, "Oh, teacher, look at this!" I was so used to that. And they said, "Oh, no, fifth graders won't do that." And I said, "Oh, wow! I am the kind of person that has to touch." And so, with last year's class I would not touch because I did not know them, but towards the middle and end of the year, they were coming up with hugs and just, "I think you are neat" and "How are you? Can I help you?" and just these little gestures. Even facial expressions, to me, meant, "Hey, I'm getting across to them."

These teachers speak of students being successful when students learn to "love," to "get along" socially, and to be "respectful" of others. Mrs. I [C], an Asian-American, says,

> The one thing that I want to get across to them is respect. I was brought up with that in my culture. Number one is respect, and if you have respect you can accomplish anything and everything. So, in our classroom it is a give and take kind of thing. Respect for each other and adults, parents, anyone that they come into contact with, because I felt that with the class I had last year ... boy they were bombed out and we really had to harp on this thing of respect. This year it is not so much, but that is not my bag. That is how I get to

them. My personality is loving, respect, love. And they all think love is — when I say, "Love," they go "Blahh." Now, that's not the love you are thinking about. Love isn't just holding hands, it could be saying "Hi! Good morning." So, this is how I just get down to the roots of things.

The coaches believe that kids are successful in classrooms where they are made to feel comfortable rather than pressured, and excited rather than bored. These teachers follow Mrs. J's [C] approach to lesson structure and development:

I feel that I have to start wherever the child is. I have been in classrooms where the material is too hard or it's too easy for a student. You can tell right before I ring the time, about three or four minutes before, they start moving around, they are done, they are ready to move. They have been there 20 minutes and so I feel that it's important to keep the level of teaching to the individual.

The most distasteful and persistent problems for these teachers are the distractions of useless meetings and paper work demands. Mrs. G [C] has the following to say:

I still love teaching — if that is what I get to do — when I'm with the children, which is what you saw me do today, that is what I love. I love it. But that is what I would like to do all the time. I don't like all these other things. Things that are going along with teaching, the mandated, the meetings, the writing, the records, all these things that we have to do without — all this writing down. It is taking a whole lot of time that could well be spent working with children. My feeling is that we have gotten away from the things that I feel a teacher should be doing, is meant to do — that is really being with children, working with children, preparing the children.

And the hardest thing about their work is the emotional energy it requires. Mrs. I [C] describes this problem:

It is very hard because it takes a lot out of you, and I am really dedicated. My aide tells me, "You go above and beyond." And I say, "I can't help it. That is how I am. I have to." Even if I have used my last ounce of strength I still crawl, I still go and I think my class knows this.

Mrs. I [C] is not suggesting that this emotional drain is destructive or unmanageable. Quite to the contrary, responding to the challenge to be emotionally available to the children is a measure of one's heroic stature as a teacher. All of the coaches like this emotional relationship with children. And all view it as a measure of their professional competence and dedication.

The mystery for these teachers is the growth process itself.

The children unfold before them. The "hormones" flow, "maturity" develops, and new abilities emerge from within the children. For the coaches, teaching is an art form. Children's emotions, attitudes, and abilities are molded and shaped as they learn to participate in the classroom culture and activity system of the school. The teachers direct and coordinate their activities, and call them to perform, but the accomplishments are the children's own.

Group 4. The Helpers

The last group of teachers in our sample are those who accept child nurture goals but adopt a school keeping strategy for teaching. As we noted earlier, this group is made up entirely of the weaker teachers in our sample. These teachers define their work roles as "helping" students to deal with the demands of schooling, which are equated with the demands of life.

Mr. K [H] summarizes this group's overall orientation when he says the following: "The most pleasant part of the work is being able to work with somebody that, maybe, I can help. I really like kids a lot." Mrs. N [H] affirms their nurturing orientation, saying "The most pleasant thing about teaching is the growth of children." Mrs. M [H] also affirms this helping orientation in the following comment: "I enjoy the interaction with the kids. I enjoy knowing I can positively influence some children. I expect to be doing this for about three years. Then I'll take off to have a baby. However, I'll return and I expect to stay in this field."

Mrs. L [H] merges the helping orientation with a commitment to keeping children engaged in the district's established curriculum: "Today we will work on spelling, we'll work in our spellers. We will have our test tomorrow, so I try to help them in any way they need to get through their spelling unit. Some of them are independent and can do it quickly, others need a lot of help." Finally, Mrs. O [H] reiterates this school-keeping emphasis on helping students to fit into preset curricular patterns:

> The class is varied, naturally. Some are very active and some are rather quiet. Some are well disciplined and some are not. I think they are nice students. Some have different problems. I can't diagnose their problems because I'm not a psychologist. So, I would not dare to start diagnosing their problems, but some seem to have some problems. I could not go into what their problems are. I work with them to the best of my know-how and try to get them to function as a student.

These teachers all believe that student success is measured by how well they "function as a student." They often speak about students performing "up to grade level," and affirm, with Mrs. L [H], that if kids were screened and grouped according to their test scores, the job would be easier.

> This would make my job more rewarding. I would have children who could understand what they are supposed to do at the third-grade level. It would make every teacher — do more, not in a total group, as I said, but you could at least subgroup with the feeling of some success in doing it. As it is now, in this "One to Grow On" group I have one third grader in the second-grade group, and she was the diehard. She can do the work, but she is just an antsy, hyper type kid and school is the last thing on her mind.

The helpers are generally suspicious that a substantial number of their students are either unwilling or unable to cope with the schooling program. For them, the most persistent and distasteful problem in teaching is the number of children who are resistive and noncooperative. Mrs. M [H] says the following of her learning handicapped class: "Almost half of them don't want to be here. They want to play. Basically they don't want to work. It takes thinking and work and they don't want to do it." Mrs. L [H] has the following insight: "The children are more alert in the morning hours than in the afternoon. Because, generally in the afternoon, they are just about exhausted, tired, so that I feel that their minds are fresher in the morning. More time would be on actual work in the morning hours when they are more alert and their minds are fresh and they are not tired." She goes on to say that her ability to teach is limited by the student's capacity to participate:

> Part of it depends on, I guess, the children and their application. When they are "with it" we accomplish more. The days that we've got an itchy or crabby or a tired, or even the days when I burn out, we don't get much covered. But I think that because I am trying to build on their own work they persevere, they "hang in" there for a couple of days and still catch up on the things they need to do.

Mrs. M [H], a special education teacher by her own choice, nevertheless says the following: "Teaching is rough. I've wondered what I'm doing. When you see children learning you don't feel the same way. You see, the children have to have behavioral problems to be in here. The biggest problem I dread is a behavior problem."

For these teachers, the hardest thing is to get the classroom organized and running smoothly. Mrs. O [H] finds that classrooms are "overcrowded," that reading levels are too disparate, and that even her blackboards are inadequate, forcing her to use newsprint papers instead. Mrs. N [H] attributes her organizational difficulties to the changing times: "I like working with kids. Once I quit working, but returned during the same year. It is harder than it used to be. Maybe it's because of the parents. You feel pressures. Today there are too many. Last year it seemed that we were continuously testing."

For these teachers, there is little wonder and mystery in the learning process. It is more a matter of routine, almost dull, a matter of plodding through the curriculum and trying to reach the kids with what they need to pass tests and move along through the school program. Mrs. L [H] even says the following:

> I guess one of the things that goofs me up is that I try to respond to every child on a different chord and that is hard. I think that is one of the things that wears me thin, because I know some children's situations are very difficult and I know that they live in a hard situation. And therefore, while I want them to learn for their sake, I don't feel that they need to be pushed or shoved any more. Because they are shoved by life, where their parents are stuck.

She continues:

> I'll tell you honestly, I feel that we are not reaching children. I have all the misgivings parents have about the schools today. It is not that the teachers are not working, but it seems that — I don't know — it seems that administrators and supervisors push all of the superficial things and the actual basic working with kids things are the things that are last on the agenda. Now, maybe I am wrong about that.

The closest thing to wonder we hear from the helpers is Mrs. N [H]'s following statement: "Sometimes kids come up to you, as one girl did recently, and say, 'I love you like my grandmother.'" When these teachers do experience mystery, it is usually in the form of someone appreciating their efforts. Apparently they feel most of the time that they are not likely to be appreciated for the work they do. And, of course, we found that they are not generally appreciated as competent teachers by either their principals or their fellow teachers.

SUMMARY AND CONCLUSION

In this chapter the work orientations and incentive systems of fifteen teachers have been examined. These teachers were found to be clustered into four basic orientational groups. The first group, consisting of teachers A, B, and C, holds the view that "producing achievement" is the school's primary mission and "keeping school" is the appropriate work style for pursuing that goal. They manifest this work orientation by defining their role as "master teachers." Bringing students "up to grade level" is their primary goal. The mark of excellence in teaching, for this group, is bringing this about in "tough kids."

Group 2, consisting of teachers D, E, and F, shares the first group's commitment to producing achievement but relies on "teaching lessons" as the primary work style for pursuing this goal. As "instructors" they place primary emphasis on executing excellent lessons. Described as "solo" teachers because of the performance characteristic of their lessons, they adopt the most technical view of their work and expect high achievement from children.

Group 3, consisting of teachers G, H, I, and J, relies on the teaching of lessons to pursue the goal of "child nurture" or development. As "coaches" they seek to evoke or educe performance and social skills from children. These teachers concentrate on providing stimulating classrooms for their students. They also strive to be emotionally available to their students and view this availability as a mark of great teaching.

The fourth group, teachers K, L, M, N, and O, use the school-keeping strategy in an effort to stimulate child nurturance. These "helpers" make up the weakest group of teachers in our sample. They attempt to follow district curricular guidelines in the conduct of their work. Believing that learning is to be evoked from children, but still tending not to initiate activities for their students, these teachers are most likely to feel that children are difficult to organize and to teach.

CHAPTER IV

Teaching Lessons: The Cultural Enterprise of the Classroom

From a cultural perspective, the defining features of schooling are embodied in the conduct of lessons. Lessons are the unique and universal cultural activities to be found in all schools, and only in schools. More precisely, if lessons are encountered in any other social institution or context, they are interpreted as "like being in school" or "playing school" and are referred to school experiences for interpretation and evaluation. It is within the enactment of lessons that the social purposes of schooling are defined and the interpersonal relationships among teachers and students meaningfully structured.

It is, of course, true that both children and teachers engage in many other activities while at school. These other activities are, however, always problematic. They are perpetually, and appropriately, in need of justification (or criticism) on the basis of whether they support or interfere with the conduct of lessons, which are the ultimate raison d'être of school life. (Some cynics might argue that schools exist to provide child care or group play opportunities in an advanced industrial society. Such a view receives absolutely no support among the participants in this study, however, and will not be taken seriously here.)

To assert that lessons are the defining cultural events of the school is to infer that they perform the two basic functions of a culture identified by Winter (1966): (1) defining the collective project or mission of schooling, and (2) providing the typifications of action and norms of behavior needed to create meaningful interpersonal relationships. In specifying the purposes of classroom life, lessons provide teachers (and students) with organization-level, purposive incentives for participation in the school. And in generating shared meanings and social norms, lessons provide group-level solidary incentives for those who participate within them. Thus it is through the development and enactment of lessons that teachers concretely experience these basic work incentives.

Moreover, as we have previously observed, distribution of the most potent rewards for teachers (student achievement and student warmth) is controlled largely by the effectiveness with which they are able to engage students in lesson activities. Several researchers have dealt with lessons as theoretical units. In this chapter we will draw heavily upon Mehan's (1979) theoretical framework to analyze classroom lesson structures among the fifteen teachers in our sample. Our analysis is divided into two parts. First, we examine the basic structural characteristics of all lessons — identifying the universal or archetypical elements that underlie successful lessons and the distinguishing features of four basic lesson types found in the data. Once these structural characteristics have been described, we will examine the relationship between individual teacher work orientations and their approach to the development and enactment of lessons. This analysis reveals that members of each of the four basic work orientation groups described in Chapter III (master teachers, instructors, coaches, and helpers) share common views regarding the nature of lessons.

LESSON STRUCTURES: ARCHETYPES AND VARIATIONS

Classrooms are crowded, turbulent, complex social systems (Jackson, 1968). Traditionally, classrooms have been largely self-contained social systems consisting of a single adult and many children (Waller, 1932; Parsons, 1959). Most analysts have recognized that this structure strongly influences the events that transpire within them. Dreeben (1970, p. 51) offers the typical view when he says teachers are divided "into isolated classrooms, each containing an aggregate of pupils (from about ten to fifty at the extreme, and averaging near thirty) under the direction of one teacher." He concludes that "this fact in itself determines much of what happens in schools."

The frequency with which more than one adult is present in the classroom has increased greatly during the past two decades. At the same time, the isolation of the classroom group has been significantly reduced by the development of specialized programs which temporarily bring new participants into the classroom or take some (or perhaps all) of the regular students out of the classroom group.

Within this context of crowded complexity, frequent interruption, and potential competition for leadership, teachers are required to establish meaningful cultural systems which can guide student participation and enable them to realize educational goals. The critical ingredient in this process, as Dreeben (1970, p. 83) and Smith and Geoffrey (1968, p. 68) have recognized, is the creation of a set of beliefs — beliefs which make it seem natural for the teachers to give directions and the pupils to follow them. It is essential that these beliefs, and the behavioral rules which they support, like all cultural systems, be largely tacit rather than explicit. Otherwise, the cultural system loses its power to stimulate, guide, or inspire spontaneous cooperation and degenerates into a coercive and alien environment.

Mehan (1979) provides a cultural framework for interpreting typical teacher-led lessons. He refers to them as "speech events," and describes four elements which govern their development: (1) the child must respond appropriately in time and form, (2) the child must respond correctly in content, (3) the activity must provide for the child to be less frequently sanctioned over time, and (4) the child must gradually become more successful in initiating the sequences of interaction (verbal and otherwise). As can be seen, these elements are grounded in certain fundamental assumptions. First, they presume that the school is a cultural milieu into which the participants are continuously and precariously socialized. Second, they identify classroom management and lessons as closely interdependent processes. Third, they presuppose that classroom management is intentional. The classroom management aspects of this cultural system will be described in Chapter V. The remainder of this chapter examines how the cultural milieu of typical lessons evolves and how it expresses basic teacher work orientations.

In specifying the context in which lessons and classroom management processes occur, Cazden (in Mehan, 1979, p. x) states the following: "None of the participants in the lesson knew the structure explicitly, the children had to learn it as they learn language, without explicit tuition. As with language, they learned more than anyone could have explicitly taught. This is the kind of subtle progress during the year that a teacher can rarely hear for herself."

There is another reason why lessons have special significance to teachers. Lessons are the vehicle through which the teaching role is enacted. Lesson structures, therefore, determine whether teachers will perceive their work as presenting opportunities for self-fulfillment or demands for self-denial or even self-destruction.

What does a lesson structure consist of? First, it provides for the sequential organization of teacher and student behavior; that is, the flow of the lesson unfolds through time from a beginning to an ending. Second, there is a hierarchical organization within which the lesson is assembled from its component parts — from the most important to the least important elements. Third, interaction sequences are tied together by reflexive structures (Mehan, 1979, pp. 75-76) in such a way that the actions of one member of the class call forth responses from the others. For example, typical teacher elicitations and student responses are reflexively structured. They are tied together by teacher evaluation processes to form one complete unit of interaction.

Mehan, looking at teacher-led lessons, suggested that lessons have five basic structural components. They begin with a set of unique interaction activities aimed at separating the lesson proper from other classroom events. This "demarcation" activity is required to "set up" the lesson. Once the lesson is set up, it is organized sequentially into an opening phase, an instructional phase, and a closing phase. Since activities within each of these phases are given formal and frequently symbolic meanings, there are distinctive ritual components within each of these phases.

The ritualistic character of the early phases of the lesson clarifies the meaning and intended sequence of events within the lesson proper so that students are able to focus their attention on the central instructional phase. Not only are the demarcations which set lessons apart from other classroom activities generally ritualized, but to a lesser extent so are the opening and closing phases of the lesson itself.

The demarcation rituals usually involve obvious physical movements or specific teacher remarks. The function of these demarcations is to indicate the end of one lesson or activity or the start of another. The opening and closing phases of the lesson are directive or informative: that is, during these phases, the teacher either directs the students (to open their books, for example) or provides them with information (about main topics covered in the lesson, for example, or procedures to be used in formulating their responses). These phases serve to prepare students for the instructional phase, and to bring it to a close.

Once the opening is completed, the instructional phase begins. This phase involves an interaction sequence between the teacher and the student. The lesson closes with a similar directive or informative ritual. Finally, an ending demarcation ritually separates the lesson from subsequent classroom activity. Figure IV-1 graphically depicts the flow of these events.

Figure IV-I

LESSON STRUCTURES ACROSS TIME

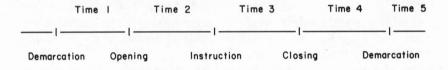

Mehan's (1979) work was devoted entirely to teacher-led verbal lessons. The fifteen teachers in our study used three additional types of lessons: (1) activity lessons, (2) drill and practice lessons, and (3) test lessons. As described more fully below, all four of these lesson types embody the same five-part structure; that is, each consists of a core sequence of instructional activities surrounded by an opening and closing and set apart from other classroom activities by beginning and ending demarcation rituals.

Before examining in detail each structural element of a typical lesson, it might be well to look at a few examples in which all of the structural components appear as an integrated whole.

The Teacher-Led Verbal Lesson

The following sequence, taken from our field notes of December 3, 1980 on a fifth-grade spelling lesson, contains all of the elements of a teacher-led lesson in nearly ideal or typical form. We pick up the observation protocol as the teacher, Mr. E [I], is out of the room escorting a group of students to the math lab.

TIME 1
BEGINNING
DEMARCATION

8:55 A.M. The aide is in the room and walks from the back of the room, stopping at the left side of the room to observe for a moment and then walks to the front. She does not need to say anything. She just observes. The students, in a fairly orderly manner have gotten out their spelling books and get to work. It is quiet in here. Mr. E returns.

TIME 2
OPENING
DIRECTIVE

Mr. E [I]: "You need to open to page 34. I want everyone to put their finger on the first word, look at it, and then look away. Make your mind work just like a camera and make a mental picture of the word."

TIME 3
INSTRUCTION
BEGINS

Mr. E [I]: "Let's begin." The first word is *less*. They go through the group of words and spell them out in unison. Mr. E talks in terms of consonant clusters and diagraphs. They are on the word *rush*. Mr. E [I]: "This has a consonant diagraph. What is it?" The class responds, "sh." Mr. E turns to the blackboard. Mr. E [I]: "Remember, there are three main diagraphs, *sh*, and *ch*." He writes them on the board. Mr. E [I]: "Okay, let's go on."
ADDITIONAL INSTRUCTION FOLLOWS FOR SEVERAL MINUTES. (It will be examined below.)

TIME 4
CLOSING
DIRECTIVE

Mr. E [I]: "I want you to write an original sentence for each word on your dictation sheet. You need to take them home tonight and study. You also need to do your handwriting assignment on page ???. Some of you are having a problem with the letter *a*. It is looking like a *u*." He shows them how to make it and says what he is doing as he does it.

TIME 5
ENDING
DEMARCATION

9:25 A.M. Mr. E [I] turns to the fifth graders. Mr. E [I]: "Fifth graders you need to take your spelling books out, please."

In this classroom, the starting demarcation ritual was well established. The aide had only to make her presence obvious for students to know that lessons were about to begin. As soon as Mr. E returned from escorting a group of children to the math lab, everyone in the classroom knew that a lesson was about to begin. The ritualized opening phase of the lesson was also easily recognized by all participants. In this well-organized classroom, opening rituals were frequently reduced to a single sentence with such widely recognized phrases as "open to page 34."

Once lessons are under way, the primary activity is the exchange of academic information. The instructional phase is structured into three recurring parts: elicitation, response, and evaluation. The teacher initiates, the student responds, and the teacher evaluates. The following excerpt is taken from the midsection of the instructional phase of the lesson presented above.

TIME 3
INSTRUC-
TIONAL PHASE

Elicitation	Mr. E [I]: "These words have a long vowel sound. What is it?"
Response	"ea. The e is long."
Evaluation	Mr. E [I]: "right."

This sequence — elicitation, response, evaluation — is repeated again and again as the lesson moves through various materials. The student's replies are evaluated as "right" only if they are properly timed and correct in both form and content.

The Activity Lesson

Before presenting an example of an activity lesson, two additional analytic concepts — *disruption* and *extension* — must be introduced. One of the ways in which our work differs significantly from Mehan (1979) is the frequency with which our teachers were forced to deal with substantial disruptions of their intended lesson structures. Mehan studied the work of highly trained, specially competent teachers engaged in time-bounded experimental teaching activities. Our teachers represent a broad range of skills, training, and experience levels and were not asked to alter their daily routine in any way for our benefit. We were especially impressed by the vulnerability of our teachers to both internal and external disruptions by events which were unpredictable and difficult to control. We found remarkably few lessons which proceeded as smoothly as Mr. E [I]'s presentation of diagraphs to fourth and fifth graders.

The second new concept, *extension*, refers to the fact that teachers frequently extend the directions or the information provided to students at the beginning of the lesson, altering either the focus of the lesson or the basis on which students are expected to respond when elicited. (Mehan treats this notion of extension, but he does not seem to recognize that extensions are — in both form and function — extensions of the opening phase of the lesson.)

The following lesson, an activity involving getting and reading library books in Mr. D [I]'s second-grade classroom, illustrates how disruptions and extensions complicate typical elementary school classroom processes. Mr. D [I]'s beginning demarcation, as is so often the case, involves physical movement. We pick up the observational protocol at 10:38 A.M., just as morning recess is ending. Mr. D [I] elicits information, and the children respond.

TIME 1	
BEGINNING DEMARCATION	The children line up and walk into the room. "Is Miss Claire here today?" a student asks. "Yes," Mr. D [I] responds.
TIME 2	
OPENING	"When we go in, put your library books on the top of your desks and then go sit on the rug."
Disruption	"Richie, you chose not to be able to sit there on the rug because you moved...Where is Sandra?" A student: "She just left." Mr. D [I]: "Was that she who just went out the door?" The child nods "yes."
TIME 3	
INSTRUCTION	Teacher addresses one of the tables in the classroom.
Elicitation	"Let's start with that table over there."
Response	The children at that table get their books and go to the library.
Disruption	"Do you have any reason for hitting Sarah? Are you Sorry?" Student: "I am sorry. I was just playing."
Elicitation	Mr. D [I] reads one of the library books that is going to be returned. He also shows them the pictures. "What is Gordon?"
Response	"He looks like a bear."

Elicitation	The story is read.
Response	A student asks, "Would you read my book, Mr. D [I]?"
Extension	"This is a Walt Disney story. This is a section of a bigger story."
Elicitation	"OK, let's try this table, quietly."
Response	They go to the library. The children are coming back from the library, and they have put their new books on the tables and then sit down on the rug again. When they sit down, they make sure they do not block someone else's view.
Elicitation	Mr. D [I] finishes reading the Bambi book.
Response	A child gives him his new book.
Elicitation	"How many children are left in the library?"
Response	"Three."
Elicitation	"OK, you may go now."
Evaluation	To the student with the new book: "I will not read any Christmas ones yet." The student has responded inappropriately and the teacher corrects the response.
Elicitation	Mr. D [I] takes up another book. "This one doesn't have very many words in it so you will have to look at the pictures very carefully." [He hands the book to our observer to look at.]
Elicitation	Mr. D [I] reads another book. "Can you see?" he asks the class.
Response	They say they can see it OK,
Elicitation	and he reads and shows it to them. A student asks, "Will you read my book?"
Evaluation	"Is it a Christmas book?" "Yes." "I will read Christmas books after Thanksgiving."
Response	"How about *Gregory*?"

TIME 4

CLOSING	"OK, but it is long and we may not have time to finish it." The children enjoy the reading of *Gregory*.

TIME 5

ENDING DEMARCATION	"Veronica, take the math cards around please."

Activity lessons are particularly vulnerable to the disruptions encountered by Mr. D [I] in the above example. Children are much more likely to break with behavioral norms during an activity than when participating in a verbal lesson. They frequently develop their own goals for participation and attach their own meanings to them.

Nevertheless, Mr. D [I]'s use of the library activity follows the same basic structure as Mr. E [I]'s diagraph lesson. First, a demarcation ritual signals that it's time to "get to work." Then, the activity opens with directions telling the students what is going to happen and how they are expected to behave. During the lesson proper, the teacher elicits student engagement and expression. These elicitations are followed by student responses and, ordinarily, by teacher evaluation of those responses. In the case of activity lessons, the elicitations generally call for nonverbal student responses.

Activities are differentiated from teacher-led verbal lessons in the frequency with which they require extensions of the opening in the form of new directions or new information. Activity lessons, like their verbal counterparts, have a closing which signals the end of the lesson and focuses the students' attention on its meaning or purpose. An ending demarcation ritual releases students from an obligation to participate in the activity and signals a transition to a new lesson.

The Drill and Practice Lesson

The third type of lesson enacted by teachers in our sample is the drill and practice lesson. Lessons of this type differ from teacher-led verbal lessons in that the teacher presumes that the students know what responses are required of them and the proper form to use in order to obtain positive teacher evaluations. Drill and practice lessons are aimed at improving the speed and accuracy of student responses — not at formulating original behaviors.

In the following example, Mrs. N [H] demonstrates that even a stylized drill and practice session, paced by means of a phonograph, must incorporate the basic structural elements of all lessons. It is 10:33 A.M. on a morning in November, and the protocol for Mrs. N [H]'s observation reads as follows.

TIME 1

BEGINNING	The children have come in from recess and sit
DEMARCATION	down at their tables. They have pencils in their hands and paper in front of them.

TIME 2

OPENING   Mrs. N [H] says, "Number your papers from 1 to 25."

Disruption   "Lucy, don't you go to reading now? Janice, Mrs. Travis will work with you."

TIME 3

INSTRUCTION

Elicitation   Mrs. N [H] has put a math record on which is giving the children math addition problems $(6+8=, 7+5=, \text{etc.})$.

Disruption   Mrs. N [H] says to our observer: "They have to pass adding and subtracting on a timed basis to get out of their grade, so we use records. They are dictated 4 1/2 seconds apart. Daisy has been here only two weeks so she is having to get used to this."

Elicitation   She repeats the record and says, "You can check and see if you got them all right, and fill in any you did not get.

Extension   Then we will check them." The record tells them to stop and put their pencils down. There are 25 problems.

Elicitation   The record says, "Get set for the answers. Here we go ... No. 4 is 11, No. 5 is 18, etc."

Extension   Mrs. N [H] puts addition problems on the board while they are correcting $(56+39, 76+37, 62+78, \text{etc.})$.

Elicitation   "Now count the right answers and put the number on the top of the page."

Response   "I got them all the first time."

Evaluation   "That's good. That's much better than you used to do."

Elicitation   "Now we will have a three-second drill. I will give you three times on the record."

Response   "Oh, Oh," comes from the class.

Extension   "When we finish the addition then we will do the subtraction."

Response   "Oh, Oh, Oh."

Elicitation   "Number 1 to 25 on the other side of the paper. Ready?"

Evaluation   Mrs. N [H] walks around to see how they are doing. Working at this speed has confused many of them and they are doing less well this time. They are being allowed three chances,

however, and for some it makes a positive
difference.

Elicitation   "Get set for the answers."

Response   "I got them all right!" "I missed only one
                       wrong."

TIME 4

CLOSING   "Put the paper in your desk. Put your crayons
                       in your desk."

TIME 5

ENDING   Referring to the work Mrs. N [H] has put on
DEMARCATION   the board, one student asks, "Are we going to
                       have to write it all down?" [The class then
                       begins new work based on Mrs. N [H]'s board
                       assignment.]

In this drill and practice lesson, as in most such lessons, speed
and accuracy are not enough. Students are also closely monitored
to ensure that they follow proper form — starting and stopping as
directed, numbering their answers, checking for errors, and record-
ing the results at the top of the page. These students are not only
practicing their math; they are also practicing the process of having
the quality of their work evaluated and recorded. Such practice
prepares them for the fourth type of lesson — the test.

Tests as Lessons

Generally speaking, the observation protocols written during
test episodes are brief and sparse in detail. Despite this brevity,
however, test taking is easily recognized as a lesson structure,
regularly embodying all but one of the basic elements found in
other lessons. The exception is in the evaluation of student
responses. This activity is typically postponed until the end of the
lesson, and may be delayed for a much longer period. The delay in
evaluation is more than offset, however, by its heightened saliency.
Students generally recognize that evaluation of their responses is
especially important during test lessons.

The following test-taking episode, observed in Mrs. A [M]'s
fourth-fifth-grade classroom, is typical of this type of lesson.

TIME 1

BEGINNING
DEMARCATION   "Fifth graders,

TIME 2

OPENING   we are going to do your spelling test. Charles, pass out the papers, please. Number your papers from 1 to 20. Fourth graders, I'll get to you in a moment."

TIME 3
INSTRUCTION

Elicitation   Mrs. A [M] dictates the words; "...Number 6 is *fetch*. He asked his dog to fetch the bone." She dictates the spelling in that fashion. Gives the word and then gives a sentence which contains the word.

Disruption   A child enters the room and hands Mrs. A [M] a note. "OK, get your stuff," she responds. The child gets her things and leaves the room.

Response   After the last word a child raises his hand.
Elicitation   "Charles?"
Response   Charles asks Mrs. A [M], "May I collect the papers?"
Extension   Mrs. A [M] responds, "Not yet. Let's see if there are any questions."
Elicitation   She allows for questions

TIME 4
CLOSING   and then says, "OK, Charles, you can collect the papers now."

TIME 5
ENDING   She then turns to say to the fourth graders,
DEMARCATION   "Fourth graders, get your papers ready."

The examples presented above illustrate the four basic lesson structure types (teacher-led verbal, activity, drill and practice, and tests). As these examples suggest, the typical lesson in each type involves a sequence of five structural elements. The five elements — beginning demarcation, opening, lesson proper, closing, and ending demarcation — define the classroom culture and provide meaningful ways for students and teachers to interact within it. In this way, lessons create classroom incentive systems. At the organizational level, they embody the purposive character of classroom participation. And at the group process level, they provide the basic vehicles for creating group membership or solidarity.

In addition to identifying the basic structural components of all lessons, the samples presented above indicate that lesson structures are frequently complicated by disruptions and extensions. Internal or external disruptions threaten the integrity of the lesson, while extensions elaborate, enhance, redirect, or reorganize its core sequence of teacher-pupil interactions.

Of course, in asserting that the archetypical lesson contains each of the five basic structural elements (often modified by disruption and extension), we do not mean to suggest that all teachers always succeed in incorporating each element. To the contrary, we found that lessons are frequently deficient in one or more structural element. By looking at the data from our teachers, however, it can easily be seen that these deviations from the archetypical form threaten the integrity of the lesson and thus weaken the classroom culture. Generally this weakness encourages student disruptions and confronts teachers with disciplinary problems which otherwise would not arise.

BASIC ELEMENTS OF THE LESSON STRUCTURE

In the next few pages we examine in greater detail the form and function of each element in the lesson structure. By looking at both successful and unsuccessful examples, it is possible to see what contribution each element makes to the classroom culture and to recognize the alternative forms of each.

Beginning Demarcations

One nearly universal characteristic of the school which is often remarked upon by visitors is the tolling or ringing of bells. To signal the start of the school day, a bell is rung across the campus. Hearing the bell alerts everyone that the school day has begun. Regular participants in the school rarely remark on it; their usual response is simply to move to the appropriate work place. If they ignore the sound of the bell, however, the school routine is generally disrupted. A group's failure to respond to the bell signals a serious breakdown in the social system of the school. If individual children fail to respond, they are viewed as being personally deviant and in need of correction.

The bell is the ultimate example of a demarcation ritual — signaling the start of something different. It says, "We are now in school," or, "It's time to change activities." Demarcation takes many forms beside the ringing of bells. Physical movement from one location to another by either the teacher or the students is often used to separate lessons. Changing books (for example, from a math book to a speller) serves a similar function. In Mrs. A's testing lesson, described above, demarcation was reduced to two words.

When she said "Fifth graders," she signaled the onset of the lesson and focused their attention on upcoming activities.

Normally, demarcation periods are short; they serve only as transitional phases. Since demarcations produce no instruction, they are more effective when they are highly ritualized and nonverbal. The following are examples of effective demarcation rituals.

In Mr. D [I]'s second-grade class, following the pledge to the flag:

"Don't get any books. We are going to get into our groups."

In Mrs. B [M]'s fifth-sixth-grade room:

Mrs. B [M] writes on the blackboard: "If you are reading this do the following: 1. Tidy Up! 2. Get things out for U.S.S.R. 3. Heads down!" Those who look to see what she is writing follow the directions immediately. Those still deeply immersed in their work do not but they are soon nudged by their classmates.

In Mrs. G [C]'s kindergarten class:

"Now let's see who is sitting up nice and straight before we have the musical instruments." [Observer: You could hear a pin drop now.]

In Mrs. I [C]'s fifth-grade room:

A student passed out work sheets to the class while Mrs. I [C] talked. Mrs. I [C] is now writing on the board and the children have moved around to various parts of the room. They are moving into work and reading groups.

As these examples suggest, a beginning demarcation serves two basic functions. it synchronizes students' behavior and focuses their attention on the upcoming lesson.

Not all demarcation rituals succeed in performing these two functions. Every teacher occasionally fails to get some students to attend to the demarcation ritual. When that happens, the missed students generally do not fully engage in the lesson and tend to become disruptive. A good example of this occurrence was seen in Mrs. L [H]'s classroom.

Attempted demarcation	Lunch is over. The children return to the room. Mrs. L [H] stands in the front of the room. She has written material on the board.
Attempted opening	"All right, children, we have one of our states on the board. We will read it and then copy it. We will have just enough time to do it before

New demarcation
we go home." Some children are still outside eating their ice cream. Mrs. L [H] herds them into the room.
"Everyone sit down."
Two further disruptions occur. After several minutes the class begins to discuss the information that Mrs. L [H] has written on the board.

Sometimes teachers succeed in synchronizing children's behavior but are not able to direct their attention to the lesson because the demarcation ritual is flawed. Mrs. N [H] illustrates this problem in the following episode.

The children are returning to the classroom from recess period. "Lay your heads down." Mrs. N [H] turns off the lights. There's a bit of small talk going on. "Barton, is that your voice I hear?" Another student responds, "Barton is crying, teacher." Duane, another student, was hurt at recess. His classmates are concerned and curious. Mrs. N [H] says: "Mr. Q is taking care of it. We don't need to be concerned." She did not try to find out why Barton was crying. "Shh." The children haven't quite quieted down and she says "Shh" a number of times. She is talking about ordinal numbers today. "I want ten good citizens at the board."

When starting demarcations are unsuccessful, lessons are postponed or abandoned altogether. When ritualization is inadequate, teachers must spend valuable time gaining students' attention with elaborate, self-conscious, but noninstructional activities.

Lesson Openings

The second structural element in a lesson is the opening. As noted earlier, openings orient students to the lesson proper by providing needed information or giving directions. The information and directions provided serve any or all of three distinct functions. First, they can orient students to the subject matter to be covered and procedures to be used in presenting the lesson. For example, at one point Mrs. N [H] says the following: "Let's look up here at the board. We are going to do some alphabetizing." In so doing, she is both directing and informing the students about the lesson procedures. A second function often served by the opening is to inform the students about how they are to respond during the lesson proper. Mrs. J [C] illustrates this function when she opens an activity lesson with the following: "Center 2, you have been working on your squirrels and some of the work is really pretty.

You have extra time to get it done today. Use your heads and think. Don't do just as your neighbor does." So does Mrs. L [H] when she says: "All right children, we have one of our states on the board. We read it and then copy it." The third function served by the information and directions provided in the opening is to let the students know the basis on which their responses will be evaluated once the lesson is under way. This function is being carried out, for example, when Mrs. B [M] opens a math lesson with the following: "Not only will you be graded on the right answers, but you will be graded on getting right letters in this name. [Sometimes] you get the right answers but you don't get the letters in the right place."

If both the starting demarcation and the lesson opening have been successful, children *disappear as individuals* with unique needs, meaning systems, and ways of acting. They then reappear in the teacher's perceptual field as *students* — playing a prescribed role in which their every action can be interpreted as an indication of whether or not they are successfully learning the lesson which is being taught. Once the lesson proper begins, teachers find individual student needs or demands for attention to be disruptive. They look upon any failure of the student to understand what is called for or to respond correctly in both form and content to be either a sign of nonlearning or of disengagement from the lesson.

The Lesson Proper

As suggested earlier, the lesson proper consists of one or more complete interaction sequences involving teacher elicitation, student response, and teacher evaluation of that response. Each of the three elements in this sequence appears in a variety of forms.

Elicitations

Mehan (1979) identifies four types of elicitations in the teacher-led lessons: choice, product, process, and metaprocess. Our data reveal that teachers regularly elicit at least two additional types of students responses: curiosity and confirmation of the behavior of other students. The following are examples of each of these six types of teacher elicitations.

First, there is the *choice elicitation*: a request by the teacher for students to agree or disagree with a statement or to pick the right answer from among several options presented to them. This process was exemplified in Mr. E [I]'s protocol.

Choice elicitation:	Mr. E [I]: "In the first ten words you are looking for words with the *ch* sound. What is

	this sound called? We had it this morning in spelling. It is a diagraph."
Student choice reply:	Mr. E [I] reads the words out loud. They say "Yes" or "No" to each word. Some do have the ch and some do not.

Mr. E [I]'s evaluation in this instance takes a novel turn:

Teacher evaluation:	He goes over words No. 11 to 20. At No. 17, he gave them a nonsense word. They said "No" and then looked at him as if he was crazy. Mr. E [I] said, "No, you are right. That is not a word and it is not there in the list."

Mehan's second type of elicitation is a *product* elicitation. This is when a factual response (such as a name, place, date, color, or other information item) is sought from the student. For example, in Mr. E [I]'s morning lesson the following exchange occurs.

Product elicitation:	Mr. E [I]: "If you want to show real emphasis, what mark do you use?"

Student response:	"An exclamation point."

In this case, Mr. E [I]'s evaluation was nonverbal — he merely went on with the lesson while nodding approval of the response.

A *process* elicitation, as described by Mehan, asks for respondents' opinions or interpretations about the form of the lesson.

Process elicitation:	Mr. E [I]: "How many people think they understand what we have been doing?"
Student response:	Most think they do.
Teacher evaluation:	Mr. E [I]: "I will give you the assignment and will let you see if you do. If you have any problem, come running up and I will give you help."

Mehan gives the name *metaprocess* to those elicitations which ask for the students to describe the basis for previous responses or the grounds of their reasoning. For example:

Product elicitation:	Mr. E [I]: "Do not look at your book. What does this word sound like?"

Student response:	The students respond, "Peak."
Metaprocess elicitation:	Mr. E [I]: "How do you know that?"
Student response:	A student answers, "It has a long vowel sound."
Teacher evaluation:	Mr. E [I]: "You guys did very well on that. Very well."

Among the teachers we observed, we found frequent use of elicitations aimed at getting students fully engaged in the lesson. These elicitations, frequently nonverbal, arise through activities or events within the classroom. We came to call them "curiosity elicitations." In Mrs. G [C]'s room, for example, one child, whose father works in a dental lab, was encouraged to share a set of laboratory teeth with the class. The other children, intrigued by the realism and variety of the teeth, asked: "Where did you get them?" "Are they real?" and "Do we only get one?" Another example came from Mr. E [I]'s class, where children were encouraged to express and explore their curiosity about election processes and meanings as they undertook to hold a mock election coinciding with the national election.

The last of the six basic types of elicitations found in our data arises when teachers ask children to judge each other's activities or previous responses. Mrs. H [C], for example, elicits *confirmation* in a reading lesson when, after asking a child to take a word from a word chart, she says the following:

Product elicitation:	"You look at it and tell us what you think it is. Then you put it back into the chart. You may choose any word you like." The first child takes a word and tells the class what it is.
Student response:	"It is tied."
Confirmation elicitation:	Mrs. H [C] says, "See if everyone agrees." To a particular child, "Do you agree with her?"
Confirming student response:	"Yes."
Teacher evaluation:	"Alright, you can put it back in the chart."
Product elicitation:	To another child, who has taken a second word, "You tell us what you think it is."
Student response:	The child responds.
Confirmation elicitation:	Mrs. H [C], "Is she right?"

Confirming *student response:*	"Yes."
Product elicitation:	To another student, "It is now your turn to choose."
Student response:	"Duck."
Confirmation elicitation:	"You show it and see if they agree."
Confirming student response:	The child does so. The class indicates agreement.
Teacher evaluation:	"That's right? No, I don't think it is."
Confirmation elicitation:	"Look at it again."
Corrective student response:	Students say, "Look."
Teacher evaluation:	"That's right. I get to hold that word."

Teachers differ substantially in the frequency and clarity with which they use the six different types of elicitations. Our data confirm Mehan's finding that there is a correspondence between the types of elicitations used and the types of responses made. As Mehan puts it, "Particular replies follow particular kinds of initiation with great regularity." In the conduct of lessons, this fact is important because the responses of students must remain faithful to the teacher's elicitations in order for the lesson presentation to move forward.

Mr. E [I] used a large number of product elicitations during our observation of his class: "What is it?" "I want you to give me a sentence using the words." "What does that end in?" "If you want to show real emphasis, what mark do you use?" These are typical examples of this elicitation style. Mr. E [I] also used a fairly large number of metaprocess elicitations, such as "How do you find out what it means?" and "How do you know that?"

The behavior between students and teachers is reciprocal and unidirectional: that is, teachers and students exchange elicitations and responses on a relatively equal basis, and the sequence of their exchanges moves forward from its starting point toward a conclusion. Any failure, by either the teacher or the student, to adhere to the reciprocal sequence and the unidirectional flow jeopardizes the quality of the relationship and the conduct of the lesson. Note, for example, the following entry in Mr. E [I]'s protocol:

Mr. E [I] is standing at the blackboard . . . he turns and writes a name on his "uncool" list. Mr. E [I]: "It is very important when we are doing math that it is all you are doing. When I am explaining a concept, I need your complete attention or you will miss something. Then it fouls you up and I have to spend extra time trying to straighten you out. And that takes away from everybody."

Responses

As with teacher elicitations, student responses fall into distinct categories. Sometimes teachers elicit responses from the whole class, and sometimes they pick out particular children. When the whole class is elicited, the teachers may be satisfied with a response from a single child who "represents" the class in responding, or they may expect every student to make the required response. When individual children are being elicited, the teachers may let any child who is rawdy respond, they may identify a specific child by name (nomination), or they may invite all children to "bid" for an opportunity to respond (usually by raising their hands).

Mehan (1979) refers to the response system as the "turn-allocation" machinery of the classroom. He means that the interaction is sequential: the teacher elicits, students respond, the teacher evaluates, and the process begins again with the teacher eliciting. The sequence specifies both the nature of the responses which teachers are seeking and the population of students who are to reply to any particular elicitation.

Mr. E [I]'s protocols provide examples of virtually all of the important variations in the allocation of student responses. He begins with an elicitation aimed at the whole class.

All students elicited:	Mr. E [I]: "I want everyone to put their finger on the first word. Look at it and then look away... What is it?"
All respond:	The class responds, *"sh"*.

In the same lesson, Mr. E [I] also uses elicitations in which students are identified by nomination (names), by invitations to bid, and by invitations to reply without first being recognized.

Invitation to reply:	Mr. E [I]: "These have a long vowel sound. What is it?"
Individual replies:	A child answers, *"ea, the e is long."*
Invitation to bid:	Mr. E [I]: "What is the first sound in *elephant*? Let's see some raised hands — bunches and bunches." The children smile when he says that.

Shift to group   Mr. E [I]: "Okay, everybody." They respond in
turns: unison.
Nomination for a   Mr. E [I]: "Would you like to read the direc-
turn: tions, Cordell?" Cordell reads them.

Students gradually learn to master this process. When students first attend school, their skills in lesson participation are absent or very minimally developed. Through time and practice, their skills develop so that their classroom participation is expected to increase in both quality and quantity.

Students learn this process by having their infractions corrected. The most common infractions which occur in classrooms are content-without-form and form-without-content responses to teacher elicitations. When students present content without form, they are giving correct responses at the wrong time or in the wrong way. When they present form without content, they are giving erroneous responses to teacher elicitations but giving them within the expected form and at the proper time (Mehan, 1979, pp. 136-137).

Student contributions are incorporated into the course of the lesson in three different ways. First, students may "get the floor," that is, they may complete an interaction sequence already in progress within the lesson. This interaction usually involves an immediate response to the instructional topic. As illustrated above, students help fulfill the intent of an ongoing lesson by this mode of participation.

The second way in which students contribute is by "holding the floor." In this instance, students pick up on the ongoing lesson but extend it by adding something new to the discussion. The timing in this case is critical. An example is from Mr. E's protocol (coming right after the "first sound in elephant" interaction sequence).

Jim brings up his dictionary and shows Mr. E [I] a page. Mr. E [I]: "Remember yesterday we talked about the pronunciation key at the front of the dictionary. Well, in Jim's dictionary it is at the bottom of each page." Jim returns to his seat.

The third way in which students contribute is by "introducing news": that is, by making original contributions. This type of contribution is most likely in more advanced classrooms. A critical component of this interaction is that the original contribution is acknowledged by the class. The acknowledgment serves to reinforce the contributor and also to facilitate further class discussion. Indirectly, this process would also contribute to motivating other members of the class to make their own original contributions. Our data indicate that this type of student contribution is rare. The factors which inhibit it include limited teacher competence, limited student maturity, limited student body composition, and a limited topic.

Evaluations

The third element in the lesson proper is the teacher's evaluations of student responses. These evaluations serve to reflexively link student responses to the teacher's original elicitations by declaring them to be appropriate or inappropriate to the lesson. Evaluations may be either procedural or substantive in content and may be either rational or moral in tone. Procedural evaluations focus on whether student responses are given at the proper time and in the proper form. Substantive evaluations declare whether the content of student responses fits the teacher's expectations.

Generally speaking, teacher evaluations are very brief and frequently nonverbal. A smile, a nod, "Right," "OK," "Beautiful," "Great" — these are the basic tools of positive evaluation. Frowns, "Are you sure?" "Look at that again," "Someone help her or him," are the most frequent negative evaluation tools. Activity lessons tend to call for more elaborate evaluations, like Mrs. G [C]'s, "You have cut too much. I will get you another one," to a kindergartener making a Santa Claus figure.

Moral evaluations are generally used to reinforce the propriety of the lesson structure or the rule structure of the school. Hence moral evaluations tend to be focused on children's procedural compliance. Children easily attach moral overtones to their substantive work as well, however. Notice, for example, how moral self-evaluation by one child is handled by Mrs. G [C].

> Nina begins to cry. "I just messed up," she says. Mrs. G [C] says to her, "I don't want you to worry about that, that is what you have an eraser for. I am glad you can see your mistakes."

Teachers sometimes capitalize on this tendency of students to respond to moral evaluation of the content of their work. For example, at one point Mrs. O [H]

> looks at the work of the girl sitting near her desk. "That is beautiful, little girl. Really beautiful." Mrs. O [H]'s voice changes as she says this — she is really pleased with what she sees.

Sometime later, however, we see that

> a child has spent a great deal of work on a drawing. She shows it to Mrs. O [H]. "That would have been beautiful if you had not put that

scrawly printing at the top of it." The child sits down and her smile is no longer on her face.

The use of moral evaluations to control student behavior is described in more detail in Chapter V. The point being made here is that moral evaluations can be effectively directed toward either procedural or substantive student responses.

Lesson Closings

Unless the classroom is disrupted or the teacher is deficient, lessons do not just end. They are brought to a close by specific forms of teacher behavior (usually a fairly brief soliloquy). Mehan (1979, p. 46) suggests that the closing of a lesson is "a mirror image of its opening." His conclusion is supported in our data in the sense that closings, like openings, are either directive or informative in character. The closings also serve another function, however. They typically refer to the content and procedures of the lesson proper in order to either summarize the work which has been done or to assign future work on some lesson objectives.

Mrs. A [M] executes a typical closing when, following a test lesson in which students exchange papers, she says,

> "Stewart, have you got your score? Will you collect the papers?" Mrs. A then says, "Starting tomorrow you are going to get a mixed drill with your times tables — a five-minute drill."

Mrs. G [C] closes an activity lesson with

> "When you are finished please come up to the rug and sit down so I can give you your jobs." She sits down in a little chair at the front of the room. "Good," she says to two boys and six girls ready for their jobs.

And Mrs. I [C] gives the following closing soliloquy at the end of a drill and practice lesson; she has just finished writing on the board, begins walking around the room, and says, "Study your multiplication tables. Remember, we are going to take a test on them. It is going to be a timed test. Your knowledge has to be all up here [pointing to her head]. It is going to be a five-minute timed test. And as long as you are with me you are going to be at the top."

These lesson changes serve two basic functions. They underscore the role of the lesson in moving children toward the goals of schooling (toward achievement or development), and they bring to consciousness the activities and behavioral norms viewed by the teacher as leading to those goals. Thus closings serve a vital function in articulating and legitimating the classroom culture.

Ending Demarcations

After the teacher closes the lesson, it is still necessary for students to be ritually released from their obligation to follow the behavioral rules implicit in the lesson proper. These ending demarcation rituals, like the starting ones, very often involve physical movement. In a typical form of this controlled release from the lesson, Mrs. G [C] ends a craft activity lesson when she

> sounds a chord on the piano. "Will you all stop please. Stand still. The boys and girls in Mrs. N [H]'s ... class have to leave us now. Put your things away and line up at the door." They do, and then Mrs. G says, "Thank you for coming," and they leave.

Mr. K [H] demonstrates the vulnerability of these ending rituals to disruption when he executes the following lesson closing and ending demarcation:

> "Put your papers away, we're going to try to get ready for lunch." A student walks over with lunch tickets. The students start to walk around, talk, and slam their desk tops. Mr. K [H] asks them to look around their desks in order to clean up. The students pick up their lunches. Some talk, others walk around, and the room gets noisy again. "We'll see who's going to be ready to go for lunch. Maybe, no one will go ... David's row can go now." The bell rings. "Manuel's row ..." They walk out as they're called.

WORK ORIENTATIONS AND LESSON STRUCTURES

The foregoing discussion has examined the basic structural elements in all successful lessons. We turn now to a brief exploration of the ways in which the teacher work orientations described in Chapter III serve to shape the use of these universal lesson structures. As indicated in Chapter III, the fifteen teachers in our sample fall into four distinct groups (master teachers, instructors, coaches, and helpers) based on their organization-level (purposive) and group-level (solidary) incentive orientations.

Individual teachers enact work roles consistent with the incentive orientations they have adopted. As they enact these roles, they tend to give greater attention to certain structural features of their lessons and to emphasize particular forms of each structural element. Analysis of a typical lesson found in the data from each teacher group will help to clarify the linkages between work orientations and lesson structures.

The Master Teachers

The two most prominent features of the lessons taught by the master teachers (Mrs. A [M], Mrs. B [M], and Mrs. C [M] are elaborate complexity and an emphasis on procedural evaluation of students. The lessons found in Mrs. B [M]'s protocols illustrate this point quite clearly. The following example of a math lesson occupied approximately 45 minutes (from 10:45 to 11:30 P.M.). Mrs. B begins with her typically terse and precise demarcation and launches immediately into an opening soliloquy aimed at reinforcing procedural expectations:

> "We have the Black American Puzzles. I will work a couple with you and then we will work them after lunch. What is the first thing we do in this classroom?" Students respond, "Put your first and last name on your paper."

Since the demarcation is successful and complete with the uttering of her first sentence, Mrs. B [M] has no need to use the physical process of passing out the puzzles to synchronize student behavior or to focus their attention. Consequently, she has time for a minilesson on body language which takes place entirely within the time required to pass out the math puzzles. With students already geared for a lesson, she needs no demarcation ritual and thus goes directly to the lesson proper, eliciting student responses with a question:

> "Why is body language so important?" A student responds, "It could make a difference when we are trying to get a job, or you can tell what we are thinking." Mrs. B [M]: "Your body language communicates to me your attitude. In this classroom we strive to be flexible and positive and your body language tells me what you are thinking."

As is typical of the master teachers, Mrs. B [M] has reversed the opening and the elicitation phases of this lesson. She elicits a response first and then adds the lesson opening to her evaluative response. Her homily on body language instructs, but only after students have already been invited to respond.

A major part of the opening phase of the main lesson has been postponed until the end of this minilesson on body language. The protocol reports the following:

> Have completed passing out the papers, Mrs. B [M] says, "Not only will you be graded on the right answers but you will be graded on the right letters in each name. You sometimes get the right math answers but you don't get the letters in the right place."
> "I will work with you on letter A. Pencils down. I really need your attention now."

Note that Mrs. B [M] has recognized that the physical activity of passing out papers and the minilesson on body language have endangered the success of her opening demarcation. Hence she reinforces with "I really need your attention now."

Her next step is to engage one student as her partner in eliciting other student responses. She

> asks Carlton to go to the board and she does the problem with Carlton. She has Carlton explain everything he is doing. "Carlton, you did a beautiful job explaining that."

Like a typical master teacher, Mrs. B [M] publicly evaluates Carlton procedurally rather than substantively. She is most intensely concerned that the other students learn the form of expected responses. She extends this point immediately:

> "Boys and girls, I want you to do your best work. I want you to show your work the way Carlton did."
> 10:55 A.M. "You should work at your own speed. If you get finished I have some more at this table here for you to do. Some of you will only do one, some will do three or four. We will be sure to correct puzzle No. 25 after silent reading this afternoon."

Now Mrs. B [M] is ready for all students to begin responding, confident that they will be trying to produce in exactly the right form.

> Mrs. B [M] then begins to walk around the room, checking to see how the students are doing. "You know this breaks my heart. Your first set of instructions was to put your name on your paper and I am afraid to look. And what about talking?" "We are to whisper." "And if I can hear you, is that whispering?" "No."

She is immediately disappointed — not by wrong answers, but by wrong procedures. And she evaluates the students immediately, eliciting confirmation that they now know what is required. Having done this, Mrs. B [M] retires to her desk.

> 11:05 A.M. Some of the students come up to Mrs. B [M] and ask questions. Mrs. B [M] is checking math packets while they are working on the math puzzles. Then she gets up and asks, "Is there anyone who is stuck on one and would like me to work it out?" A student wants help with letter M. She and the student do it on the board.

She recognizes that retiring from the lesson has endangered group solidarity and the dedication to mission needed to keep the lesson intact. Thus she returns to elicit active responses from students once again.

The lesson is then disrupted by the return of some children from a special "pull-out" program. Mrs. B [M] is faced with the task of integrating these newcomers into an ongoing lesson.

> 11:17 A.M. The children return from the E.S.A.A. lab. Mrs. B, who has been working on the math packets at her desk, stands up. "You know I really like the way Dwight came back from the E.S.A.A. lab, sat right down, and started to work."
> "Puzzle No. 25 we will be doing after silent reading this afternoon, and the others we will do later on . . . Is there anyone besides Laura who did not get puzzle No. 25?"

A second disruption occurs three minutes later when students who work in the cafeteria must leave to perform their duties. Mrs. B [M] handles this interruption in the following manner:

> 11:20 A.M. "Cafeteria workers, get your silent reading things out and get ready to go to work." They do and then line up. Mrs. B [M] goes to the door, opens it, and they leave.

Finally, the lesson period draws to a close as Mrs. B [M] needs to take a few minutes before the lunch hour to deal with noninstructional matters.

> 11:25 A.M. Mrs. B [M] surveys the room. The aide is helping one child with her math. "OK, boys and girls, we only have a few minutes left before lunch time and we have a very important matter. Leave your math and silent reading on the corner of your desk and put everything else away. Have your silent reading ready for after lunch. Pencils put away. Math papers to the corner of your desk."

From beginning to end, Mrs. B [M] insists on strict adherence to procedural expectations. The substantive content of the lesson is generally embodied in the materials and in responses to student queries — not in information Mrs. B [M] presents directly. Mrs. B [M], like the other master teachers, clearly believes that the best way for children to learn is for them to engage in curricular materials and to ask for help when they need it. Her concentration is on getting this engagement organized in such a way that she can quickly and easily tell which students need her help.

The Instructors

Mr. D [I], Mr. E [I], and Ms. F [I] constitute the group we have called "instructors." They are strongly oriented toward the production of achievement through the teaching of lessons. Their work orientation leads them to elaborate the opening phase of most lessons and to focus their evaluations on the substantive content rather than the procedural propriety of student responses. Mr. E [I] provides the following example of a typical instructor's lesson.

Like the master teachers, the instructors tend to have short, precise starting demarcation rituals. Mr. E [I] begins with the following statement as he addresses the two reading groups in his class. "I will take 'Inside Out' back here and the 'Lizards' will go outside."

As soon as the group is assembled, Mr. E [I] gives a very brief opening and plunges into a long elicitation and response sequence during which most of the student responses are inaudible to our observer, who is seated across the room from the student group.

> To the reading group that Mr. E [I] is working with, "I have a list of words we need to go over."
> 1. Island. "What does it mean? How do you spell it? What two words make up this word?"
> 2. Dragon. "Where do dragons usually live? We were talking about dragons in history the other day — where were they then? Who was the sailor who was not afraid of dragons? How do you spell it? What are the two words in dragon?" Students respond to these questions, but it is difficult to hear their answers distinctly.
> 3. Neither. "The long e and silent vowel partner coming behind it."
> 4. Minute.
> 5. Fierce. "Let's all spell it together."
> 6. Creature. "What is a creature? Name some creatures for me. I saw dozens of creatures the other day [Halloween]. Think about Halloween." A student tells what happened on Halloween. "We went trick or treating and then we went to Long John Silver's to get something to eat. A guy came in dressed like the K.K.K. with a shotgun. Everyone got a little nervous and my aunt did not want to stay there, but the manager came over and told her they were going to get him out of there. And they did."
> 7. Moment.
> 8. Giraffe. "That is a tricky one and I will spell it and then we will spell it together."

Mr. E [I] extends the lesson, moving from discussion to oral reading, saying "Now we will read. If some one has trouble with a word, don't help them out. Let them work it out by themselves so they can learn the word."

Like other instructors, Mr. E [I] vigorously pursues the class after each reading segment, eliciting information and metaprocess reflections from numerous students.

> "What kind of job did Maria's father have?" "He was a fisherman." "Where did they live?" "On an island." "Does anyone know where the

West Indies are?" No one does, and Mr. E [I] gives them a short geography lesson so they would know.

The next child reads. "How many of you lay in bed and listen to the sounds? What do you hear? When you are home alone, you always hear all kinds of weird sounds. Why do people always run to bed and pull the covers up over their heads? Does it make you feel safe?" There was a "yes" response in unison. "It makes me feel safe too."

The next child reads. "How does the ocean sing? What is the title of this story? Everybody. Why do you think she is lonely?" "No brothers or sisters." "She lives on an island." "No friends on the island."

The next child reads. "Why was she growing tired of the game she was playing? With other people you can change the game a little." Benton tells the group that he plays "poison" differently when he plays with some of his friends.

The next child, Theresa, reads. A boy began to help her, realized it and covered his mouth.

The next child reads. She got stuck. No one said anything and she figured the word out by herself. "What is Maria using?" "Her imagination."

The next child reads. "That is a hard word. It is Spanish, *blanca*. They pronounce their vowels differently."

As indicated in this extended sequence, Mr. E [I] tends to use open-ended elicitations, seeking whole group or bidding responses from students. If no responses are forthcoming, he tends to extend the lesson with brief homilies on the subject at hand. Mr. E [I], like the other instructors, appears to believe that lessons are group events; if any student responds, he is able to move on without becoming overly concerned that each individual student is getting all of the information being presented.

Instructors tend to have very brief closings, as is shown in the following excerpt:

"We will start here tomorrow. Get out your Skilpaks and finish up." One child says, "We did get it finished up." "OK then, you can work on your homework for the last 10 minutes."

One reason for this brevity is that the instructors tend to be successful in setting a businesslike tone in the classroom and therefore tend not to feel the need to either justify or elaborate on their classroom norms and requirements.

There is no clear ending demarcation for this lesson. As the protocol reports, children tend to remain within the framework of the instructor's lesson structure even after it has formally ended.

There are very few children in the room right now. Some are still with Mrs. Martin (a specialist), some are with the aide outside, and some are at music. Mr. E [I]'s reading group has gone to work on either their homework or their Skilpaks (a few did not have them finished). They are all working, some together, some separately.

The Coaches

Our third group of teachers — the coaches — view the school as an agency of child nurture rather than achievement, yet see the teaching of lessons as the primary means of pursuing that goal. This approach leads the coaches to be much more concerned than the master teachers and instructors about the attitudes students display toward their schoolwork. As a result, the coaches tend to open and close their lessons differently, to elicit a broader array of student responses, and to offer moral as well as substantive evaluation responses. Mrs. I [C] is representative of this group. The following lesson is taken from her protocol.

As is typical of the coaches (and the helpers described below), Mrs. I [C] opens her lesson by asking to look at students' homework assignments. The demarcation for this lesson is quite unusual. Mrs. I [C] has two students who have gotten into a fight. They have gone outside the classroom to try to talk out their differences with the aide. Mrs. I [C] asks the class to get out their homework while they wait for the trio to return. Thus when the two students return to class, indirect entry to the lesson has already occurred. We pick up the protocol just after the aide has explained that the warring parties have declared a truce. Looking at homework papers, Mrs. I [C] says to one student,

> "Is that an incomplete paper?" She asks the same question of some others. They speak to her quietly. "Did you make an attempt to take this book out, or did you just play?"
> "I forgot to bring my violin, guys. Most of us associate a violin with smooth, slow music. But I could play sad little tunes on it for your sad excuses." (She mimics the motions of a violin player.) Some of the students have just not done the assigned work. "Maybe you two just gave up. You are not being fair to yourselves. I will just close the book and play all weekend and come in on Monday and give Mrs. I [C] an excuse."

Mrs. I [C]'s moral extensions are actually more important to her than whether the students have achieved mathematically. She goes on:

> "What was the solution I told you last week? I tried explaining why homework was important. I feel a little bit of homework is not going to hurt anyone. I give you only 20 minutes and I even give you some

time in class. You are now fifth graders. I push and pull and with some of you, you are doing it. You people that put in the effort, you will excel and get ahead."

Mrs. I [C] sees that the real lesson of homework lies in its contributions to character and self-discipline.

Next, Mrs. I [C] extends the lesson by giving what might have been the originally intended directive opening. She begins by giving answers to the problems. Then she continues.

> She explains that n or x is a symbol for the answer. "If you have the incorrect answer, don't erase, just put the correct answer alongside it. You don't have time to erase."

Mrs. I [C]'s lesson suffers an internal disruption because a child who normally is out of the room for special instruction at 11:00 A.M. is back in the class this day. She takes time out of the lesson to assign this child to the aide for special attention. Within a few minutes she is back to the lesson. Now reinforcing the substantive opening and refocusing the class's attention she writes two words on the board.

> "When you see this word *sum*, what do they want you to do?" The class responds, "Add." "When you see this word *difference*, what do you do?" "Subtract." "To find the difference, you subtract. To make it a challenge, they put the *n* in there."

Note that she uses emotional, rather than cognitive, language to describe the substitution of letters for numbers in this pre-algebra exercise. She calls the process a "challenge" rather than a new way of formulating numerical operations. This approach is typical of the coaches, who want students to feel excitement and opportunity in school, not just to know facts. She goes on:

> "Remember, I told you we were jumping from here to there, to go through the fifth-grade test materials. What is this section?" "Graphs." "Where do you find graphs?" Various students respond. "The Church of Scientology has a bunch of graphs on the wall." "The blood bank." "The spelling chart." Mrs. I responds to that answer, "Not exactly, but we could graph it." And she shows them how.
> "We could also graph the hair colors, the number of boys and girls in the class." "Look at page ??. Oh, I should have you look at the easier ones first." "Yes, let's do the easy ones first. Turn to page ?? first. When you look at a graph you have to look at the key first so you know what the graph is telling you. Remember, I will not always get to give you the directions. You will have to read the directions for yourself." The class then goes through a problem about snowmobiles.

Here again, the coach tries to make an experiential linkage and to do "the easy ones first" so as to give students an easier access to the alien world of graphs.

Shortly, however, the flow of this lesson is disrupted when Mrs. I [C] becomes upset with one student who has not been following directions. The protocol reports:

> "Now turn to page 348. This time the key has changed ... 200 times."
> "Wayne? Are you with us on page 348? ... I don't need to see that sassy face. I could track up a ten in comparison with you."

Balancing her frustration, she tries to restore the lesson flow with "I like the way you guys are raising your hands." The disruption ends as quickly as it began, as the elicitation, response, evaluation cycle continues with the following:

> "Let's go on to page 349. They have taken away all the pictures. What does this graph work with? "The subjects of fifth-grade students." "The numbers are going from left to right in a row. The numbers going across indicate what? Pedro?"
> "The green bars stand for what?"
> "The subject with the greatest number of students?"
> Everyone wants to answer that question.

Other disruptions occur, however, as Mrs. I [C] tells the children that they can get sweaters if they wish because it's cold, moves a child who is talking loudly and distracting others, and stops another child from making a disruptive thumping sound.

Despite elaborate concern with attitudes and social processes, the coaches retain a vital interest in children's learning. Mrs. I [C] concludes this lesson with a test patterned after the district proficiency test, which all her children must pass before being promoted to the sixth grade. Thirty-seven minutes after starting the lesson, Mrs. I [C] starts the closing process:

> "Put your math books away. As soon as you get your paper, put your name and the date on it and go immediately to work. This is not a timed test, so don't rush. Read carefully and work carefully." Mrs. I [C] hands out the papers and they set to work immediately.

Three minutes later:

> "When you finish your math, work on your spelling on p. 29. I will write your homework assignment on the board while you are doing this."
> 11:35 A.M. The children are quickly finishing the math paper and they are taking theirs up to Mrs. I [C]'s desk. "I see that Dean's ready and so is Tania. They are following directions. Some of us are still taking the test, so let's be considerate and not get noisy."

She finally offers her closing soliloquy as she

> finishes writing on the board and then begins walking around the room. "Study your multiplication tables. Remember, we are going to take a test on them. It is going to be a timed test. Your knowledge has to be all up here (pointing to her head). It is going to be a five-minute timed test and as long as you are with me you are going to be at the top."

The Helpers

Those teachers who see the school as an agency for nurturing children (while maintaining a classroom process orientation that emphasizes keeping school) enact their work roles as "helpers." The five teachers in this group — Mr. K [H], Mrs. L [H], Mrs. M [H], Mrs. N [H], and Mrs. O [H] — display the least-well-structured lesson sample. It should be noted, however, that they do attempt to preserve some structure in order to maintain classroom order — an objective which is prominent in their thinking. The classroom cultures created by these teachers are quite different from those found in the other classrooms.

We have called this group of teachers the "helpers" because they view themselves as facilitating child nurturance by assisting students in coping with school program and curriculum demands. The helpers tend to be less well organized in their approach to teaching than the other three groups, partly because they feel less competent and less in command of their work roles.

The following lesson, taken from Mrs. N [H]'s protocol, illustrates the typical pattern of teaching behavior by the helpers. Mrs. N [H] starts with a brief demarcation between the departure of a classroom visitor and the opening of a language arts lesson. She says, "Let's look up here at the board." Note that, like other helpers, she speaks in the first-person plural, "let's," in an effort to strengthen a social bond with her students.

The opening phase of her lesson is very brief, given the complexity of the events which will be unfolding over the next twenty-five minutes. She says only, "We are going to do some alphabetizing. Let's look at these words and try it." The lesson proper begins with a series of nominated responses. Mrs. N [H], using a typical helper approach, calls on many different children by name:

> "Are there any *a* words, Gina?" "*Air.*" "When you put it on your paper you put a No. 1 by it. Are there any *b* words, Carlos?" "*Boat.*" "And what do you put beside it on your paper?" "No. 2." "What about *c* words, Betty?" "There are two words." "What are they?" "*Clean and*

cream." "What do we do then? Jamey?" "We look at the second letter."
Mrs. N [H] continues through the list. "When you are finished you
should have fourteen words on your list. If you do not have fourteen
words, you need to check and see what happened."

At this point the lesson is extended and reorganized. The
students are broken up into groups, and there is a transition period
while Mrs. N [H] passes out papers and directs children to their
groups. We pick up the protocol at the following point:

Mrs. N [H] is working at the blackboard with her group. They are
going over some words on the board. "What kinds of shoes do we
have?" Children give a list of various kinds of shoes. "What kind of
leather do we have? Does all leather feel soft?" One child says, "Some
leather feels hard."

A brief disruption is handled and the lesson is extended to include
oral reading.

A child, not in the group says, "Teacher, Raul is talking to me." "Raul.
You know better."
"Now we will read the sentences on the board. Arnold?" He reads the
sentence. Another boy reads the second sentence. "Which one could
really happen? Frank?" "The second one." They do the same thing
with another set of sentences. "We could imagine the first sentence,
but we could not do it."

Again, individual nomination is the prevalent turn allocation
mechanism and is typical of the personalistic style of the helpers.
A brief period of total group elicitation follows, and the lesson
is again extended as children are asked to turn to prepared
"Skilpak" curriculum materials.

"What about the test I took?" a child asks, "I did not pass it." Mrs. N
[H] responds, "Mrs. N ... (the aide) will work with you on Monday."

Notice, again, the ease with which this lesson is interrupted by
children expressing special needs. Mrs. N [H] tries to give attention
to individual children while simultaneously directing the activities
of the entire group. She is not always successful, however.
Mrs. N [H] ends her active involvement with this small-group
lesson by saying, "When you finish this you will begin your
alphabetizing." She returns to the group after briefly attending to
the needs of another child. She checks on their progress and then
executes an ending demarcation for them and a starting demarcation for another group by asking, "Those of you in 'The Dog Next
Door,' would you come up quietly?"
The most prominent features of the helpers' lesson structures

are their lack of clarity and precision in the openings, closings, and demarcation rituals. These teachers apparently feel that classroom cultural norms are self-generating and do not need ritualization or explicit articulation. The result is high vulnerability to disruption as children do not segment their personal needs and interests from the lessons and do not "get down to business." The helpers respond to this vulnerability and consequent high noise level in two ways. First, they personalize interactions with the children, trying to engage them one by one in the lesson process. Second, they rely on curriculum packages, workbooks, and other structured learning activities to give continuity and direction to the lesson, rather than imposing their own demands and directions on the students. The typical result is a low level of student engagement and high rates of classroom disruption.

SUMMARY AND CONCLUSION

In this chapter we have examined how teachers engage in their fundamental work responsibility: teaching lessons. We have noted that there are five basic structural elements in all successful lessons and that the lesson proper is characterized by a reflexive sequence of teacher elicitation, student response, and teacher evaluation. This sequential structure can expand beyond the original lesson objectives or redirect the focus of the lesson through the incorporation of teacher "extensions" which are in form and function like the original lesson opening.

We examined typical lessons from our fifteen teachers and concluded that each of the four subgroups in our sample (the master teachers, instructors, coaches, and helpers) emphasize specific aspects of the lesson structure and tend to rely more on some forms than others within each structural element. In this way classroom cultures come to reflect the work orientations and incentive systems of the teachers who organize them.

CHAPTER V

Managing Classrooms: A Cultural Perspective on Rules and Their Enforcement

Whereas lessons embody the essential purposes toward which classroom cultures are directed, classroom management defines the operational character of these cultures by structuring social relationships among teachers and students and by assigning meanings and values to various classroom activities. Teachers manage their classrooms through the creation, interpretation, and enforcement of moral and behavioral rules.

While the fifteen teachers in this study can be classified into four distinct groups with regard to their lesson structures and teaching activities, their divergent approaches to rule formation are best described in terms of a single broad continuum. At one extreme, we found tension-laden and chaotic classrooms with unclear and unenforced rules. At the other end of the spectrum were classrooms with well-defined and broadly accepted rules — rules so well understood and internalized that overt enforcement was unnecessary. Most classrooms, most of the time, lay somewhere between these extremes. Rules were obvious, reasonably explicit, but support for them was limited and enforcement was problematic.

Problems of classroom management confront teachers the moment they enter the school. Students are initially assigned to

118

them as disparate individuals representating a wide variety of backgrounds and subcultures. To undertake the task of instruction, teachers must transform these individuals into a unified group, a cultural unit. They must bind individual students together, organize their behavior, and establish a shared frame of reference or common point of view. The capacity to do this depends primarily on establishing effective rules which students come to accept as natural, necessary, and meaningful. Benn and Peters (1959, p. 18) note the following:

> What we call human society is a number of individuals bound together by ... an order of normative rules. They behave predictably in relation to one another because of this normative system. These rules define the rights and duties which they have toward one another, the ends which they may pursue, and the ways in which it is legitimate to pursue them.

Social order is possible because human beings have an inherent potential for following rules. They perform predictably in relation to one another and form what is called a "social system," to a large extent, because they accept systems of behavioral rules which are binding on all, yet alterable by human decision.

At the beginning of each school year, teachers create classroom order by developing and articulating enforceable rules, rules which seem natural and do not have to be explicitly remembered, rules that specify legitimate activities and define both social and academic responsibilities for all students. Although the rules in any given classroom may be virtually identical from one year to the next, they must be established anew for each class so that each new group of individual students can be integrated into a cohesive social group.

Data from the teachers in our study show that teachers are not equally successful in creating and maintaining a classroom culture or incorporating students into it. Life in the classrooms we observed ranged from virtual chaos in one room, to rooms with highly visible rules and overt systems of enforcement, to ones which were culturally directed by social norms that needed little interpretation and almost no enforcement.

Interview and observation data obtained from twelve of our fifteen teachers clarify the nature and importance of rule formation and enforcement. The classroom environment of one teacher, Mrs. O [H], is examined first. It reveals just how fragile the establishment of a classroom culture can be. Her failure to establish and enforce rules or to ensure regularity in student behavior led to the most chaotic classroom in our sample. Dissatisfied with her classroom experience, and encouraged by her principal to do so, this teacher retired at the end of the year.

Against the background of Mrs. O [H]'s extremely weak classroom management, other teachers' efforts become more understandable. Life in most of the other teachers' classrooms includes substantial periods of effective social organization, but some of them do not fully comprehend how classroom cultures are established. In these cases, classrooms are orderly at some times while verging on chaos at others.

Most teachers do understand the necessity of rules and readily articulate them for the students. Frequently, however, their students do not "own" these rules and thus tend to either misunderstand them or obey them only to avoid punishment. When this happens, the students tend to view the rules as arbitrary, capricious, or without fundamental purpose. Even when teachers are successful in formulating rules which are, on the whole, seen as legitimate, there are times when it is necessary for them to use overt power strategies to maintain order.

Kindergarten teachers apply a special rule in the development of classroom subcultures. Among our respondents, Mrs. G [C] illustrates how teachers introduce the youngest students to the universal rules of the school and prepare them for the years to come.

Our discussion of classroom management concludes with a look at teachers' responses to the intrusion of the schoolwide rule structures into the classroom.

Data from three teachers in our sample are not included in this analysis. The resource specialist (Mrs. C [M]) has been omitted because her work was with individual students rather than with groups during the various observations. Ms. F [I], the aphasic teacher, had a class that was so small (five students, the teacher, and the aide) that a true tutorial relationship was possible. In a third class, composed entirely of below-grade-level students with behavior problems, there were multiple authority figures, including a totally inexperienced teacher (Mrs. M [H]). Attempts at rule formation in this classroom relied heavily on a somewhat confused form of Skinnerian behavior modification — the hoped-for results were constantly in doubt, however.

THE FRAGILE CHARACTER OF CLASSROOM ORDER

In the most chaotic of our classrooms, ostensibly being directed by Mrs. O [H], it was virtually impossible to discern through either observation or interview data what rules were supposed to exist. If they did exist, it was equally difficult to see how they were being enforced. Shouting, threats, repetition of requests, and sending students to the principal appeared to be the most common methods used by this teacher in trying to maintain order.

For example, while Mrs. O [H]'s class, like every other class, lined up and waited for her to meet them at the playground, they were often noisy as they walked to the classroom. On one particular morning, as they entered the room and went to their seats, Mrs. O [H] stood at the rear of the room and said,

> "Boys and girls, will you take your seats, please?" A moment passes.
> "Boys and girls, will you take your seats, please? Boys and girls, will you take your seats, please? I sound like a broken record."

Despite her repeated requests, the students were slow to quiet down and get their things organized to begin the day. Over five minutes passed before there was sufficient order to say the pledge to the flag.

No group teaching was done during this observation. The teacher spent time searching for pencils for students and telling various ones to stop talking. She actually worked with only two children before the morning recess period. Comments such as these were heard during the morning:

> "Tom, I am going to have to send you out of the room if you don't stop talking. Is that the biggest pencil you have? I will get you a bigger one."
> "Nancy, you just get here! Now sit quietly and get to work." Nancy stopped talking with her girlfriend and began talking to one of the boys at the table instead. "We can't have all these people walking around," the aide shouts. Mrs. O [H] responds, "I just told Lynn to sit down a minute ago."

During this period the aide works with a large reading group. Their work is interrupted when two members of the group started kicking each other. The aide turns to them and says,

> "Jim and Bob, you won't be able to sit back here." Mrs. O [H] then says, "Go back to your seats, please." The boys stay put, the aide again tells them to leave and Mrs. O [H] adds, "you are to go back to your seats." Jim returns to his regular seat at this point but Bob remains at the table. The aide resumes working with the group but ignores Bob's desire to participate. He does not like this and becomes annoying again. This causes the aide to say, "Bob, go back to your seat right now. Mrs. O [H] told you to go back to your seat." Bob still

does not leave. "Will you get your work done? We have given you another chance." His response was not audible but he remains with the reading group and does the material in his workbook with the rest of the group.

There was only one direct mention of a common classroom rule during the various observations in this classroom — and this was by the aide. Two boys leave their seats and walk to the aide to speak to her.

> She turns to them, "You are going to have to stay in your seat and raise your hand. If one more person gets out of your seat to tell me you are not sharing the eraser you will have to stay in at recess on a nice day." [Due to inclement weather recess on this particular day would be indoors for everyone.]

These boys return to their seats, but other children get up without raising their hands and walk around, and no further effort is made to enforce the hand-raising rule.

One afternoon Mrs. O [H] decides to read to the class. She announces her intention to do this and asks them to quiet down. However, she begins reading before she has their complete attention. A number of children continue talking, and after a while she stops reading to say, sarcastically, "I expect you to disrupt me, Bob. I don't expect you to do anything but disrupt me." The situation does not get better, and Mrs. O [H] finally acknowledges that the class is not involved in the story. She stops reading, looks at them, and angrily states, "OK, get your spelling books out please. Get your spelling books out. I'm finished trying to read to you. Come up here, Lynn, to where I told you to sit." Mrs. O [H] then walks to her desk, gets her thermos, and returns to the front of the room. She opens it and pours a cup of coffee. She looks around, sees Bob's back, and says,

> "Turn around, Bob. I will wait until I see you people are ready to work and then I will go on with your lesson. I will put the page number on the chalkboard."
> While the children got out their spelling materials Mrs. O [H] wrote "Spelling. Begin on page 48" on the board. Many of them, however, were rather noisy as they got ready, Bob among them.
> "All right, Bob, you have to go to Mrs. S [the principal]. Come here. I am going to write a note. All right, Bob, go to Mrs. S. Leave the pencil, Bob." "It is my pencil." "Give it to me Bob. *Give it to me, Bob.*"

Bob leaves the room but returns a few minutes later with a note from the principal. Mrs. O [H] walks to her desk, gets out note paper, and returns to the front of the room. She writes another note and sends Bob back to the office. Bob returns about seven minutes later, goes directly to his seat, and sits down. He is very quiet and does not misbehave in any observable way. As soon as he gets seated, however, Mrs. O [H] says,

> "Come on Bob, you have to go back to Mrs. S." Bob, very bewildered, responded, "Why? I didn't do nothing." "Come on." Mrs. O [H] began writing another note and suddenly stopped. "I will talk to Mrs. S after I get out of class so go sit down." Bob, who had been standing near Mrs. O [H], returned to his seat. "I will talk to Mrs. S after class."

Observations in Mrs. O [H]'s classroom remind us that classrooms do not necessarily get organized at all. Even children who are ordinarily well behaved can become disoriented and noncooperative in this classroom. Mrs. O [H]'s failure to establish orderly social relationships demonstrates that no teacher can depend entirely upon the work of previous teachers to establish class rules. Without a rule-making and enforcement strategy of her own, Mrs. O [H] spends much of her time struggling for control.

USING REWARDS TO ENFORCE RULES

Even when teachers are aware of the importance of classroom organization, they may not understand the internal dynamics necessary for success. Mrs. L [H]'s class, for example, was orderly and controlled on some occasions but verged on chaos at other times. Although there was evidence of the existence of some rules, Mrs. L [H] relied primarily on a token economy of "red marks" and "green marks" (as well as actual material rewards) as her primary tool for maintaining order. Little effort was made to produce a satisfactory classroom subculture.

When asked how she arrived at her way of doing things, she stated it was "strictly hit or miss." She added, "I have never been taught." She had initiated the use of her token economy strategy several years previously while teaching in an isolated, atypical rural school as a way to motivate her students, and because she had found the results personally satisfying, she decided it might solve her problem of maintaining order in this urban classroom.

On a particular day her classroom begins in an organized, orderly fashion. The children enter, put away their things, and sit down. The opening exercises include group instruction, which involve the entire class followed by the pledge to the flag. The birthday of a child is acknowledged. The class wishes Mark

"Happy Birthday" and Mrs. L [H] presents him with a special birthday card.

The sense of groupness and order are soon shattered, however, when Mrs. L [H] goes to the "red and green marks" chart to reward or sanction students for doing, or not doing, various assignments. Between ten and fifteen minutes are spent at this task. Meanwhile the students are told,

"While I am checking spelling you can do your other work." And the aide stating, to a child who had gotten out of his seat, "Everyone should be doing their reading or something."

The children's names are called; some respond by bringing up their spelling work, while others give excuses for why they do not yet have it in. Others simply do not respond at all. The conversation during that episode include such statements as the following:

"Rose gets green marks for spelling."
"Carl, you get two green marks."
"Joanne, your writing is getting so good I am going to give you an extra green mark for that."
"Chuck, you forgot your spelling. If you do not bring your spelling tomorrow you will have to get a red mark. I will trust you to bring it tomorrow."
"Tina, you did your work very well. I really like the way you are doing your work. And you did it so well you will get an extra green mark."
"Paul, I hope you are working because you only got five points last week. Paul, do you see where you are? You do not have any this week (no red marks either)."
"Sally, you get a treat and two green marks for (completing your reading book). Do you want a treat now or later?" "Now." "You people who passed to a new book get a treat." [Lollipops were given to the children who passed into a new reading book in the last few days].

With the exception of the opening exercises, there are no large- or small-group instructional activities until after 10 A.M. Just before morning recess Mrs. L [H] meets with a small reading group for about fifteen minutes. She tells them she would meet with them again after recess. Although they reassemble as instructed, she never gets back to them. Instead, Mrs. L [H] spends the remainder of the morning with individual students, calling them in informal groups to her desk to check their math folders, assigns them further work, and answers individual questions. Some children do not even have tutorial contact with her. And not all of those who are summoned heed her call. Andy, for one, does not get out his math folder when he is told. He just sits doing nothing. As a result, Mrs. L [H] states, "Andy, what did I ask you to do? Andy, if you do not get to work you will be in real trouble." To Tim, she says, "OK, Tim, move yourself to the back table. Get your things. Are you working? I would never know it."

Carl, who had earlier received two green marks for his spelling homework, becomes disengaged from the classroom activities once he is left to his own devices and ignores orders to become involved. Sitting at his desk doing nothing, he is told, "Carl, come here. Bring some of your books and come back here" [to the work table by Mrs. L [H]'s desk]. He slowly arrives, is assigned work to do, and is then told to return to his seat to get to work. He returns to his seat but does not get to work. Shortly thereafter he begins wandering around the room, erasing the birthday boy's name from the blackboard as he passes by. The following exchange occurred:

"Mrs. L [H], Carl erased Mark's name." "Carl that is IT for you."

Mrs. L [H] then goes and puts a red mark by Carl's name. That action, however, does not faze him in the least. He finally goes back to his seat and turns the pages in one of his books, but still does not work. Instead he gets up again and wanders over to Peter's desk to observe an older child working with Peter. When Mrs. L [H] notices where he is, she calls to him:

"Carl, come here and bring your math book. Where is your math floor plan? Didn't you get one yesterday?" "No." "Carl just didn't go up and get one" [said another student]. "Carl, you have got to come in from outer space and get your mind working. You can't go wandering around like a little lost boy."

Mrs. L [H] goes to get him a math floor plan, and while she is doing that Carl wanders off again. "Carl, where are you?" she says when she returns to her desk. Carl then comes back to her desk, listens as she assigns him his math work, and once more returns to his seat. Four children have lined up at Mrs. L [H]'s desk while she is directing Carl, and they carry on a social conversation while they wait. Carl glances at the work assignment but does not do it. Instead he gets up, joins Peter, who has also left his seat, and the two of them stroll around the front of the room. Mrs. L [H] looks up from her work with a student, notices them, and says to Carl, "Carl, you take your book and go outside and work at the table." He leaves the room and stays outside until it is lunchtime. Then he returns to the room to get his lunch ticket and goes to lunch recess.

After lunch Mrs. L [H] conducts a geography lesson with the whole class, and during that period of time the class is orderly. When the day ends, Mrs. L [H] goes to one child and gives her enough money to buy an ice-cream cone. She says to her, "You have been very well behaved all day and did good work. This is your reward."

Mrs. L [H] does not understand the difference between rewards and incentives. She believes that material rewards rather than cultural incentives control behavior. Her public display of distributing red marks, green marks, lollipops, and ice-cream money is made in the often vain hope that students will not only comply with her present expectations but will also achieve a deeper commitment to orderly participation in the days to come. She really believes that today's ice-cream money will buy tomorrow's good behavior.

Another classroom, Mr. K [H]'s, displays organizational problems similar to Mrs. L [H]'s. In his case, however, he uses personal appeal rather than monetary or token rewards in an effort to maintain order. He, too, has been largely unsuccessful in the development of a satisfactory classroom subculture. Part of his difficulty springs from a sense on the part of some students that their whole group is without legitimate meaning. One student confides the following to an observer: "We're the 'leftovers.' The best students are in Mrs. X's room, the second best in Mr. Y's room and the leftovers in our room. About five or six of us are good students but the rest are not. This is a weird class." Even Mr. K [H] has some doubts about the authenticity of this group. He says, "It is a very lonely group. They don't take directions very well." His strategy for coping with this problem reflects, however, an essentially rational (rather than a cultural) perspective. He says, "I try to change everything every day so they'll follow directions." By trying to change things rather than unifying his students into a system of shared meanings and purposes, Mr. K [H] further weakens their already deficient culture — exacerbating the very problems of loneliness and alienation he seeks to cure.

Mr. K [H] does attempt more group instruction and teacher-directed activity than either Mrs. O [H] or Mrs. L [H]. And he works to gain complete student attention before conducting a lesson. He also provides considerably more teacher elicitation and secures more student responses. He displays an understanding of the tenuousness of classroom social order during one lesson. When the class shouts out an answer, Mr. K [H] responds with the following: "Sh. Sh. Don't let me lose you. You're doing fine." On another occasion when students are restive, Mr. K [H] states, "I'm not going any further unless you get yourselves under control ... In order to pull this off everyone will have to do their part." And because some students still do not respond, he says the following:

"We are not going to go on until everyone quiets down. Bill, turn around. I am somewhat ashamed of you. Maybe you can't handle activities. Maybe we shouldn't have them. I've spent a lot of time preparing this. Sit down in your seat, Joan. I did not say anything about running for anything. First thing we are going to do is read this sheet. It makes sense to follow along. Candy, you can't do it by talking with Wendy. Follow along fellows."

The class finally does quiet down and the students read the material aloud. Some of the students raise their hands so that they can get a chance to read.

RULE-BASED ORDER: OVERT POWER STRATEGIES

The majority of our teachers did recognize the importance of establishing rules. They generally managed rule-bound classrooms. Of these teachers, only two tended to rely primarily on overt power-based enforcement strategies rather than on rule enculturation to maintain order.

One of these teachers, Mrs. N [H], mixed the use of legal and moral rules, not only to control behavior but also to control the rewards and honors she had to bestow. She was prone to begin teaching some lessons without having the complete attention of all her students.

On one occasion, after recess, she began the math lesson before everyone was quiet and also failed to give explicit directions about the work assignment. this beginning resulted in confusion and talking. Hoping to reduce the talking, she states, "I like the way Luke is working, so nice and quiet." Donald, however, is not quiet, does not take the hint, and is told the following: "You are making too much trouble up there. Go sit in the back of the room in that chair." Donald changes his seat as he is told, but instead of participating in the learning activity, he rocks back and forth in his chair, plays with paper, and then with his hands. Being moved to the back of the room quiets Donald, but he never becomes engaged in the math lesson and it does not quiet some of the other children. There is a good deal of "Sh, Sh" going on.

The chair to which Donald has been moved actually belongs to another child, Davy, who is in the lab. When he returns to class, another disturbance occurs. Seeing Donald in his seat, Davy goes to him and said: "Why are you sitting in my seat? You don't belong there. Get out of my seat." Mrs. N [H], who hears Davy's comment, responds: "Davy, I told Donald to sit there. You may sit in the chair next to him." Davy grudgingly complies with Mrs. N [H] but vents his displeasure on Donald by giving him a shove in the side with his elbow. He remains annoyed with Donald the rest of the morning. By this time, however, Donald is interested in the lesson that is under way and, after glaring at Davy, just ignores him.

The most pervasive concept behind the rules in Mrs. N [H]'s classroom is "good citizenship" — a concept which she developed in an attempt to control attitudes as well as behavior. Mrs. N [H] would say such things as the following:

> "Susie is being a good citizen. She is sitting in her chair nice and quietly."
> "I want ten good citizens at the blackboard."
> "Let's see which good citizens go to lunch first. Table 2, you are all very good citizens. You may go to lunch."
> "Since I do not have enough [math problems] on the board, I will choose who goes up on the basis of good citizenship — how well you are sitting and watching."

Identifying the good citizens is not a class decision; this power belonged exclusively to Mrs. N [H]. And it is not always clear what behavior constituted good citizenship. For example:

> Mrs. N [H] is preparing to show a film and says to a student, "Andy, you have your head down. You are being a good citizen. Would you like to pull the screen down?" However, when [the film ended] another child, who has been sitting quietly and paying attention, raises his hand and asks, "Can I take the projector to the office?" Mrs. N [H] tells him, "No, because you asked. I pick good citizens that *don't* ask."

The inability of the second student to do the right thing is the result of (a) Mrs. N [H]'s inconsistent use of the notion of good citizenship to establish classroom control and (b) her view that students threaten her control if they try to lay claim to rewards, no matter how well behaved they are. On some occasions, raising one's hand when Mrs. N [H] asks for "good citizens" to go to the board, etc., is accepted as appropriate behavior. Thus, her claim that "good citizens don't ask" violates a rule which the student had good reason to believe would govern the classroom. This episode also reveals that Mrs. N [H] had no intention of sharing her right to distribute special privileges or honors. Indeed, Mrs. N [H] frequently invents new rules when she feels her ability to maintain control over the distribution of rewards is being threatened.

Mr. D [I], the other power-oriented rule enforcer, strongly supports the use of rules and the development of a classroom culture. In addition to seeking control over his children's behavior, however, he tries to use rules to control their attitudes and goals.

His classroom reveals the difficulties teachers encounter when trying to use rules for these purposes. When disruptions occur or children disobey a rule, they are often charged with disloyalty to the class (culture). The charge is articulated through his special use of the word *choice*. For example:

> "Julie, are people back there [at Table 1] choosing to put their heads down?" "No." "Then you need to choose to be quiet."
> "Julie, you have chosen to move to the closet because you are talking too loud. I am very sorry you have chosen to do that, but when you talk too loud, you don't let other people do their work."

On another occasion, he says, "Richard, you chose not to be able to sit there on the rug because you moved." On still another occasion he says: "Those of you who passed out books, please collect them. Arnold, you chose not to collect any more books. Collectors have to be very quiet."

So that he can provide small-group instruction, Mr. D [I] assigns two groups of children to independent work projects and work with the third group. (A fourth group always works with a tutor assigned to his room.) Sometimes children working independently have some problems which they can not solve working alone. On one occasion, the following interchange occurs:

> Tania has a problem with her independent assignment and goes to Mr. D [I]. "I need some help." "I am working with this group. You may find someone in your group to help you." She returns to her seat and asks for help but no one is able to provide satisfactory assistance. As a result she returns to Mr. D [I], who responds, "I cannot do anything for you. You may not interrupt the group." She returns to her seat but is unable to complete her assignment.

On another occasion, when Mr. D [I] walks by the two groups working independently, making sure they are doing their work, a student at Table 2 says, "Mr. D [I]?" He responds, "No, I am just passing by. I am not answering any questions."

Mr. D [I] clearly wants to encourage students to work independently as well as to not interrupt his working with a particular group. However, he does not provide sufficient alternatives for students to solve problems when they arise. Not all children are willing to sit quietly and wait for his attention when they get "stuck."

During a teaching session involving teacher elicitation and student response, Mr. D [I] rearticulates a common classroom rule: "Remember you raise your hands to answer." Later in the lesson this rule is referred to again, this time with the threat to punish: "I see Erick has his hand up quietly. I am not going to listen to anyone speaking out of turn." At other times during the observations the following comments are made to reinforce appropriate behavior:

"Laura is working so quietly. That is so helpful. She does not bother other people who are working."
"I see Chachi is sitting very quietly and so is Pedro."
"MaryJane has her pencil ready and is sitting quietly."
"Ross is sitting very quietly waiting for directions. He knows if he listens he will know exactly what to do."

Occasionally, Mr. D [I] employs an exchange mechanism which at first glance looks something like that employed by Mrs. L [H]. In reality, however, he unilaterally sets the terms of what he calls a "bargain" with the children, who are given no say in the matter.

During a teaching lesson that involves the use of brand new books Mr. D [I] says to one student, "If you do not want to participate, maybe you don't need a book. You should be on this page and not looking through the book. Remember at the beginning [of the year] I said you could look through the book all you wanted so when we are working in the book we could stay at the same page. I kept my part of the bargain, what about you?"

There are substantial costs associated with Mr. D [I]'s power-based rule enforcement strategy. Although his room is generally quiet and although considerable teaching goes on, there are often tears and a sense of frustration on the part of various students. Mr. D [I] has rules, but he has not moved from enforcement to enculturation.

RULE-BASED ORDER: NORMATIVE STRATEGIES

The majority of our teachers developed normative, explicit rules, rules which could be understood and obeyed without the continuous threat of enforcement.

A second-year teacher, Mrs. J [C], demonstrates one typical mechanism for the development of classroom cultures. Gathering her class at the rug, she leads them in singing, "You are my Sunshine." She interprets this activity to first graders by saying, "We have gotten to sing that two days in a row because there are no names on the board." Such celebration of cooperative behavior is a common occurrence among our teachers. This teacher adds verbal reinforcement to this ritual celebration when she says such things as the following: "Center 2 looks super. Center 3 does too. Center 4 is ready."

If children still have trouble with self-control, however, Mrs. J [C] is willing to use public shame as an enforcement mechanism. For example:

> Two children working on their number sheets got each other into trouble. Bernard takes Jennifer's eraser from her and she tries to get it back. Mrs. J [C], seeing the struggle, says, "Jennifer and Bernard, put your names on the board."

Mrs. J [C] sometimes adds personal appeal to her repertoire of devices for getting student compliance. She is going to be out of the classroom one afternoon to attend a meeting and informs the class that they are going to have a substitute. She says that when she comes back she does not want to find any names written on the board. She says, "It makes me sad and I don't want to be sad." She also tells them that she always comes back to school after her meetings so that she knows what is going on.

Specific class rules are not posted in this room, but their presence is felt and the children know what they are. In Mrs. B [M]'s fifth-sixth-grade class, a list of rules is posted on the bulletin board. This class has a number of students with serious problems, including two who have been expelled from other elementary schools. But, as Mrs. B [M] says, "I can't dwell too much on their problems at home. I can empathize ... but when it comes time that they are in this classroom, then by gosh, at that time I must insist we get on with the lessons."

One strategy she uses to facilitate "getting on" with the lessons is to begin her class by

> leading her students in a discussion concerning why they are in school and why they should do their best work. Following that they also review the class rules. These rules are (1) no inappropriate talking, (2) keep hands, feet, objects, etc., to him- or herself, (3) remain seated unless permission is given to do otherwise, (4) follow directions the first time, and (5) no cussing or teasing.

According to the class discussion, the purpose of these rules is to provide a safe, orderly environment in which conversation, time, and energy are directed toward getting an education.

Positive social and academic behavior in Mrs. B [M]'s class is often publicly reinforced through praise, having one's name put on the *cool* list, or occasionally with rewards like posters. Negative behavior is usually dealt with privately or with a minimum of fanfare. Sometimes it is necessary to put names on the *uncool* list. The following excerpts are examples of both events.

> The students come into the room. "I like the way Reggie came in, sat down, and knew right what to do. Karen knew right what to do. Jeremy looks good. Edward looks good." Mrs. B [M] put their names on the board under *cool* and put a star beside each name.

During a reading session she says, when the first reader has finished:

"That's a real good job. You can be proud." When the second reader has finished, she says, "I like the way you are really using periods to help give good expression." To the group who was listening to cassettes at another table, she says, "I want to compliment the Octogons for the nice way you were at the listening table." On another occasion, as it is drawing close to recess time and students are busy working at their desks, Mrs. B [M] goes to the blackboard and writes the following:

> If you are reading this, do the following,
> 1. Tidy up!
> 2. Get things out for U.S.S.R.
> 3. Heads down!

Those who look up to see what she is writing follow the directions immediately. Those still deeply immersed in their work do not, but they soon are nudged by their classmates. Then they too look up, read the message, and do the same. There is absolute silence in the room, and Mrs. B [M] says, "Thank you for doing that so promptly." They are dismissed for recess a few minutes thereafter.

There are students, of course, who forget the rules occasionally, who do not get to work as quickly as they should, who get to talking when they shouldn't, or whose whispering becomes too loud.

> A group of children is supposed to be doing an assignment listed on the board and one of them hasn't yet gotten to work. Mrs. B [M] notices that and writes him a note, which another child delivers, stating "Get to work." A short time later when she notices he is working she sends a second note which reads, "Much better, Damien. XO, Mrs. B [M]." When Damien's reading group meet with Mrs. B [M] he returns her second note, with a note written on the back stating, "Thank you, Mrs. B [M] XO."

Some time later, she stops working with a reading group, rings a bell, and says,

> "Freeze! I can see you are all doing good work but the noise level is

getting too high. If you are working together what are you supposed
to do?" The students respond, "Whisper." "If I can hear you, you are
not whispering." With the exception of two students the voice level
drops immediately. Mrs. B [M] gets up and says to them, "I resent
having to get out of my seat." She speaks quietly to them and gets
them back to work.
Sandy, another student, misbehaves one morning and gets her name
put on the *uncool* list. As time goes on and Sandy has been working
along quietly, Mrs. B [M] says, "Sandy, keep up the good work" and
erases her name from the *uncool* list.

On only one occasion during our observations does Mrs. B [M]
use an overt power enforcement strategy. During a math lesson, a
large group of students are sent to the board to do some of the
problems given in Puzzle 25. The others remain at their seats. One
of the students at the board has trouble solving his problem and
becomes a bit noisy trying to get help from his classmates. And
some of those in their seats begin working on other classwork
while they wait for those at the board to finish writing. One boy
takes out a comic book to read. This student disengagement angers
Mrs. B [M]. She stops everyone and states,

> "I will wait till everyone has pencils down and eyes up here. Tommy,
> why don't you join us? Spelling books away. Comic books away.
> Rick, the only thing we are working on is math. I should see Puzzle 25
> right in front of you." Having said this Mrs. B [M] walks around the
> room and checks to see if her directions are being followed.

To further emphasize her displeasure with such conduct, Mrs. B
[M] says to the class monitor for the day,

> "Lucius, will you get that suspension form from my desk and bring it
> to me? Also will you go to the office and get me one more?" Lucius
> follows her directions. There is dead silence in the room. The math
> lesson is resumed, the students doing the problems and completing
> the assignment.

No student is actually suspended, but Mrs. B [M]'s implied threat is
understood by her class, and there are no further problems that
afternoon.
    In another fifth-grade classroom, the rules reflect the teacher's
belief in the importance of relationship and respect. This teacher
believes that students who respect themselves and others function
better in the classroom. Her reminders and enforcement strategies
for her students who "forget" or lose their self-control reflect this
belief. Three of the rules in this class are (1) no rocking in your
chair, (2) no name calling, and (3) no hitting. The students
understand and accept the need for these rules and sometimes

participate in deciding how a rule offender would be disciplined. Often, however, only a reminder is necessary.

> While working on a problem, Jeff leans back in his chair and begins rocking. Mrs. I [C] says, "Remember, you are not to lean back in your chair and cause it to rock. What will happen if you keep that up?" Jeff responds sheepishly, "I could fall over and get hurt." He stops doing it immediately and then continues with his work.

Later that day a name-calling and hitting incident occurs on the playground between two members of this class. Mrs. I [C] is informed of the incident, and when class reconvenes, the episode is discussed and dealt with immediately. Members of the class contribute to the discussion and agree with Mrs. I [C]'s proposed means of solving it without formal disciplinary action. (On other occasions the students had suggested other informal ways of dealing with classmates who had broken the rules.)

> During the discussion Mrs. I [C] says, "Jill, you have been calling people names. You called Ronny a 'black nigger' and Vicky a 'white honkey.' These kids do not like it when you call someone a name, especially if it refers to color. Do you understand?"

Indeed, the overwhelming majority of the students in that class believe in the "no-name-calling" rule and have, on other occasions, verbalized their sense of outrage when name-calling has occurred. Even Jill, herself a relative newcomer to the class, has been working on controlling her tendency toward name-calling.

> Andy has done the hitting and Mrs. I [C] says to him, "Andy, hitting is not good. You may have been taught to hit at home but we just can't have hitting at school." She then comments that Andy is sorry for what he has done.

Just before lunch that morning, Mrs. I [C] publicly awards imaginative certificates to various students for improved academic or social behavior. She gives *boned up* awards to two students with the following words: "I am proud that Tamika has *boned up* on her spelling." "Shirley and Tamika have really done well. I congratulate you. That is what really counts, trying." When Mrs. I [C] finishes presenting those certificates, she then gives the *hang in there* awards to various students. The protocol reads as follows:

> "You have not made as much progress but we are aware that you have been doing better. And you are doing better." The students clap for the winners. "That's what I like about you guys, you always clap for people who get awards."
>
> Mrs. I [C] then presents a certificate which she reads: "A special

award is presented to Jill for outstanding improvement in her attitude and behavior at N...School. She has shown a terrific attitude for the past two weeks." The class applauds with vigor when Jill receives her certificate.

The hand-raising rule is frequently reinforced in this classroom by positively evaluating such behavior. During a math question-and-answer session, for example, Mrs. I [C] says "I like the way you guys are raising your hands."

As students get older, teachers find that they must insist that attention be focused on the subject at hand and that students not work on any other materials or assignments. Mrs. A [M], a fourth-fifth-grade teacher, forces such attention in the following episode.

The math lesson is going on and students are doing work at the blackboard. Mario is asked to go to the board to do a problem and while he is there Mrs. A [M] picks up a book that he was working with and sits on it. The book related to another assignment and not to math. When he finished at the board he returned to his seat and found his book missing. He began looking for it. Saying nothing, Mrs. A [M] watched him hunt. She then asked, "What is the matter?" "I can't find my book." She doesn't tell him she has the book but says instead, "You don't have to worry about your book now. We are right in the middle of this lesson. You'll find your book when the time comes and you need it."

During this math lesson Mrs. A [M] also makes explicit the generally invisible structure surrounding the process of teacher elicitation, student response, and teacher evaluation process described in Chapter IV. The observation protocol reports the following:

Mrs. A [M] selects one of the boys in the class to be "teacher" and he calls on another student to come to the board. The person he assigned does the work correctly. Mrs. A [M] says to the "teacher," "Aren't you going to tell him what a wonderful job he did?" Some of the children laugh. Mrs. A [M] says, however, "Seriously, if you do a good job you should be told so." Another "teacher" is selected, he calls some students to the board, gives them problems to solve and when they do them correctly, he compliments them.

Like the other effective teachers, Mrs. A [M] regularly reinforces and evaluates student behavior with such comments as the following:

[After passing out papers to the class to begin a work session] "You have five minutes. Tomas's ready, Jay's ready and has his pencil all sharpened. Peg's not making a sound, Joline's ready, she's looking at

me, Penny's ready, she's sitting up. Hot dog! You are all doing a good job today."
[When it is time to check the spelling assignment] "OK, exchange your papers. Dawn is ready, Juanita is ready, Penny's ready. I know that Chad is ready because he has his pencil in his hand and he's not making a sound. [At the end of a small group reading session] Thank you for remembering to push your chair in, D.D."

One morning the principal comes into the room and speaks with Mrs. A [M]. She also speaks with the class for a moment before she leaves the room. Mrs. A [M] then says the following to the class:

I'd like you to know that while Mrs. P was here there was one person in the back of the room that was really listening, yet continuing to do his work. I'm really pleased with you, P.T. You have done a complete turn around from last year and are really being a good student. Even his mother realizes and is so pleased.

During all of the observations of Mrs. A [M]'s classroom, there is only one explicit reference to a specific rule, and that concerned hand raising. During most of the morning, children raise their hands for permission to get materials they need or to get help from Mrs. A [M]'s aide. However, during one work session, while Mrs. A [M] is busy with a reading group, Andrea and Penny get up from their seats without raising their hands and walk back to the aide's desk. The protocol reports:

"You go and sit down. You didn't raise your hands," says the aide. Mrs. A [M] adds, "I think maybe we need to have a talk at lunch time if you are not going to remember the rules."

Whereas some of the teachers permitted students to help each other with decoding problems in reading, Mr. E [I] did not. The following is an excerpt from a reading session.

"Now we will read. If someone has trouble with a word don't help them out. Let them work it out by themselves so they can learn the word." Therese begins to read and has a problem decoding a word. A boy starts to help her, realizes what he's doing and covers his mouth. Another child reads the next paragraph. She gets stuck, no one says anything and she figures out the word by herself.

Students in this class are often publicly honored and rewarded for their good behavior, as happened in the following episode.

"Whatever you are working on now, you have two or three minutes to finish up and then it will be time for lunch." A small amount of socializing begins and Mr. E [I] says, "OK, listen up! Everybody back to their seats. Everybody back to their seats immediately. Excellent, Megin, excellent." Megin's name is written on the *cool* list on the board. Mr. E [I] writes some other names also. "OK, everyone's head down." Some more names are added to the *cool* list and get stars put beside them. "Looking good. This afternoon I will teach you to play 'Steal the Bacon.' Remind me." It is now time for lunch. The names of the students who are on the *cool* list are called first and thus first in the room's lunch line.

Mr. E [I] also uses the *uncool* list when necessary. He is especially likely to use this rule enforcement strategy to secure complete student attention during a lesson.

"Today we are starting double divisors. Turn to page 78." Mr. E [I], who is standing at the blackboard when he says this, turns and writes a name on the *uncool* list. "It is very important when we are doing math that it is all you are doing. When I am explaining a concept I need your complete attention or you will miss something. Then it fouls you up and I have to spend extra time trying to straighten you out. And that takes away from everybody."

Mr. E [I] uses an exchange mechanism of control on another morning when members of his class fail to comply with the rules.

The class is told to get ready for lunch and some of them get too noisy. Mr. E [I] just stands in the front of the room and soon it is absolutely silent. "As you can tell, I am not real thrilled right now. I had to spend too much time talking about people who were not quiet. So it is lunch time now and I get to waste your time for a few minutes. So if you waste my time then I will waste yours." He lets that sink in. Then he walks around and hands out the lunch tickets. "There are no cuts in line. Some of you are doing that and it is not cute. You are to walk out like ladies and gentlemen. After recess there will be a line, a neat line." He calls the names of the various students and they line up at the door. They are very subdued. "Now, like ladies and gentlemen, we will walk down to the lunch line." They leave the room and go to lunch.

KINDERGARTEN: WHERE THE SOCIALIZATION PROCESS BEGINS

For most students, socialization into the rule structure of the school begins in kindergarten. The typical kindergarten teacher spends a great deal of time preparing students for entry into the culture of the many different classrooms they will encounter over the years.

Mrs. G [C], the kindergarten teacher in our sample, uses an

intriguing array of techniques to develop her classroom culture. On the opening day of school, Mrs. G [C] had all of the children sit down together so that she could talk with them and explain what they were permitted to do at the beginning of each day. She explained that there were various activities for them to work on until the bell rang to start the school day. She provided them with a large number of activities at first and then limited the number after a few days. She explained to them that some activities would no longer be available because "it takes too long to clean them up before school starts." Unlike the older children, kindergarteners go directly to their classrooms when they arrive at school, and Mrs. G [C] would greet each of them as they entered the room and direct them to the extracurricular activities until the bell rang. She called each of them by name and insisted they call her "Mrs. G [M]," not "teacher." She also checked to make sure they put away their personal belongings before becoming involved in an activity of their choice.

An episode which occurred one morning, shortly before Halloween, illustrates Mrs. G [C]'s most powerful socializing tool: the rationalization of rules.

> Mrs. G [C] has brought a pumpkin into class and placed it on the table. When the children arrive they spot it immediately and go to the table to handle it, feel it and move it around. Mrs. G [C] walks to the table and says to them, "I would not lift it up. I would hate to have it fall and land on a foot and squish some toes." The children continue to enjoy the pumpkin but no one attempts to lift it.

By offering a meaningful rationale for the rule "don't pick up the pumpkin," Mrs. G [C] is able not only to get compliance with this specific requirement, but also to make rules appear natural, reasonable, and an appropriate part of school life.

On another occasion, Mrs. G [C] demonstrates that rules can be made to seem more reasonable if teachers anticipate their effects and help children cope with any problems they encounter when trying to comply. Just before the bell was to ring, Mrs. G [C] says the following to the students who are busy playing in various sections of the room: "I think it is time for you to put things away now. I think the bell is going to ring." The children heed the warning and start putting their things away. The bell rings and Mrs. G [C] says: "All right boys and girls, the bell has rung. Come and sit down please." Only three children do not immediately respond as they are reassembling the puzzles so that they can put them away. The task is taking a bit longer than expected, so Mrs. G

[C] calls to them: "Earl, Jose, Barry, put the pieces down. You can finish putting them away later."

Mrs. G [C] routinely expects the children to sit up straight with their hands in their laps and legs crossed when she assembles them for group instruction. On one particular morning, she reminds them of that expectation: "Now let's cross your legs and put your hands in your laps. Good morning, Megin Mitchell." The child replies, "Good morning, Mrs. G [C]" Each child in the class is greeted in this fashion, and only one needs correction because he says "teacher" instead of her name. Each time the children gather at the rug, Mrs. G [C] uses her second most powerful socialization tool — positive attention — to reinforce their compliance with the sitting rule: "I like the way Amy sits. I like the way Kerry sits. Kirby has his hands folded and is sitting up straight. Donald's sitting so nicely. You make me feel so good."

Mrs. G [C] is also quick to act if behavior outside the bounds of her simple rule structure is in evidence. When, for example, she is discussing the math work to be done and two boys are not completely attentive, she stops and says the following: "Donald, I would like Bob to sit someplace else so you two won't talk so much. You can be friends on the playground."

There are times when personal conversation is acceptable in the classroom, but Mrs. G [C] expects the children to be quiet when she is teaching or giving directions and takes immediate action when she does not have their complete attention. In the following example, she points to the collective purpose or mission of the classroom as the justification for her demands:

> Mrs. G [C] is working with phonic sounds with the children and some are still a bit too wiggly. "I think we are going to have a little talk. I am having to spend too much time talking to you about what we are doing. Will you not talk unless I ask you to? I think this lesson is the most important thing you are going to do today."

When they are supposed to be doing followup work, Mrs. G [C] publicly rewards as well as reinforces appropriate social and academic behavior:

> "OK, let's see who is going to be the first one to get their name on the board. Carlotta is busy, she gets a smiling face. Gina gets a smiling face. Cassie. Ginny." [The name of each child mentioned is written on the board and a smiling face is drawn next to it]. The children are quiet and busy at work almost immediately.

As was mentioned earlier, a nearly universal rule requiring students to write their names on all papers — first thing, so they won't forget — is usually introduced in kindergarten. At one point, when the children in this class were at their seats doing a math assignment, one boy vividly portrayed the socialization process at work when he said aloud to himself, "I have got to write my name first."

Mrs. G [C] relies on a less universal but still widespread rule for determining when children have completed their seatwork material so that she can begin checking it. She does not require children to come to her to tell her they are finished or to raise their hands and possibly distract others still working. Rather, she has them turn their papers over and place them on their desks. One morning she notices one boy who has finished but has failed to comply with this rule:

> "Walter, when you are finished, what do you do?" As Walter demonstrates what he's supposed to do, Mrs. G [C] says, "You turn your page to the back and then I can see you are done and can come and check your work."

As other children finish their work, they follow the directions given in Mrs. G [C]'s reminder.

SUCCESSFUL ENCULTURATION: DIRECTION GIVING RATHER THAN RULE ENFORCEMENT

When a teacher successfully enculturates the rules for all students, their idiosyncratic behaviors blend into the classroom subculture to become unobtrusive — almost invisible. As this happens, student behavior can be viewed as a part of that culture and the teacher can rely on "giving directions" rather than "making rules" in order to control student actions. Moreover, virtually all student behavior, because it is guided by the classroom culture, then becomes an occasion for teaching.

The observations of Mrs. H [C]'s first-grade classroom reveal such a culturally directed order. Mrs. H [C] tells parents about her behavioral rules in an in-service session:

> It takes me about six weeks to get to know your child. What they can do and what they can't, whether they will settle down or won't settle down. First, we have some classroom rules and the children are expected to follow them. We have gone over them since the first day of school and if I call you, it is probably because they are not following these rules. The rules are posted there on the bulletin board.

And she indicates that the rules are important to her when she states that an important consideration in teaching is "maintaining good discipline in the classroom so that everybody is functioning and doing and having a good time, but still learning without a whole lot of haphazard activities going on." She adds, "And I don't think a classroom has to be absolutely quiet but I think it has to be meaningful talk."

When we observed her classroom we found it quiet; her students worked with the aide, independently, on assigned materials, or with Mrs. H [C] herself. There were almost no references to requirements or rules in evidence.

Mrs. H [C]'s ability to give directions rather than make rules is illustrated in the way she works with a reading group one morning. She tells the reading group that they can choose any word from the chart that they want and then tell the rest of the group what it is. If someone does not get the word right, Mrs. H [C] gets to hold it so that they can do it again after they have gone through all the words once.

> "You may look at it and tell us what it is. Then you can put it back into the chart." To the first child: "See if everybody agrees." The child answers, "It is *tied*." "Do you agree with her?" "Yes." "Alright, you can put it back on the chart." To another child: "you tell us what you think it is." "Is she right?" "Yes." "It is your turn to choose." The child responds, *"duck."* "You show it and see if they agree. That's right? No, I don't think it is. Look at it again." *"Look."* "That's right. I get to hold the word." The child hands her the word. Mrs. H [C] then points to the chart. "Oh! Oh! You see something wrong with that A?" One of the children answers, "Oh, I see. I put it upside down," and she goes and turns it right side up.

This lesson requires the students to cooperate with highly developed social rules, but Mrs. H [C] has so successfully socialized these children that they no longer see her as forming rules. She only directs their activities within a framework of fully accepted but virtually invisible rules.

A little later Mrs. H [C] directs these first graders' attention to a bathroom use rule as she dismisses them for recess: "Let's put your things down. Now stand up and then line up. Remember you are to use the bathroom first." Even this explicit rule, however, is not articulated as a requirement, only as a reminder to follow what is culturally defined as the natural order of things.

Following recess the children begin their math. One child has a problem and Mrs. H [C] again invokes classroom rules in a natural way:

> "You come up here and I'll work with you. It looks like you are having

a problem with subtraction. Read your number sentence again. What does it say?" Desmond follows her directions and while he works on his paper Mrs. H [C] checks the work of another child. Then Mrs. H [C] looks at Desmond's paper again and says, "Hurrah! You have gotten it all right. Now let's do the next page. But you check the signs. They are all mixed up now. Look at all the pictures very carefully." "Tyrie. Tyrie." Tyrie has been busy working away but he has been talking to himself about his work and his voice has gotten a bit too loud. He lowers his voice and continues working.

Clearly the most important element in Mrs. H [C]'s ability to transform rules into directions is her ability to continuously monitor all of the children and quickly spot any trouble they have complying with expectations. She displays this skill repeatedly. For example, one day as she watches the class at work she calls various ones up to the front table to check their work or to give them help if she believes they look puzzled. She also checks Desmond's work again:

"We have gotten three oops! here." She erases the three answers and he goes right to work on them.

Patsy gets most of her work done but then has trouble with the money section. She stops working and looks out of the window. Mrs. H [C] sees her:

"Patsy, what are you doing?" "I don't know how to count money." "You had better come here." "How much is a nickel?" "Five cents." "How much is a penny?" "One cent." Patsy then works on her math sheet right in front of Mrs. H [C] and gets it completed. Mrs. H [C] checks it and marks it. "What is that?" "A C for correct." Patsy proudly returns to her seat and says, "Now, I can work on sets."

Though the observations in Mrs. H [C]'s classroom, as with all of the teachers in this study, were limited in scope, we were impressed by the effectiveness and consistency with which she is able to rely on culturally supported directions rather than rule enforcement to guide student behavior. We were also impressed by the extent to which this shift from rules to directions turns all classroom activities into learning experiences for children.

THE INTRUSION OF THE SCHOOL'S RULE STRUCTURE

In addition to classroom rules, there are also schoolwide rules, and the school's rule structure sometimes intrudes into the classroom. When this occurs, teachers sometimes direct their disapproval at breaking a school rule both to the particular offender(s) and to the entire class in the hope that it will not be repeated in the future. The following excerpt illustrates this process.

> Mrs. I [C]'s class returns from recess. There has been a problem during recess and Mrs. I [C] says, "Before we can get to work again we have to talk about some things. I have gotten a referral slip. What grade are you in?" This question is directed toward a specific student, who responds, "Fifth grade." "This referral says you were writing on the bathroom stall. Do you have to clean it off or does the custodian have to clean it off? If you need to write during recess I have plenty of scratch paper. That's just not done. That belongs to everyone. What would happen if you weren't caught? The third graders could see it and add to it. I don't think it is very funny. This is the second referral slip. Are you trying for one next week?" Mrs. I [C] is really annoyed. "Remember, I read the rules. I think instead of giving up my lunch time you will stay after school with me. You will lose your lunch recess and spend it with [the aide]. After school, you and I will discuss the consequences. Mrs. I [C] is not going to let you get away with it. I am going to deal with it."

While only the offender is going to be kept after school, the whole class is being informed and warned of the unacceptability of such behavior.

In another instance a notice has been given to the teaching staff by one of the principals concerning student behavior on the playground. Some of the older students have been involved in a throwing incident, and a child has been injured. Earlier in the year the teachers had taken class time to discuss appropriate playground behavior, and although none of this class' students were actually involved, Mrs. J [C] views the offending students' conduct as being potentially contagious and wants to make sure her students do not become infected.

> Mrs. J [C] takes attendance and then says to the class, "Look at the clock. We are supposed to be reading now but we have to take time for scolding. Do we have to make a long list of what we can't throw? We can't throw sticks. We can't throw anything. An upper grader was saying that Mr. R [the principal] didn't say anything about throwing sand. He knew better. You know you shouldn't throw sand, don't you?" The class responds, "Yes." "Good." The teacher then begins discussing what the groups will be doing during the first work period this morning.

Occasionally, however, teachers will intercede on behalf of their students. The following is an example of teacher intercession.

> "OK, boys and girls, freeze. Every part of your body including your

mouths." Mrs. B [M] then reads a note from Mrs. S [the principal] about the new sand and the rules about sand play. The note said that yesterday Mrs. S was stopping them from playing in the sand. However, because Mrs. B [M] and Mr. E [I] said, "Please let our students play in the sand," Mrs. S was willing to give them "one last chance."

Mrs. B [M], having read Mrs. S's note, had the class pledge they would use the sand in a safe way. They had to raise their hands and repeat after her, "I will use the sand in a safe manner," then "cross my heart." "What will happen if Mrs. B [M] gets a yellow slip about you?" "You will have a fit." "Yes, and what kind of fit?" "A hissy fit." They chuckle but they know that she means business.

Having interceded with the principal, this teacher wants her students to know that she is at risk and that she expects them to act responsibly in return.

CONCLUSION

We have examined rule formation and enforcement by twelve of the fifteen teachers in our sample. Mrs. O [H]'s highly chaotic classroom lacks clear behavioral rules and consistent rule enforcement mechanisms. At the other end of the spectrum, Mrs. H [C]'s culturally directed first grade classroom also lacks visible rules and identifiable enforcement mechanisms. Thus, we find that well-organized and highly disorganized classrooms show little evidence of explicit rule making or enforcement. We conclude that overt behavioral rules form a bridge between chaos and cultural order. Teachers with less well-developed classroom cultures are required to spend more time and energy declaring and enforcing rules. As the classroom culture becomes more fully developed, rules come to be seen by the students as a natural outgrowth of the shared meanings and overall purposes of the classroom group and thus serve as the basis for teacher direction giving rather than the occasions for power struggles or psychological manipulations.

CHAPTER VI

Five School Principals: Administrative Work in Cultural Perspective

Cultural meanings — the development of a shared interpretation of social activities and a common definition of collective social projects — are just as important to principals as to teachers. As Ouchi (1981) suggests, the articulation and interpretation of cultural symbols is a powerful mechanism for social control in any organization. More importantly, principals, like teachers, can only understand and execute their work responsibilities within the framework of a comprehensive (though largely unconscious) cultural meaning system. Before principals can use available cultural symbols to influence others, they must first acquire for themselves a comprehensive and vivid way of typifying school events and defining the educational mission of the school. Observation and interview data collected from the five principals in our study reveal how principals develop and use specific cultural orientations. The most important cultural meanings embedded in these principals' work orientations interpret the relationship between personal cultures and the most prominent features of work habits or administrative styles.

Before examining in detail the work orientations of the principals studied, we should underscore the fact that only five individuals were observed and that they were selected primarily to ensure access to teacher and school variables. Hence the analysis presented in this chapter should be viewed as more suggestive and tentative than our analysis of teacher work orientations. Nevertheless, we found the principals individually interesting, and comparisons among them led to a provocative reinterpretation of many key concepts in principal leadership school management.

The principals investigated in this study revealed orientations which did not generally include either clear conceptions of their own role responsibilities or explicit attention to their influence over the teachers' incentive system. (In this respect our data echo those of Blumberg and Greenfield, 1980.) This does not mean, however, that the principals' work behavior was chaotic or unpredictable. To the contrary, by combining observation and interview data, it is fairly easy to identify a consistent pattern (we will call it a "work style") for most principals. It is much more difficult, however, to discern the *basis* for that consistency. Thus our analysis of the principal data presents a set of concepts useful in capturing the overall character of each principal's style. The concepts selected are those which address the most salient features of the work done by the particular principals participating in this study. At the same time, our analysis is broad enough to provide an overall description of the organizational and governance responsibilities of all elementary school principals.

Abstract theory and concrete data were integrated by concentrating on the application of four terms commonly used to describe the work of principals and other middle-level executives: *administration, leadership, supervision,* and *management.* In the literature on complex organizations, these four terms are used in many different, overlapping, and sometimes contradictory ways. Recent scholarship, however, has begun to distinguish more precisely among them and to describe more fully the behaviors associated with each (see, for example, Owens, 1970; Zaleznick, 1977; Krajewski, Martin, and Walden, 1980; and Sergiovanni et al., 1981). Uniform definitions for the four terms or a common set of criteria for distinguishing among them have not yet been produced, but researchers have used these concepts to highlight different aspects of middle-level executive job responsibilities and work orientations.

As described more fully below, four of the five elementary school principals in our sample can be meaningfully classified as organizing their work primarily in terms of one of these four terms: that is, the most important differences in the work styles of our sample principals are highlighted by saying that one is primarily an administrator, one a leader, one a supervisor, and one a manager. By moving dialectically back and forth between the data and the literature, the meaning of each of these different conceptions of the principalship is refined and a richly textured interpretation of the work orientations of our principals is provided.

Figure VI-1 presents the conceptual framework that best classifies the important differences among the principals we studied. As suggested by the figure, our data are more easily understood if we describe briefly how the principals differ in their approaches to defining and executing their job responsibilities.

The overall work orientations of the principals are shaped primarily by the ways in which they (a) typify teaching work behavior and (b) define the overall mission or purposes of schooling. As is shown in the rows of Figure VI-1, when thinking about the work of teachers, some principals concentrate on the level of *effort* teachers put into their work, while others focus more on the character and quality of their teaching task *performance*. When adopting the teaching effort perspective, principals tend to feel that teachers themselves know best what and how to teach and that the job of the principal is largely to stimulate, motivate, and support them. This orientation toward teaching work assumes that improved teaching depends on the development of a more fully dedicated staff who will give their utmost effort to the task. Principals who concentrate on the character and adequacy of teachers' task performance feel that teaching can be improved by prescribing more precisely the tasks to be performed and the techniques to be used by teachers. Principals holding this view emphasize the importance of taking steps to ensure that appropriate techniques are used in the classrooms.

As is indicated by the headings over the columns of Figure VI-1, principals generally orient themselves to the mission or enterprise of schooling by concentrating either on the adequacy and efficiency of the school's *organization* or by concentrating on the *execution* of its various program elements. Principals who concentrate on program organization tend to feel that educational quality depends primarily on planning and coordination — that is, on whether tasks are properly defined and assigned to various members of the staff and whether the efforts of various staff members are fully integrated and adequately supported. Those who concentrate on program execution tend to feel that educational outcomes depend more on the care or diligence with which relatively autonomous teachers discharge their work responsibilities.

As the cells of the figure suggest, the four primary concepts for describing the principalship are consistent with the alternative teacher work and educational mission orientations described above.

FIGURE VI-I. PRINCIPALS' WORK STYLES AS A FUNCTION OF THEIR ORIENTATIONS TOWARD TEACHING WORK AND THE OVERALL MISSION OF THE SCHOOL

ORIENTATION TOWARD
SCHOOL MISSION

		SCHOOLING AS THE ORGANIZATION OF PROGRAMS (SEEK IMPROVED EFFICIENCY)	SCHOOLING AS THE EXECUTION OF TASKS (SEEK IMPROVED EFFECTIVENESS)
ORIENTATION TOWARD THE NATURE OF TEACHING WORK	TEACHING AS DEDICATED EFFORT	Emphasizes Supporting Function ——— Administrator: Mr. Q	Emphasizes Motivating Function ——— Leader: Mr. R
	TEACHING AS APPROPRIATE PERFORMANCE	Emphasizes Directing Function ——— Supervisor: Mrs. S	Emphasizes Training Function ——— Manager: Mrs. P
		(SCHOOL SEEN AS THE BASIC EDUCATIONAL UNIT)	(TEACHER SEEN AS THE BASIC EDUCATIONAL UNIT)

Administration (upper left cell) is the proper label for principal work orientations when principals are concerned primarily with (a) encouraging teachers to be diligent and dedicated and (b) planning and organizing program elements. Principals adopting this style believe that their primary duty lies in *supporting* both the activities of their teachers and the program of the school district. Like hospital administrators or university deans, these principals tend to believe that the people with whom they work are professionals who need to be provided with encouragement and adequate support services, but who are themselves best able to define and execute their primary work responsibilities.

Leadership (upper right cell) is the central concept when principals see teaching as dependent upon dedication and intensity of effort and see schooling as a matter of individual excellence rather than of collective organization. These principals concentrate on stimulating and motivating teachers to execute their responsibilities energetically and effectively. They see their own jobs primarily in terms of inspiring teachers with a vision of the purposes of education and the possibilities of children. They view teaching as an art form requiring spontaneity, dedication, and sensitivity rather than elaborate organization or intense technical training.

Supervision (lower left cell) is the central term for describing the work of principals who combine an organizational view of school programs with a level-of-effort concern regarding teacher performance. These principals concentrate on controlling and directing teacher work efforts (a) by giving immediate guidance in the tasks to be performed and (b) by insisting that the planning and organization of these tasks is the prerogative and responsibility of school executives. Supervision-oriented principals tend to display relatively little trust in the motives and competence of teachers and to believe that schools cannot function without strong and direct intervention by principals.

Management (lower right cell) is the concept which highlights the work of principals who feel that schooling is dependent upon organization and that teaching quality is a matter of technical performance. These principals concentrate on the execution of programs and the task performance of teachers. They tend to believe that quality education depends upon having a highly trained staff whose efforts are carefully coordinated and integrated into specific program goals.

Of course, all principals use at least some elements from each of these four modes of relating to teachers. Nevertheless, our data revealed sharp differences among the principals studied — differences reflecting special emphasis on particular elements within the four work styles shown in Figure VI-1. Moreover, as we will describe in detail below, the principals in this study displayed certain contradictions in their work — contradictions which they intuitively recognize as limitations on their ability to fully implement their favored work style. Since these contradictions are best illustrated in the context of concrete case data, we turn now to a discussion of the data from the principals.

THE PRINCIPAL AS MANAGER: THE CASE OF MRS. P

It is 2:40 P.M.; Mrs. P sits in her office, where she has just finished talking with her daughter by phone. The observation protocol at this point reads as follows:

> She begins sorting out the paper work. She decides what she needs to take home and what she can do here now.
> 2:43 P.M. Mrs. P: "School is over already. How time flies when you're having fun."

She goes on to say: "I keep three files, one for Ed. Services [the central office division where I work half-time], one for the elementary school where I am principal, and one for my home stuff. I hold that because I can never get the concentration going until I get home."

Thus Mrs. P starts to "wrap up" her day. During this nine-hour day, she will have dealt individually (in person or by phone) with co-workers, students, parents, and others on at least seventy-four distinct occasions (including eleven different encounters with her secretary). She will have shifted her work location at least forty-one times (not counting two moves when no work was involved). And she will have worked with students and co-workers in six different group settings. Beyond the more than nine hours of observation (lasting from 7:58 A.M. to 5:20 P.M.), she will spend at least an additional two hours at the district office and will have her hair cut at 7:45 that night.

The most striking feature of the observation protocols on this principal is the picture they paint of intense and rapid-fire interactions. During our two days of observation, Mrs. P was never alone for more than five minutes at a time without being interrupted by a phone call or visit. She frequently was interrupted in the course of a conversation with one person by the telephone or by another person needing immediate attention.

At one point, talking about another principal, she voices feelings which undoubtedly refer as much to herself as to him: "He is getting burned out by too much work. The central office is rewarding good principals by giving them too much work." She illustrates her point with reference to a third principal: "Mrs. W got E school, but they increased the student population to 600 people. She now has the bilingual program for the district too, and she has no assistant principal. When we worked on the Futures Project it was Fridays from 4 to 7 and then on Saturdays too. Teachers all get paid for that, but we are 'management.' "

In addition to the rapidity with which Mrs. P moves from place to place and from person to person, three other features of her work are prominent in the data, as discussed below.

Program Planning and Personnel Problems

First, Mrs. P gives greatest attention to program planning and development but finds herself plagued by personnel problems. Her commitment to the programmatic features of her job is clearly revealed in a statement she makes about how to evaluate a principal's job performance. To evaluate a principal, she says, one should look to the following:

1. Identify what kind of expectancy there is; is there a major thrust, or is everybody doing their own thing?
2. What's going on for improvement?
3. How is student discipline handled?
4. How is parent involvement handled?

Notice that there are no references to the feelings or attitudes of staff, students, parents, or even higher-level administrators in this list. Principal evaluation, in Mrs. P's mind, is rooted in program evaluation — if the program is going well, the principal is doing well.

In both interview statements and observed activities, Mrs. P reveals a continuing interest in many different aspects of school and district-level program planning. In fact, her workload as a program planner is so heavy that she cannot trust her memory:

2:47 She says, "I write notes on everything, because I just cannot rely on my memory anymore. I have gotten a better sense about what things I can handle and what I cannot handle ... Anything I can do without thinking, I respond to as quickly as I can." She continues to go through papers. She reads files, throws away, writes a note, etc.

Although Mrs. P complains about the workload, she takes pride in her ability to cope with the myriad of details and extensive paperwork involved. Describing the complexities and difficulties associated with working half-time as a principal and half-time as a curriculum coordinator in the central office, she says.

I think I can manage any school. And I think probably do it better than most ... I think that probably I am better informed about the total district than almost anybody else. I have been able to bring some coordination and continuity between elementary and secondary [programs] ... But it's a real killer ... I don't have time to talk with my teachers informally right after school and that kind of stuff. If you just take my calendar and look at the time that is fixed by meetings — it's tough.

It's tough alright. In May of that year this principal experienced a minirebellion by key staff members. They formed a committee and complained to her superior about a lack of attention to school problems resulting from the fact that both the principal and assistant principal were away from the building frequently performing district-level assignments. Reflecting on the difficulties, the principal commented as follows:

> Probably more than anything that has surprised me is that I have never been with a group that has returned as little as this group has. I really wonder if somebody would say, you know, they have decided I am not going to be at (this school) next year, I am going to be at Timbuktu — I wonder how the teachers would feel because I don't get any reactions or "vibes" or anything one way or the other. I have always had stroking from my staff, I have been here two years now. By the time somebody has been with me for two years, usually they have learned how I stroke and they start doing it back. These people are not stroking me and I don't know why.

She links her staff difficulties with her managerial responsibilities when she says, "I think that the real crux [of the problem] is that, as we continue to cut down on the real managers [due to budget cuts] there are not going to be that many people available to deal with some real problems... I know that for some time the small schools have wanted full-time principals... I do all I can here, but I cannot do everything."

Despite tensions with her staff, however, Mrs. P continues to adhere closely to the managerial work role:

> Management consists of an assessment of a situation and the systematic selection of goals and purposes. The systematic development of strategies to achieve these goals; the acquisition of resources; the rational design, organization, direction, and control of required activities and, finally, the motivating and rewarding of people to do the work complete the role.

High Energy and Careful Work

A second notable feature of the data on Mrs. P is the level of energy and diligence which she brings to her work. For example, during a midday principals' meeting with a central office administrator responsible for the district's $6 million ESAA grant to implement court-ordered desegregation, the subject of writing letters to parents of children who were being transferred to a new school came up. The observation protocol for that day contains the following entry:

> Letters need to go out and N... [the principal whose school the

children will be leaving] wants someone else to send the letters.
[Another principal] suggests that [the central office administrator]
do the letters. [The central office administrator] indicates, however,
that the receiving schools should send the letters. [The second
principal] says, "I have a foul attitude about this." He says he doesn't
want the additional responsibility. [The central office administra-
tor] finally states that he could do it if they really want it that way.
Mrs. P states, however, that she would send the letters out and will
type [the sending school principal's] signature on them.

Thus, despite her complaint that she and other good principals are
unable to keep up with work demands placed on them by the
central office, Mrs. P responds to the tension in this meeting by
taking on a responsibility which she could have avoided. Of course,
avoiding this responsibility would have meant that the central
office administrator would be saddled with a task which he felt
belonged to the principals, but he had grudgingly agreed to take it
on before Mrs. P volunteered.

In another example of unusual work effort, Mrs. P tells the
ESAA administrator that she would prefer to have the visitation
by the transferring children occur after her school completes the
district's testing program. She decided to hold off on a final
decision, however, until after she has talked with her teachers
about their preferences. Within ten minutes after returning to her
school, she makes the rounds of all the teachers in the building and
discovers that a majority prefer to have the student visitation take
place the day before the testing program is to begin. As a result, she
reschedules the visitation according to the majority's wishes.

Repeatedly, Mrs. P was observed to extend herself beyond the
minimal requirements of her job. She took work home, she followed
up on phone calls, she wrote numerous interoffice memoranda, and
she kept abreast of the myriad of details of district and school site
programs. Her busyness, though exhausting, did not seem to be
neurotic or unrelated to specific aspects of district programs and
policies. Rather, she appeared to simply work very hard to fulfill
both her own and senior administrators' views of what the job
required.

Language Usage

The third striking feature of our data on Mrs. P is her use of
language. Her conversations with our observer, with teachers, and
especially with other administrators were frequently witty, liber-
ally peppered with slang expressions, and a bit cynical in tone. As
mentioned above, at the end of an arduous day, she says, "How time
flies when you're having fun." A little later she is talking with her

assistant principal, who says, "This has really been some day."
Mrs. P responds, "Another day of excellence, right?!" Other
examples include the following:

> [To her secretary carrying a stack of supplies]: "It's not in your job
> description to hurt yourself."
> [On the phone to the central office]: "Okay, you'll be hearing from me,
> babe."
> [To the United Parcel man]: "Have you got a million dollars for me in
> the box?" The UPS man responds, "I sure hope so." Mrs. P: "We can
> split it."
> [Responding to an interview question on teacher evaluations]:
> "[sometimes] you have got the one where you are just laying it on the
> line and saying, 'Baby, I'm documenting you.' "

This language is clearly intended to create an atmosphere of
informality and good humor. And it conveys a sense of Mrs. P's
authority and spontaneity in relation to the various staff members.

In sum: Mrs. P is the only one of our principals ever to say, "I
am a management person, and that is what determines my time." In
both attitude and work style, she fulfills the definition of management offered by Krajewski, Martin, and Walden (1980, p. 9), who
define management as "working with and through people — both
individually and in groups — to accomplish organizational goals."
They continue: "Management functions include planning, organizing, motivating and controlling." When considering how to improve instruction, Mrs. P gives primary emphasis to in-service
training for her staff, which she reports is "a real biggy" in her
repertoire of principalship strategies.

Contradictions in Mrs. P's Style

As is illustrated in the data just presented, two discontinuities
or contradictions are especially apparent in Mrs. P's handling of
her principalship duties. Both concern her relationships with
teachers. One is related to the ways in which she tries to influence
the adoption of various instructional goals and techniques; the
other is seen in her attempts to create bonds of trust and mutual
respect with individual teachers.

The contradictions in her work stem from trying to combine an
intense focus on *activity* with a desire for strong social relationships. While she wants to "work with and through people," she
intuitively recognizes Mintzberg's (1973) view that managers exert
control by using for their own ends the activities that are essential
to their work: that is, they tend to depersonalize relationships in
order to control goals.

Establishing a Presence versus Enforcing Standards

Despite expansive and detailed discussions of teaching techniques and repeated assertions that she has "pressured" some teachers to adopt specific program goals, teaching techniques, or performance standards, when Mrs. P routinely encounters the teachers in her building, she is primarily concerned to establish a "presence" and to communicate her interest and support for them rather than to interpret or enforce job performance standards. A typical example of this behavior pattern is shown in the following observational protocol:

> She indicated that it was time for her to go and visit classes, so we left her office and started toward the classrooms. "I'm not here a lot, so I like to go through the classes so the kids get to see me. It also lowers teachers' anxiety when you go in to do teacher evaluations."

After visiting several classrooms, our observer notes, "None of the classroom visits were very long — they were just as long as necessary to establish that things were OK (or not OK)."

Two reasons are apparent for the disconnection between Mrs. P's professed orientation and her actual behavior. The first is practical. In the ordinary course of events, Mrs. P is simply unable to spend enough time with any one teacher to be able to clearly judge whether appropriate teaching techniques are being competently used and adequately adapted to the unique features of a particular classroom or lesson. Given the complexity and variety of the tasks teachers are required to perform, the teacher-principal ratio in the typical public school is entirely too large to permit effective implementation of the management approach to the principalship. Both Mrs. P and her teachers know that she cannot observe them often enough or under enough different circumstances to easily distinguish incompetent or inappropriate teaching techniques from temporary disruptions or the introduction of innovations in the classroom.

The second reason for the contradiction in Mrs. P's behavior is a theoretical one. In order to effectively implement a managerial approach to the oversight of instruction, principals need more than just the opportunity to observe teachers coping with a wide variety of classroom circumstances and student needs. They also need an adequate theory of teaching which provides them with a template for explicitly assessing whether teachers are performing required tasks effectively and at appropriate times. Without such a theory for rationalizing expectations, principals are forced to rely on assessing teachers' intentions rather than their actual performances. No such theory of instruction can be found in the data collected from Mrs. P. Although she has a better sense of instructional theory than any of the other principals in our sample — a theory derived in large measure from the work of UCLA professor Madeline Hunter — she is still compelled to acknowledge the following:

> As a principal I should be able to go into the classroom and see if the teacher is teaching a lesson — whether she's using the elements of good lesson design or not...[but] we haven't really developed a standardized format for doing it. I worked with [the associate superintendent] and came up with different elements that I want to include in all of my evaluations.

Thus, although Mrs. P knows that she needs a theory of instruction in order to evaluate teacher performance, she also knows that her current ideas about good lesson elements are not yet adequately developed and do not make standardized, comprehensive evaluations of all teachers possible.

"Stroking" an Alienated Staff

Mrs. P devotes a substantial amount of time and attention to what she calls "stroking" her staff. She writes interoffice memoranda to compliment those with whom she is pleased, and stops by the teachers' lounge to socialize and discuss the feelings and attitudes of various staff members with her assistant principal in order to find better ways to establish adequate relationships with them. Her feelings in this area are perhaps best summarized in the following remarks made about her relationship to one of the teachers whom we studied:

> I think maybe part of it is developing some trust. A lot of the teachers here had no more confidence in me than a hole in the wall. N...[the teacher in question], I think, has begun to feel some element of confidence, or trust, or security, or whatever you want to call it, so far as my work is concerned and how I will respond to things and back her up.

Mrs. P then described, in some detail, how their joint efforts to cope with one particularly difficult student helped to produce these feelings of trust.

As reported earlier, however, despite this apparent commitment to the development of trust, Mrs. P finds herself substantially estranged from most members of her faculty. The reasons for this estrangement provide important insights into why a managerial approach to the principalship has real limits. The lack of teacher trust for Mrs. P springs from two basic sources. First, because she thinks of herself as a "management person" and spends at least half her time working for and with district-level administrators, her teachers are a bit fearful that Mrs. P does not give them the unqualified loyalty and support which would justify the trust and confidence which she expects them to give. Some are anxious that she might be willing to impose arbitrary work standards or force the adoption of inappropriate instructional techniques if district administrators asked her to do so. This anxiety was exacerbated during the year of our study by several weeks of tense labor negotiations during which teachers were challenged by both managers and teacher organization leaders to think about which side they would be on if a strike were called. In fact, the teachers most active in the teachers' union were also the least responsive to Mrs. P's "stroking" efforts.

A second and more fundamental cause of this contradiction lies in Mrs. P's failure to fully understand the differences between rewards and incentives in motivating teachers. Mrs. P has a tendency to "stroke" teachers by sending them notes, praising them publicly, giving them pleasant assignments, or allowing them to attend various in-service training programs. She does not seem to recognize, however, the weakness of these rewards when compared with those controlled by the students (student achievement and student warmth and cooperation). Nor does she appear to recognize that teachers are guided more by incentives embedded in the overall culture of the school than by those rooted in personal relationships with individual managers or other co-workers. Thus Mrs. P mistakenly hopes to offset her frequent criticisms of school programs and teachers' performances through the development of warm personal relationships of trust and understanding with individual teachers. Such a strategy cannot work because the teachers inevitably suspect Mrs. P's respect for skilled teaching and her own skepticism of warmth and cooperativeness which are not grounded on competence and dedication to effective task performance. Nowhere is her dedication to competence more explicit than in her evaluation of a fellow principal, of whom she said the following: "You can't count on [him] at all. He used to be a team leader...I had a purchase order that I needed him to sign; he said: 'No problem, I will have it done right away.'" Mrs. P said that it wasn't until three days later that she got the thing put through. She also seemed to indicate that this was just one case of many.

THE PRINCIPAL AS ADMINISTRATOR:
THE CASE OF MR. Q

Mr. Q sees his job as time structured. When asked to describe his typical work responsibilities, he began with "Maybe I just should start with Monday and go from there." Through the course of the rest of his answer, given from memory and covering his most recent week's work, he made twenty-one specific references to particular hours of the day during which events occurred. And he gave an additional nine indirect references to equally specific times (such as, "today I started out," "during the lunch period," etc.).

In responding to a question about whether he has control over his job, however, Mrs. Q replies as follows:

> That's a hard question . . . I have some control there as to how I will spend my time, but the demands also control the time, so I feel that, "Yes," I do have some control in terms of my own time and my structure. But there are other events that happen just throughout the course of the day that I have no control over and which then take over control of my time, and I am not very good at saying "No." I am very accessible and available.

Mr. Q sees his work responsibilities much more in terms of planning and organizing programs than of supervising or "role modeling" appropriate teacher behavior. Asked how he makes a contribution to instruction at his school, he gives the following answer:

> In this particular school it is through planning and through organization. In terms of delivering actual role modeling of instruction, I do very little of that....I guess I think that the principalship has changed, that you are more of a manager in terms of personnel. In terms of operation and instruction that is why we are here. But the demands that are on my time frequently leave little opportunity to be actually involved in modeling of instruction.

The above passage contains Mr. Q's only reference to the term *management*. It is clear he sees management as a personnel rather than a programmatic concept. Mr. Q sees himself as planning and organizing programs, as facilitating smooth functioning of the school, and as securing the cooperation of teachers. He fits closely Owens's (1970, pp. 126, 127) description of the administrative role:

> Administration is concerned with the smooth operation of an organization, here, the school. In his role as administrator, the principal facilitates the use of established procedures and structures to help the organization achieve its goals. Administrators are

properly concerned with *maintaining* the organization, with keeping its interrelated parts functioning smoothly, and with monitoring the orderly processes that have been established to get things accomplished.

Mr. Q talks about leadership only twice in his interviews. The first time is in reference to the basis of his own evaluation by central office superiors. Of his immediate supervisor, he says the following:

> He looks for leadership, responsibility, and program development. [He looks at] what role I play in developing the A-127's [program planning documents], program articulation, communication with staff, students and community. Whether the instructional delivery system is designed to increase student performance and achievement in language arts, specifically in oral and written expression and spelling. The way I evaluate certificated personnel. The methods used to carry our district-adopted proficiency requirements. Leadership in compensatory education to promote student support and community participation in district desegregation and integration programs.

The other occasion on which Mr. Q talks about leadership is when he is discussing what teachers expect of him: "I think they want leadership. I think they also want changes, at times, when it is impossible for me to deliver." Asked for examples, he continues: "I think that sometimes teachers would like to think that principals could change extremely difficult kids into model children and, of course, I can't do that. I can work with them to bring about change, but it is not going to be over night. It is probably not going to be all that dramatic either." Indeed, in the next breath, Mr. Q expresses the view that teachers probably don't really want this kind of leadership anyway. He says, "I think that they want someone to be caring and to be sociable with them, and I don't mean necessarily socializing after hours, but be friendly, and I work at that." He is not even sure that these demands for friendly socializing are entirely justified, however. As he puts it: "I guess I would say that the communications are a two-way matter. And there are some days that are really very rushed, a lot of demands and sometimes I might not be as relaxed at that particular moment as I would like to be."

The tone of these remarks reflects Mr. Q's belief that he is responsible for developing programs aimed at reaching district-wide goals and objectives. Generally speaking, he approaches program development bureaucratically, emphasizing logistical rather than technical terms. His view of leadership is dominated by routine organizational activities — facilitating and coordinating — not the "visionary" or "motivational" dimensions identified by Sergiovanni et al. (1980) as fundamental to this concept. Nor does his view encourage development of innovative new approaches to teaching. His use of the term *leadership* connotes a responsibility for being the first one in his organization to get things done right — as might be implied if one talked about being a company's "leading sales representative." Mr. Q does not fit well into the following statement by Owens (1970, p. 127):

> Leaders initiate change in the organization: changes in either its goals or the way the organization tries to achieve its goals ... In other words, leaders tend to be "disruptive of the existing state of affairs ... the behavior of leaders is probably governed more by broader, cosmopolitan personal goals than is the behavior of administrators.

Mr. Q's departure from Owens's description of leadership is nowhere more evident than in his discussion of how to get cooperation from teachers:

> Well, I think that's a matter of, if they feel that I am approachable, if I am available, accessible to them. And I try to be that. I also try to listen and hear and to be amiable. But yet I feel that there are certain decisions that I have to make and I am sorry if not everyone agrees, but I will make those decisions.

Mr. Q sees his role as a passive, coping, and supportive one aimed at facilitating rather than directing the work of teachers. He says of himself, for example:

> I guess that the thing that I feel that I have skills in is that I am a good listener and that once someone is really upset (and I had one yesterday) I listen but I hold firm with what I have done, because I make my decisions recognizing that there might be differences of opinion on it. So I tend to remain calm, particularly when I am working with parents, but if need be I will be firm. I try never to be abrasive.

Not only does Mr. Q not like to be abrasive himself, but he reports that the part of his work which he finds most distasteful is working with a

> difficult staff, where you feel that you really work at trying to communicate and you are sapped. Some kids getting treated unfairly, and you are caught ... you try to help ... in certain situations you have got to support that teacher, but you know that if she or he had used different tactics or better judgment ...

When discussing how he is able to offer rewards and incentives to teachers, he again offers a fairly passive view of his role: "I tell them personally when I feel they have done a real good job . . . I try to stroke." Somewhat more actively, he indicates that he sometimes uses more objective rewards:

> I have had some control in terms of who goes to particular in-services and sometimes I use that, because a person has really done an excellent job and is interested in growing professionally . . . teachers that I felt were really working hard and needed recognition and an opportunity to grow professionally, [I] provide the opportunity for them to visit other schools or to go to workshops, that sort of thing. We haven't had the money to do that this year, but I have done that in the past.

The emphasis, here, is clearly on maintaining a smoothly functioning unit — not on retooling the personnel or redirecting the organization's operations.

Although he views most responsibilities programmatically, Mr. Q's view of the students is given a highly personalistic tone:

> I know this is going to sound like an old cliche, but I feel that working with students is a very definite part of my job that's important to me as a person. I realize that it's very significant and important in terms of working with staff . . . but it is important to me to be involved with kids, to be out where the action is.

In observing Mr. Q, we noted three important features of his work style which distinguish him from principals holding a less administrative view of their roles.

Student Behavior Problems

First, a disproportionate amount of Mr. Q's time is taken up with student behavior problems, which arise almost constantly throughout his typical day. In part this problem is due to the size and makeup of his school — the largest in our sample. But it is also because Mr. Q views student discipline as a very important part of his job and is willing to interrupt other matters in order to respond immediately to requests for help with troubled or troublesome children.

The Nature of His Presence

Like all principals, Mr. Q moves around the building and grounds of the school quite frequently. He displays his commitment to playing a supportive role, however, by the way he presents himself in various places. For example, Mr. Q typically eats his lunch early. The protocol explains why:

> When lunch begins he can go and help get trays out in the cafeteria.

> The design of the cafeteria is such that it is hard for many of the
> smaller children to reach the trays when they are pushed through, so
> Mr. Q stands there and keeps moving them through for the children.

Thus, rather than develop a solution for this technical problem, Mr.
Q takes the occasion to make himself useful to the children and to
visibly demonstrate his willingness to be supportive and responsive to their needs.

Scheduling Problems

Mr. Q encounters a continuous stream of scheduling problems.
These problems involve demands for his own time and attention,
but they also reflect his need to make decisions about program
activities, teacher conferences, and meetings with other administrators. He is the only principal whom we observed who moved or
canceled more than one appointment or who arrived late for more
than one meeting in the course of his workday.

CONTRADICTIONS IN MR. Q'S STYLE

Three important contradictions are revealed in Mr. Q's administrative style. Two concern limitations on his ability to control
events which he believes to be central to his work. The third
concerns the contrast between his interest in programs and his
interest in children.

Responsibility Without Power

The most obvious contradiction in Mr. Q's principalship is his
extremely limited capacity to effectively structure programs and to
secure teacher cooperation. His was the only school in which a
teacher whom he had asked to cooperate with our project refused to
participate in order to demonstrate her low regard for his authority. He had the greatest difficulty with teacher organization
activists among our principals. And he reported the least direct
impact on the ways in which teachers define or execute their work
responsibilities. Thus, despite his apparent commitment to administrative program development, Mr. Q found his power to secure
cooperation from teachers quite limited.

While this contradiction should be viewed, to some extent, as a
matter of Mr. Q's own personal weaknesses, it also reflects a
theoretical contradiction within the administrative approach to
the principalship. By assuming that teachers are professional
workers — responsible for the organization of their own work —
Mr. Q renders his own work relatively unimportant. If teaching
activities were more specialized, administration would be then

more important. Indeed, it is with the specialist resource teachers that Mr. Q spends most of his planning and organizing time.

Leadership without Vision

A second obvious contradiction in Mr. Q's administrative style is his attempt to provide leadership without having an adequate vision of the mission of the school. His concern with problems of leadership are confined largely to meeting the expectations of central office executives, yet he shows little evidence of having internalized those expectations. Thus he seems to be always trying to get his staff to meet goals and pursue projects which are not really his own.

This contradiction springs largely from the fact that, as Charters (1964) has noted, schooling is not a particularly specialized industry. Since schooling is not specialized, effective leadership would seem to be one requiring vision and purpose. Instead, the sort of leadership which Mr. Q envisions for himself is important when individual workers' efforts are linked to the overall productivity of an organization. By assuming that teachers are professionals, responsible for defining and controlling their own work performances, Mr. Q vitiates the little administrative leadership that would otherwise appear to be needed in the unspecialized work of elementary school teaching.

Personalistic Relationships and Planned Programs

The third important contradiction in Mr. Q's administrative style is that he desires personalized, affectively warm relationships with teachers and students while at the same time insisting that rational planning and affectively neutral organization are the bases of effective educational programs. He sounds, for example, like an executive decision maker in a classic bureaucracy when he says the following:

> I would like very much to have four-hour aides (for each teacher), but, curriculumwise, we need two resource teachers. Now their time is negotiable and we'll look and see, do we want them doing remedial work? We operate a math lab . . . [and] we may have to say [the lab teacher] needs to do more remediation and work more directly with children. That may be true of the reading resource teacher also. But the two positions are not negotiable. That is a decision I am having to make. My parents support me in that, I think some teachers do — but some do not.

When asked what he enjoys most about his job, however, he does not talk about taking pride in the effectiveness of this sort of tough decision. Rather, he says the following: "The thing that I enjoy most...[is] working with teachers that really are enjoying what they are doing. And then I enjoy the kids too."

Mr. Q was genuinely anguished by this contradiction between what he enjoys and what he feels is necessary — between his personal desires and his bureaucratic responsibilities. He frequently felt impelled by district policy or budgetary necessity to make decisions which strained relationships with various members of the staff. And he was truly distressed by a running battle with several teacher organization activists on his faculty.

This contradiction is, we suspect, fairly widespread among older and more experienced elementary school principals. It appears to reflect the disruptive impact of recent developments such as specialized teaching roles, categorical programs, and innovative curricula, which have substantially increased the organizational complexity of the traditionally patrimonial, extended-family atmosphere of many elementary schools.

Mr. Q's administrative style requires the presumption that teachers are capable of truly professional work roles. He can succeed in creating the warm, communal ties with which he is comfortable only if he can (a) trust the teachers to take full responsibility for the quality of their own work and (b) view himself as a supporter and facilitator rather than evaluator and director of their efforts. The recent flood of mandated program and policy changes imposed on the schools by public policy makers who suspect that educators are failing to produce either equal opportunity or excellence of outcomes creates a special problem for administrators with Mr. Q's orientation. They are forced to recognize their inability to support teachers' professional autonomy or to protect them from pressure and criticism. Mr. Q's anguish and the resulting contradiction in his work result from the collapse of the professional conception of teacher work roles which received widespread support during the 1940s and 1950s. Mistrust of school performance makes administrative support for teacher professionalism impossible to sustain.

THE PRINCIPAL AS LEADER: THE CASE OF MR. R

Our third principal, Mr. R, is somewhat more difficult to interpret. He is the only Hispanic principal in our sample (one of two in the district). He serves two small, predominantly Hispanic elementary schools. The school in our sample has a visibly lower income clientele than his other school. We observed Mr. R at both schools because he tends to divide his time each day, spending mornings at the more affluent school and afternoons at the sample school.

The data regarding Mr. R illustrates how the principalship provides an opportunity to "put on a show" to provide a "drama" of school life. For example, he tended to turn observation time into a sort of "guided tour" of school life as he thought we ought to see it. Many times his interview responses were frequently colored by a tendency to give little lectures about an idealized view of his work rather than open discussions of the actual issues and events which he confronted. For example, when asked about a typical work week, he replied as follows: "With two schools it's about a twenty-four-hour job. It keeps you busy. I probably average ten to twelve hours a day. In a typical week I average those hours, plus I probably have at least two night meetings of some kind, either school advisory committee, PTA, or something. That's a typical week." The question "What duties are characteristic of the typical week?" elicited the following reply: "Everything, everything that goes on in a school. From staff development, dealing with teachers and aides to parent communications, to discipline problems, plus the normal reporting. The school principal is involved in everything that goes on in a school." Probing again for a clearer picture, we asked, "Does your job change at different times of the year, or is it just the same job all the time?" He replied as follows: "No. I am assigned for the full year. It doesn't change. We normally are assigned at the end of the year. Usually in the spring time. This year they held it up because of the school closure issue."

Interview difficulties like this were compounded by Mr. R's tendency to treat our observer as a guest who needed to be given little homilies about everything that was taking place during the observation period. At 7:45 one morning, for example, our observer reports going to the playground with Mr. R and then reports as follows:

> He stands to greet the kids as they come on campus. The kids are very glad to see Mr. R. Not a single child walked by without saying "good morning." Most of them come up and give him a hug. The kindergarteners give Mr. R the special kindergarten handshake. For the males, grades one through six, he gives them a "high-five." Later, Mr. R plays a clapping game with a song with four of the girls. Mr. R greets kids everywhere and where he is the kids are.

In typical form, the protocol then continues:

> Mr. R tells me that it is very helpful for him to be out on the grounds where the kids are, because he finds things out that could develop

into problems between kids. Mr. R says a lot of problems are prevented this way.

Some of our difficulty in gaining access to Mr. R's cultural meaning system might be the result of inexperience on the part of our field observers. (Unfortunately, we had a personnel change affecting continuity in observations and interviews with Mr. R.) For the most part, however, these difficulties spring directly from Mr. R's views regarding schooling, teaching, and his role as a principal.

Atmosphere is the key term in Mr. R's approach to his work. When asked about how he could tell if he was being successful, he put this term in context in the following manner:

> You can feel it from the atmosphere at the school. You can feel it in different ways. You know you are being successful if there is discipline. You know you are being successful if there is a fair amount of parent participation, and you know you are being successful if your scores on students are on the move, or improving. You know you are being successful if these things are happening... The teachers tell you, teachers keep you posted if it's going good or not.

This theme recurred several times in his discussions of teachers and students. Of his teachers, he said the following: "They appear to be very comfortable working under me, I guess you would say. They have a very, very relaxed feeling, so I guess this is what a teacher really looks for, to work under a relaxed atmosphere." Or again, in talking about his role in providing teachers with rewards, he said the following:

> I guess the best way is to constantly reinforce the teachers. You know, a pat on their back if they are doing a good job. I think that's the best way. Then, of course, teachers are evaluated every two years, so they look forward to this evaluation — sometimes as a fear type of thing — but then when they receive it, if this reinforcement has been going, it's a real happy feeling.

And, in another interview several months earlier, he said this of his school: "N... is an up-and-coming school where there are a lot of positive signs of academic achievement. This leads to a sense of enthusiasm by the staff." Or again: "There is a high level of team spirit here. I think that my attitudes affect the staff very positively."

Mr. R's commitment to providing students with what he views as an appropriate atmosphere showed through in his typical opening remarks when he was counseling a student who had been referred to him for noncooperation in a choral music class:

> "You're not in trouble. I am just worried about you. You know I think pretty highly of you. Now think for just a minute ... what kind of bad habits do you have ... can you tell me? ... [pause] ... Well, you're stubborn aren't you? Can you tell me another weakness you have?" The kid said: "Well, let me see." Mr. R then said: "I may be wrong, but I think I know you pretty well — I think you always want to be first."

Mr. R then went over the "three things that are most important at this school": (1) "pride," (2) "hard work," and (3) "happiness." This statement parallels Mintzberg's (1973) observation that the purpose of *leadership* is to effect an integration between individual needs and organizational goals. Throughout his dealings with this student, as with everyone we observed, he stressed the importance of social obligations. The protocol reports the following conclusion to this session:

> "Now is the time to set your habits — now there are people who depend on you and you can't be proud and happy if you let people down. And I know you wouldn't let me down on purpose. My boss tells me to do things and I don't want to do them, but I do them anyway because I don't want to let my boss down. Now after our talk I can't let you do this any more. If you don't think you can sing, then just move your mouth, then everybody will be able to participate without worrying why you're not singing. I only want to help you. Talk to your Mom about this, I know you can do it and you won't let me down." Mr. R gave the boy "high-five" and he left.

After the boy was gone, Mr. R turned to our observer to interpret his actions with "You have to leave them a way out — have to let them get out with dignity."

This emphasis on atmosphere is given formal expression in Mr. R's discussion of how his role is differentiated from that of his assistant principal. The assistant principal, he says, "is mostly in charge of parent groups and instruction at the school." Mr. R, on the other hand, considers his own role to be concerned primarily with "staff management and counseling." He elaborates: "I let the staff take care of instruction the way they want, this is what works out best for the program." Mr. R's concentration on atmosphere also leads him to concentrate on keeping in touch with the feelings of staff and students. In addition to the playground surveillance described earlier, this concentration is revealed in the frequency with which he moves in and out of classrooms. He also says the following:

> In a large district like ours we have way too many meetings. You can't do a job if you are away from your building. You have got to be at your building. So in the last few years I guess I have been selecting the meetings that I attend. I can't attend them all and still do a good job, especially with two schools. I put a premium on being at the school site.

He reports the following: "In my particular style I am in and out of all of the classrooms so I know what's going on and, from that sense, I can make a lot of referrals to teachers to either put program development or individual help in — so I'm on top of everything." And when asked about the most unpleasant aspects of his job, he continues to reveal a concern with the establishment of a relaxed atmosphere, saying that "usually the most unpleasant things are unsupportive parents, or parents that come in barking at the principal for things that kids have done, sort of defending wrong." He sums up his views, saying "I'm a humanist, and under that system, it's a very happy, relaxed atmosphere — so I'm pretty comfortable with that." He also has this to say: "I always operate on a team approach. Everyone is part of the ball team."

Because atmosphere is so important to Mr. R, it is easy for him to feel that there are too many programs:

> We have too many programs in this school. I am basically a reading, writing and math type and I believe that with a strong basic program you don't need any new programs. Because we have way too many, they don't give them a chance for success. If you are meeting success at a school, why change? Keep doing what you are doing if you are meeting success. You don't need new programs.

And, despite the fact that this is a low-achieving school, Mr. R clearly feels that success is present in the form of enthusiastic and dedicated staff efforts.

This concentration on staff enthusiasm as the criterion for school success means that, when he is doing teacher evaluation, Mr. R should concentrate on positive rather than negative aspects of each teacher's work. As he puts it, "Basically my evaluation is to write up the strength of that teacher."

Believing so firmly in the importance of atmosphere, Mr. R treats every social contact with students and staff members as an occasion to build feelings of cooperation, loyalty, and enthusiasm. This, he believes, will result in an effective school program. He even treated our interviewers and observers as people to be incorporated into this atmospheric system.

There are, of course, some problems with this strategy. First, it requires Mr. R to maintain a kind of energetic, enthusiastic, problem-denying facade so that he can present himself as the originating source of what he hopes will be a set of contagious good feelings. Consequently, he only praises the strengths of teachers — overlooking or denying the existence of weaknesses. And, while achievement scores in the school are in the bottom 2 or 3 percent on national norms, he takes an upbeat view, saying that these scores are "on the move" and "progressing upward." Although this attitude might be really helpful to staff and students, it leads Mr. R to respond to queries about problem areas with the following vague assertion: "There are some problems. I couldn't name any at this point, but there are problems that never get solved, but I can't pinpoint any." One suspects that this is more than just a manipulation to encourage our interviewer to concentrate on positive aspects of the school. This remark probably betrays Mr. R's own tendency to suppress any awareness of potential problems in order to keep them from dampening his enthusiasm and making him negative. But the result, no doubt, is that Mr. R finds himself always "putting out grassfires" at the school because, as the protocol reports, "there's always a backlog of problems by the time he gets to [the sample school] from [his morning school]" Mr. R rationalizes these problems, attributing them to the socioeconomic conditions of the children, saying "A lot are from broken families and don't get nearly as much affection as they need."

The emphasis also leads Mr. R to see district-level management primarily as a major source of pressure on his principalship. Responding to a question about the most important sources of job pressures, he says the following: "From downtown, all the reporting and time-lines that we have to meet, those are the pressures. You have to get in a report this Thursday and they let you know, like Tuesday, that type of thing, so those are very unpleasant pressures, I guess."

Mr. R recognizes that his style is not going to lead him to higher management positions. He sums up his feeling about his job with the following: "I enjoy it. I tell everyone that the site principal is the only way to go. You can't do what you want to do unless you become a principal. I would never think of going to the central office, this is where the ball game is."

Mr. R's emphasis on site-level conditions is not widely appreciated by central office managers. Mrs. O articulates, rather harshly, feelings about Mr. R which we heard from others when she said, "Mr. R's people orientation is better viewed as 'here's a piece of candy, we'll talk about it later.' "

Though Mr. R's execution is not always sophisticated, his approach to the principalship represents an important option for school executives. He embodies the visionary and symbolic approach to organizational control which Sergiovanni et al. (1980), Owens (1970), and Ouchi (1981) equate with leadership. His concentration on the "atmosphere" of the school, the "enthusiasm" of staff, and the "pride," "hard work," and "happiness" of the students reflects a belief that intentions, efforts, and feelings — rather than program structures or teaching techniques — are the key ingredients in school success. It would be easy to criticize Mr. R's psychological manipulation of students, his tendency to ignore teacher shortcomings and programmatic inefficiencies, but it is more important to recognize that these are the most likely points of ineffectiveness for anyone who tries to stimulate and encourage rather than organize, supervise, or direct subordinates. Moreover, an individual with more expansive skills and a better sense of the specific requirements of good teaching could probably use Mr. R's style in ways that would yield a far more effective channeling of teacher and student energies.

Contradictions in Mr. R's Style

The most obvious and distressing contradiction in Mr. R's approach to the principalship is the persistent tension between his professed interest in a relaxed, friendly, open, and cooperative atmosphere and his tendency to manipulate the feelings of both students and teachers by appealing to their sense of social obligation and loyalty. He acts as though relaxation could be produced while maintaining a social distance between himself and others. His physical presence is intense, his verbal and physical contact with children expansive, and his friendly dialogue with teachers quite evident, but he attempts to impose his own enthusiasm and sense of commitment on others rather than allowing them to develop their own. This process is easily recognized in his way of relating to our research team. He interprets, but does not disclose, the interior space of his own cultural meaning system. In the same way, he concentrates on student and teacher cooperation and overt attitudes rather than attending to their teaching and learning activities.

This contradiction appears to be the direct result of Mr. R's belief that he personally must originate the good feelings which he believes are the source of adequate motivation and rewards for teachers. By believing that the appearance of success is the starting point for high performance, he is forced into pretense and away from the analysis of issues and problems in his school.

THE PRINCIPAL AS SUPERVISOR: THE CASE OF MRS. S

Our fourth principal, Mrs. S, is a black woman in her second year as principal of a predominately black elementary school. In addition to her responsibilities as a principal, she is a team leader for the district's court-ordered desegregation (D&I) program. The combination of categorical programs at this school and her D&I responsibilities means that she has three essentially full-time classified employees under her immediate supervision: the regular school secretary, a community aide, and the D&I program secretary. She also has regular interaction with a teaching assistant principal and two resource teachers. In addition, the site has the services of a counselor, a speech and hearing specialist, a half-time learning disabilities teacher, two part-time music teachers, and a part-time psychologist, with whom Mrs. S works less closely. Her office is positioned in such a way that the regular school secretary and the D&I secretary are accessible through different doors.

A little time spent in her office quickly highlights differences between the work style of this principal and those of the others in our sample. There is more paper shuffling in this office, since D&I projects compete for attention and decision-making time with the usual flow of student, teacher, and parent visitations to the school office. Unlike any of the other principals we observed, Mrs. S keeps her calendar on a large chalkboard prominently displayed in her office. Meetings, deadlines, and other important events are noted on this chalkboard for anyone who enters the office to see.

The general impression conveyed by this office is that of a job shop in which projects are constantly being scheduled, worked on, and completed. Mrs. S, who serves as the shop foreman, concerns herself with whether work is properly scheduled and whether the workers are attending to their responsibilities in ways that keep the shop running smoothly. Her two secretaries are trusted lieutenants in this process — providing information, pursuing details, and following up on projects in progress. The extent of her trust for the D & I secretary is revealed in the following excerpt from an observation protocol:

> Before she leaves the office Mrs. S checks in with the D&I secretary again and asks: "Do you have the letter all done?" "Yes." "Why don't you type it up then, so we can see what it will look like?" This is a letter that Mrs. S has been dictating to parents concerning the special programs. She dictates the main body of information and then lets the secretary fill in accordingly. She and the D&I secretary work together off and on all day, and from an outsider's view, it appears they have an excellent relationship here. To a degree, Mrs. S depends

on this secretary to use her own judgment in doing some of these things. She gives her the basic outline of what needs to go into it and then the secretary is permitted to have some degree of creativity in writing such a letter.

This same trusting relationship is revealed when Mrs. S talks to the regular secretary about a substitute who will be taking over the teaching assignment of her assistant principal for a few days. Early in the morning, before most of the many staff members have arrived, the secretary comes into her office on another matter and the following exchange takes place:

> Mrs. S asks about the substitute scheduled to arrive that morning: "Does he look strong or am I going to be in for a very rough day?" The secretary responds: "Well, he has subbed at the high school for the last three months." Mrs. S says, "I guess I had better make a trip down to the classroom. I think I had better see what he looks like and get [the assistant principal's] impression."

A little later she says, "We don't need any interruptions from that class today."

Mrs. S's close working relationship with the secretarial staff extends to her community aide and her assistant principal. Her relationships with several teachers and with numerous students stand in rather marked contrast to her relationship with this close-knit office staff, however. The following remarks — which sound a bit strong because they are here taken out of context — reflect an underlying tone of social distance between Mrs. S, the staff, and student body of her school. In a general way, she says the following:

> Being a principal means that you've gotta be the mommy most of the time — or the daddy — you've gotta be a know-it-all, you've gotta have the answer to everybody's problem, including teachers and anybody who comes through here. Most of the teachers are just like children, they tattle on each other.

In more specific terms, she says the following of one teacher:

> If I let her, N...will teach to the absolute minimum. So I have to know what she is planning to do. What kind of order they will be working on to obtain their goals. Some people seem to jump around from here to there and the learning process gets all mixed up.

The protocol reports the following remarks about another teacher:

> "Mrs. N...is sure to need help. She doesn't understand at all. She needs help just to stoop. We are going to have to hold her hand and baby her through because she is going to have to do it." Mrs. S's voice

and demeanor show her frustration and anger as she talks about dealing with Mrs. N.

Of substitute teachers Mrs. S says, "Substitutes have problems with most of the classes in the district — indeed, some of the substitutes that the schools get are very poor specimens." And of a janitor who does not want to set up the furniture for a special program at the school, our observer reports the following: "Mrs. S is most unhappy with him. She informs me that he is being lazy."

The direct, almost belligerent, manner reflected in these remarks should not be taken to mean that Mrs. S fails to respect the rights of employees. In fact, as the following episode clearly demonstrates, she has a very high regard for employee rights and is just as aggressive in defending those rights as she is in criticizing staff members who are lax or incompetent. In this episode she is trying to arrange a luncheon meeting with teachers from another school. The secretary from that school calls to say that the teachers are not permitted to leave the campus during the lunch hour. Our protocol picks up the story:

> Mrs. S informs the secretary to tell them they certainly can get off. They have a duty-free lunch and they are free to leave the school for that luncheon if they wish. The person at the other end of the phone implies that the principal of the other school will have a fit if they do this. Mrs. S's response about the other principal's attitude towards teacher lunches is that "He's a . . ., anyway." She feels as though [the other principal] is probably making those teachers' lives miserable. She goes on to talk about the fact that those teachers have a right to a duty-free, playground-free, lunch. It's part of the contract and he has no business trying to give them a hard time about it. It is obvious that Mrs. S does not object to the idea that the teachers' lunch time is their own.

This belief in the fundamental rights of teachers is accompanied, in Mrs. S's mind, with a belief that they need to be given very explicit, almost legalistic, directives about what is expected of them in their jobs. In talking about what to send out in a bulletin to teachers regarding materials covered in a recent staff meeting, she says to her assistant principal, "Put it in print so the teachers can't say, 'We didn't hear about it,' or 'Did we talk about that?' "

The piece which she then dictates to go into the bulletin reflects the general tone of her relationships with many students:

> We've been working with a lot of kids lately who have been disrespectful of adults — they probably need to be counseled — there might be more than we're aware of, so be sure to let us know about

any additional instances so that we can support you. We can't do anything about it if we don't know about it.

This tone is reflected in her playground surveillance behavior. On one occasion she makes the following remarks to our observer about her playground duty: "One teacher and I usually come out to make sure there's no pushing. There are normally very few problems." Within a few minutes, however, the observer reports that she "chewed out a little girl for not coming in when the bell rang," and "on the way back to the office she spoke to a couple more about 'getting to class' and hurrying up with milk." On another occasion, Mrs. S heads for the playground with the following remark: "I think I'll go outside and supervise the troops." Once on the playground, our observer reports the following: "Various children are walking far too fast for her and she tells them to slow down. She calls to two children that are running and also tells them to walk."

In the class where the substitute teacher whom she discussed with the secretary is about to take over, our observer reports the following: "She expects them to behave and does not want to have any of them sent to the office. She states that she knows they can behave and she doesn't see it necessary for them to try to give the substitute a hard time." To a group of children about to leave the campus to attend a play performance, she says that "if they cut up at the play she will come and get them." The protocol continues:

> She does not expect them to misbehave in any way but she has her car and she'll be happy to take them from the scene.
> Back on the playground, on still another occasion, she takes a position close to the basketball area. Mrs. S states that most often it is in the area of basketball playing that a fight may arise during play. One student is apt to decide that someone else took his shot and that's where a fight can occur.

As the bell rings, Mrs. S blows her whistle and says to the students, "Come on, let's go." The protocol continues:

> She has to speak to a half-dozen people or so about moving along. She calls each of them by name. There's no "Hey you!"; the children who are dawdling she knows and calls directly. The students line up and the teachers come and get them to take them back to class.

This extensive concern with orderly behavior and student discipline certainly has some justification. We observed more than one student altercation on the playground of this school. And Mrs. S has at least one teacher whose ability to maintain classroom order is exceedingly weak. In this classroom, our observation protocol for one early afternoon reads as follows:

> At 12:51 Mrs. S stops in at Mrs. N . . .'s classroom. Mrs. N . . . is having some problems getting the class to be orderly and attentive. Mrs. S stands there for a few minutes as Mrs. N . . . repeatedly tells them it is time to sit and be quiet. Mrs. S booms forth with "I don't hear anyone paying attention to me or Mrs. N . . . She shouldn't have to tell you that every afternoon." She's referring to their sitting down and getting in order. After Mrs. S speaks, the class is very quiet and attentive. We then leave.

Mrs. S's firm, assertive manner is not always directed toward students and teachers. When one of her aides is taken home ill, Mrs. S arranges for her sixth-grade daughter to be sent home from school to care for her. She then calls the family doctor's office. At this point, our protocol reports the following:

> Mrs. S tells the doctor's nurse what has happened to [the aide]. Also that the daughter has been called to go home and that Mrs. S has told the daughter to call the Dr.'s office if necessary. She impresses upon the doctor's office that this is a child who's been put in this situation and that she's told the child that the Dr.'s office would be most helpful. Mrs. S is polite, but she is rather firm about letting the office know that she expects them to be of help in this situation.

In sum, Mrs. S's principalship is based on a fairly explicit embrace of what McGregor (1960) calls "Theory X" management. Hoy and Miskel (1978, p. 124) summarize this view:

> Theory X — the traditional view of the worker and working — holds that people are lazy and dislike and avoid work and that administrators must use both the "carrot and stick" to motivate workers. McGregor maintains that other less explicit, but widespread, beliefs are held by management or administration. For example, the average man (educator, student) is by nature indolent, lacks ambition, dislikes responsibility, and prefers to be led. Moreover, the worker (educator, student) is inherently self-centered and indifferent to organizational needs unless they satisfy motives. The worker is by nature resistant to change. Finally, he is gullible; not very bright; and a ready dupe for crusaders, charlatans, and demagogues.

The notion that people are gullible, rather than bad, is embodied in Mrs. S's views about the major problems confronting the schools: "All educators are faced with the problem of fighting the TV. While schools are being blamed for all of the evils of education, the real culprit is TV." Not only are the minds of children easily distracted and destroyed by the drivel of TV, but their parents are also gullible: "Every parent thinks their child is a perfect angel, until we prove it otherwise. So we sit and talk with parents and decide collectively what we're gonna do with Johnny's behavior." Mrs. S even views herself as easily mistaken:

> About two-thirds of the time you're right and about one-third of the time you're wrong, but you don't sit around and brood about it. You say, well if that happens again I'll know what to do. We learn every day, this is how we grow. As long as we treat each other as human beings and treat our problems as individual problems, a lot of the time you can deal with it much better.

Thus, for Mrs. S, the world of human limitations, sloth, and ineptitude forces the principal to be a strong, sometimes stern, director of the schools' affairs.

Contradictions in Mrs. S's Style

The contradictions in Mrs. S's style are less obvious than in the three principals described previously. She seems to be the hard-headed realist in the group, with few illusions or romantic dreams and with even fewer misperceptions about her own intentions or those of others. She has a real contradiction, however: it is that her style leads her to concentrate almost entirely on the formal projects and emergent problems of discipline or noncompliance even though she knows full well that it is necessary for the school to include in its "main thrust" "building student self-image as well as improving general academic performance." She also knows that when evaluating how well the school is performing one needs to look at "teacher morale" and "parent involvement" as well as discipline. Moreover, as she says, "The most important thing a principal has to do is work well with people — to interrelate with different types of people and to use this ability to have people work as a cohesive group." What we observe, however, is that Mrs. S spends a very large portion of her time working on problem children, problem teachers, and problem program components. Successful teachers, compliant children, and working programs get little attention. The result is that many of the people she works with feel that any contact with Mrs. S probably means that you are in trouble. Mrs. S was probably the only one really surprised to discover that the aide who had to go home ill did not want her to know about the problem for fear it might jeopardize her job. Although our observer could have predicted Mrs. S's diligent and sensitive pursuit of help for the aide — including her aggressive contact with the aide's physician — the aide was responding to the prevailing impression of Mrs. S as a no-nonsense, strictly-by-the-book supervisor.

THE MULTISTYLE PRINCIPAL: THE CASE OF MRS. T

The work orientation of the fifth principal in our study, Mrs. T, is more difficult to classify than the others. Mrs. T is a somewhat younger, white, female principal in her second year as an elementary school principal. She is highly regarded by senior central office administrators and impressed our field observers as bright, energetic, and fairly comfortable with her relatively new role as principal of a high-achieving, largely white, middle-class suburban school.

There are at least three reasons why Mrs. T's work style is hard to classify. First, she is relatively new to this role and is still discovering what to emphasize and what to overlook among the demands and opportunities which are presented to her. She is no newer to the role than Mrs. S, whose supervisory style is easily recognized, however. Thus inexperience in this role cannot be the whole explanation.

A second factor contributing to the complexity of Mrs. T's work style is the strength and cohesiveness of the faculty at her school. Some teachers from this school are key leaders in the district's teacher bargaining unit, and they take an active interest in seeing to it that teacher rights and interests are fully protected. These teachers are more than simply teacher rights advocates, however. Senior members of this staff have well-established personal friendship ties with one another and take an active interest in the overall climate and functioning of the school. This was the only school in our study at which a group of faculty members initiated a meeting with our research staff. At a rather informal meeting called by the most influential teachers at this school, we were first carefully scrutinized regarding our motives and methods and then expansively told about how good this school is.

A third factor which complicates Mrs. T's work role is the middle-class, suburbanized character of this school's clientele. Among the principals studied, Mrs. T was contacted most frequently by parents expressing explicitly educational rather than behavioral concerns. Families sending children to this school obviously care about the quality of their children's education — the nature and character of their educational experiences and not just their test scores or their grades. This concern for children's educational experiences is given even greater visibility because Mrs. T's school houses five special education classes for children with problems ranging from severe aphasic disorders to mild learning handicaps. These special education classes encourage increased day-to-day interest in educational achievement measures and diagnostic testing on the part of both parents and staff members.

Mrs. T sometimes displays a leadership orientation of the type characteristically seen in Mr. R's work: that is, she sometimes concentrates primarily on developing a proper climate or atmosphere in the school. This orientation shows up in her discussions of working relationships with teachers: "I try to have established a working relationship, a rapport, with teachers so that when I need something I can go to them and tell them I need for this to happen. And I try to do it on an informal basis. I try to do it one-to-one, if it's that kind of an issue." She elaborates on this process in describing how she can tell whether she's being successful:

> I think I can tell by climate. I can tell when I am out on the playground — if I am taking responsibility for student behavior on the playground at lunch time. If there's a lot of hostile behavior going on, there's something wrong, there's something that I need to do to address that question. I can tell as I am talking to teachers — if there's a lot of hostility. If they are not congenial with me, if they are not free to talk to me, that usually is an indication that something is wrong. On the contrary, if things are flowing smoothly, then I feel that things are pretty successful. If I get positive comments from parents...

As indicated in the following excerpt from an interview, her leadership concern is also evident when she talks about her participation in formal meetings with the teaching staff:

> There are times when we have staff meetings and I have things that I need to make teachers aware of. I need feedback from the teachers — and for me that's a good time to get it ... I don't like the teachers doing other work when they are sitting in a staff meeting. I like for them to participate in it, and I am fairly assertive about that.

In this context, Mrs. T is deeply committed to the belief that education requires intense communication and a shared vision of the school's purposes and programs.

This is but one aspect of Mrs. T's complex style, however, and it is difficult to be certain on the basis of our limited data whether Mrs. T's apparent effectiveness is due to her skill in the execution of this leadership style or to other elements in her overall work orientation.

At other times, Mrs. T sounds more like Mrs. O, the manager principal in our sample. This orientation is particularly evident when she is talking about the importance of staff development and her role in staff evaluation. Her interview protocols offer the following example of this technical, managerial orientation:

> Teachers can be taught to be effective teachers by learning certain techniques and, as principals, we can help teachers become aware of those techniques. We can reinforce them when we see that good teaching is going on ... We can reinforce that behavior by pointing it out to them and making them aware of why what they are doing is effective. So, as part of the evaluation process, when I go in to do an observation on the teacher, I try to write a word picture of what is going on in that classroom. And I take down as many specific kinds of things as I can and then from that I draw out the elements that fit into Madeline Hunter's concept of lesson design. I am sure that you probably have heard about the seven different elements that are found in good teaching lessons — I identify those areas that I have actually seen and reinforce them by giving positive feedback on it. And when I find that there is an aspect of good teaching that's missing, I make suggestions in that area — realizing, of course, that simply because the teacher doesn't establish an "anticipatory set" doesn't necessarily mean that she's not a good teacher. It doesn't even necessarily mean that it was needed. But if the students aren't motivated to learn and they are not paying attention, then maybe an anticipatory set might have been called for, so I would make that recommendation.

As clear as this technical basis for managing instruction appears to be, however, Mrs. T tell us the following:

> I am not very comfortable evaluating teachers. As a new principal, it is for me the most stressful part of my job. Madeline Hunter has given me a handle on it. It is much easier because of the terminology she identifies. It is easier for me to go in and feel like I am doing a competent job, picking out effective elements of good teaching and addressing myself to things that I find lacking.

In addition to the support for this technical management orientation provided by the Madeline Hunter training in teaching techniques and lesson structures, Mrs. T is strengthened in this orientation by her effective relationship with senior central office administrators. She calls the executive administration a "support group" and reports that they have visibly attended to her efforts as a new principal and have warmly encouraged her in her work.

On a few occasions Mrs. T sounds like Mr. Q, our administratively oriented principal. This is particularly evident when she is dealing with budget and reporting problems in her job. For example, when talking about how to plan her work for the coming week, she says the following:

> The main thing I am considering right now are some deadlines that I have in terms of budget. Budget cutoffs are coming up for the end of the year. As I mentioned earlier, my teacher evaluations are past due. I need to complete those. I try and keep it ongoing. As I come to something that I need to follow up on, I try and mark it on my calendar.

The main difference between Mrs. T's approach to these administrative demands and that taken by Mr. Q, however, is her sense that these requirements are peripheral and intrusive rather than central to her overall workload. She clearly has more important things to do with her time than to attend to administrative deadlines and make school budget decisions, but when forced to deal with these issues, she does so with much the same orientation and decision-making strategies as Mr. Q.

The closest Mrs. T ever comes to Mrs. S's supervisory style is when she describes how one staff member was "encouraged" to undertake a special training program:

> I have one teacher, for example, that has a problem with discipline and control. So I have suggested that he attend the assertive discipline workshops for his own professional development. In our district we have what's called Keys to Teaching; it is based on Madeline Hunter's professional development program. Some of my teachers have elected — maybe with a little encouragement — to attend.

Here again, Mrs. T's style is only vaguely reminiscent of Mrs. S's aggressive supervisory approach. She is clearly willing to take steps to "encourage" teachers to comply with her expectations. In fact, Mrs. T "encouraged" one teacher with whom she was unhappy to transfer to another site in the course of our study year. But this aspect of her work style is not accompanied by Mrs. S's pervasive sense that teacher and student disciplinary problems are about to erupt at any moment, or that there is a need to either "baby" marginal teachers or "be on the lookout" for trouble.

Flexibility Rather than Contradiction

While there are obvious contradictions between intent and action in each of our other principals, none are readily apparent in Mrs. T's style. She believes that high-quality teaching is based on both dedicated effort and specialized technique, emphases which are differentially embraced by the other principals. And her beliefs about the ultimate aims of schooling seem to include both the developmental and the achievement goals which divide the other principals. While each of the other four principals display a clear bias toward a specific combination of teaching work and school mission definitions, Mrs. T embraces a comprehensive and flexible pattern. It is a pattern which appears to provide her with the ability to alter both her work orientation and her approach to the specific requirements of her job as she moves from one problem area to another. This case is an illustration of the integration of administrative, managerial, supervisory and leadership characteristics in one person.

SUMMARY AND CONCLUSIONS

The five principals whose work orientations and executive styles have been reviewed in this chapter represent a broad range of personal background, training, and experience. Each has demonstrated an identifiable, personal, work orientation or cultural perspective which serves to define their tasks and guide their work activities. The five principals presented in this chapter illustrate four essentially different cultural perspectives.

Mrs. P has adopted a "managerial" orientation. She carries out her work in a technical manner, placing emphasis on program planning and personnel issues. She exhibits a unique high-energy level and careful workmanship. She is also different from the other principals in the manner by which she uses language, displaying a sense of wit and cynicism. These characteristics give her school an atmosphere of efficiency but also exacerbate certain personnel problems.

Mr. Q relies on an "administrator" orientation. He is preoccupied with time and scheduling. His primary concerns are to provide support and presence. He deals with student discipline; he perceives his teachers as autonomous professionals and passes along to them programmatic suggestions from the central office. This executive style results in his having a sense of managerial responsibility without adequate power, a sense of leadership responsibility without a general vision, and a tendency to personalize relationships.

We have called Mr. R's style "leadership" because of his tendency to focus his attention on the emotional climate or atmosphere of his school. This principal has a view of what schools should be, and he tries to personally infuse that view into the organization. One problem created by this leadership style is that problems are easily avoided in the rush to create a positive atmosphere. His belief that enthusiasm originates with the principal leads Mr. R to accentuate positive aspects of the school and give relatively casual attention to real conditions that may be hindering the school from accomplishing as much as it could.

Mrs. S has adopted McGregor's "Theory X" approach to management more than any others among our principals. Her attitude toward teachers and other employees leads her to concentrate attention on weaker teachers and to see close supervision of their work as a primary responsibility.

Mrs. T is a multistyle principal. She does not display a particular style consistently, but rather displays characteristics of all types. This flexible, integrative style enables her to manage her school in ways that are perceived to be effective and reasonably efficient by both central office executives and a strong cadre of teachers within her building. The school situation is unique, however, making it difficult to be confident that successful management is a result of her style or her placement in this special setting.

CHAPTER VII

Cultural Incentives and Effective Teaching

It is time to ask, "What does it all mean?" We have reviewed prior research on motivation, rewards, and incentives. And we have explored the work orientations and activities of fifteen teachers and five principals. Does the analysis yield a meaningful, consistent theory of teaching incentives? If so, what does it say about the relationship between teaching incentives and teacher effectiveness? We can address these questions best by developing a broad overview of the data and exploring its implications for theory and practice.

Obviously, our work departs markedly from the traditional literature on workplace rewards and incentives. It is equally clear, however, that the major findings of this study are broadly supported by a number of recent studies of effective management activities in industrial organizations (see, for example, works by Ouchi, 1981; Deal and Kennedy, 1982; Peters and Waterman, 1982; and Schein, 1985). Like this recent management literature, our theoretical framework asserts a fundamental and direct link between work incentives for teachers and the development of robust school and classroom cultural systems.

The cultural theory underlying our analysis of the work motivations of elementary schoolteachers is best summarized by means of a step-by-step review of key findings presented in previous chapters. In most cases, it will be noted, our findings are directly related to critical elements in the recent spate of school reform policies adopted by most states. We provide especially important support (and some cautionary advice) for the "second wave" reforms proposed in such programs as the Carnegie Task Force report (1986), California's Commission on the Teaching Profession (1985), and the teacher education reforms proposed by the Holmes Group (1986).

MOTIVATION AND REWARDS

Appropriate motivation is the bedrock of effective work performance in any occupation. In public education, this intuitively obvious fact of life is too often forgotten by policy makers, executive managers, and an impatient public as they press for educational reform and school improvement. There is no substitute for effective teacher motivation. Neither regulations nor resources, neither technical innovations nor program reorganizations, can significantly alter school performance if the teacher motivation system fails to energize and shape teacher behavior in ways that link educational program requirements to student learning needs.

Our study has helped to clarify the conceptual foundations of motivation. We note, for example, that not all human behavior is "motivated" as we are using this term. Physiological responses to loud noises or temperature changes arise spontaneously from the operation of the body's autonomic nervous system, without conscious attention. Work behavior, however — especially the complex work of teaching elementary schoolchildren — does not arise from such unconscious or automatic processes. This work activity must be motivated. Motivation involves the twin processes of stimulating or energizing human action and shaping or directing it toward fulfillment of specific task requirements. The effectiveness of individual teachers depends on both the overall *level* of their stimulation to action and the specific *form* which their activities take.

In organizational terms, appropriate motivation serves two basic purposes: securing *energetic participation* in the workplace and ensuring the *effective performance* of specific tasks. Participation is, of course, the more fundamental problem. Unless creative individuals can be motivated to seek teaching jobs, show up for work regularly, and engage energetically in their assigned tasks, no teaching will get done. But participation without adequate performance motivation is of limited value. Especially in complex and emotionally demanding jobs like teaching, it is all too easy for workers to confuse mere participation in routine work activities with their broader responsibilities for high-quality task performance.

As the data presented in earlier chapters have amply demonstrated, we cannot fully understand the motivations of teachers or administrators without carefully examining how they interpret both the participation and the performance dimensions of their job responsibilities. Educators have many different ways of orienting themselves to school and classroom work activities, and they adopt sharply divergent views of both the goals of teaching and the criteria to be used in assessing progress toward those goals.

MOTIVATION THROUGH REWARD DISTRIBUTION

Work motivation is directly linked to the distribution of meaningful rewards. This statement is more complex than it may at first appear. First, it implies that work behavior is not spontaneous. Unlike play, work activities are distinguished by the fact that they involve *accepting responsibility* for engagement in the performance of actions necessary to the completion of identified tasks — regardless of whether these tasks are spontaneously interesting or enjoyable. Enjoyable work is to be preferred, of course, but it is work rather than play to the extent that activities are valued (by the worker, that is) in terms of their contribution to job-related goals rather than to personal needs and interests.

A second implication of the link between work motivation and reward distribution is that work behavior is substantially shaped by the nature of the *reward distribution system*. As argued in Chapter II, when the distribution of rewards becomes systematically contingent upon task engagement or performance, the rewards become *incentives*. Before reviewing the system of teacher incentives, however, we need to clearly delineate the essential character of these rewarding experiences.

DISTINGUISHING REWARDS FROM REINFORCEMENTS

It may be helpful in clarifying the nature of rewards if we carefully distinguish this concept from that of reinforcement as it is used in behaviorist psychology. While *reinforcement* and *reward* are frequently used interchangeably in everyday conversation, they differ significantly in technical discussions — and that difference is crucial to our analysis of teaching incentives. As a technical term, the word *reinforcement* is universally used by behaviorist psychologists to refer to the fact that certain experiences, when closely associated with a particular activity (usually described as "emitting a particular behavior"), increase the likelihood that a person or animal will emit that behavior again. Behaviorists consider any experience which increases the likelihood that a behavior will be emitted to be a reinforcer for that behavior. They look exclusively at the *observable consequences* of behavior, ignoring beliefs and attitudes. Mental attitudes and feelings like pleasure, satisfaction, or fulfillment are seen as highly inferential concepts (some even deny that these terms have any meaning at all). Since the dictionary definition of the term *reward* includes feelings of pleasure or satisfaction, but not the likelihood that future behavior will change, these theorists generally avoid using the word altogether.

Psychological theories involving more complex conceptions of human activity — those tracing human motivation to drives, needs, or cognitive meaning systems — are much more likely to incorporate the concept of reward. They generally use *reward* to refer to the subjective feelings of satisfaction, fulfillment, or pleasure that accompany certain experiences. These affective emotional responses to experience are an essential element in the definition of a reward. The higher-level psychological theories are more comfortable with this affective dimension of human experience because they share a common belief that individual actions are directly affected by how one *interprets* past experiences and *anticipates* future consequences. Although these processes of interpretation and anticipation are mental activities that go unobserved by strict behaviorists, they are widely recognized in higher-level psychological theories as necessary elements in a theory of human motivation. They do indeed complicate the analysis of human activity, but this sort of complex analysis is certainly preferable to simplistic conclusions.

Our use of the term *reward* to describe the origins of teacher work motivations reflects our rejection of a strict behaviorist interpretation of human action. In our view, behaviorist research has produced weak and contradictory findings largely because it has denied the importance of subjective meaning systems used by individuals to orient themselves to an action system. While some behaviorist research has found significant (though usually weak) relationships between reinforcement experiences and subsequent actions, it is impossible to adequately analyze teacher work behavior without taking their subjective interpretations of day-to-day experience into account.

TYPES OF REWARDS

Work-related rewards can be divided into two basic classes or types: *intrinsic* and *extrinsic*. Two critical attributes distinguish extrinsic from intrinsic rewards. First, intrinsic rewards are *personalized psychic experiences*. They are generated entirely within the subjective experience of those who receive them and cannot be physically manipulated by others. Second, intrinsic rewards are immediately linked to engagement in the specific activities with which they are associated: that is, their distribution is immediate and direct, not contingent upon the actions of others or delayed until some subsequent experiences are encountered. Thus the link between engaging in an activity and receiving any intrinsic rewards that may come from it is created entirely by the characteristics of the activity and the actor who engages in it — it is not contingent upon the operation of some external distribution system.

Extrinsic rewards have the opposite characteristics. They are objective or material in character and are therefore subject to manipulation and control by others. Their distribution is not fully under the control of the person who receives them and frequently is imperfectly linked to engagement in the activities with which they are nominally associated.

Despite the immediate and personal character of intrinsic rewards, their flow in any given situation remains problematic. It is not unusual for an individual to engage in some activity expecting it to yield personal satisfaction, or anticipating a feeling of pride and accomplishment to emerge upon its completion, only to be disappointed in the outcome. Uncertainties of this sort are inevitable when the success of the activity is uncertain, but may also be caused by an inability to really foresee one's reactions to success or failure. Such uncertainties are intrinsic to the situation, however, and are not the result of some imperfections in a reward distribution system controlled by others.

While it is relatively easy to distinguish among major types of rewards, it is very difficult to measure their size and potency. The reward value of obviously important and widely recognized extrinsic rewards (like salaries, promotions, or tax benefits) are far from uniform for all individuals. Many researchers assign a nominal value to such rewards by measuring their cash value. But reward values often differ quite sharply from the dollar values assigned in this way. The magnitude of a reward is reflected in the extent to which it produces personal pleasure, satisfaction, or fulfillment. Hence the potency of any given reward is profoundly shaped by the subjective meanings and values assigned to it by the recipients.

All of the available evidence supports two basic conclusions regarding the value or potency of various rewards for educators. First, educators generally find intrinsic rewards more meaningful and attractive than extrinsic ones. Given that teachers are paid about 30 percent less than comparably trained workers in other fields, this finding is not surprising. It is, however, vitally important that managers and policy makers keep it in mind when trying to improve school performance. The second broadly supported conclusion is that educators rely on sharply divergent subjective meaning systems for interpreting their work responsibilities and experiences. As a result, different teachers seek and respond to quite different intrinsic rewards within their work. This finding means that the impact of any system of rewards aimed at enhancing teacher effectiveness will be complex and difficult to predict — requiring managers and policy makers to understand the subjective dimensions of teacher value systems and work orientations as well as the objective characteristics of schools and classrooms if they hope to develop a reward system capable of supporting strong teaching.

DISTINGUISHING REWARDS FROM INCENTIVES

Rewards become incentives — that is, acquire the capacity to modify work behavior — only when they are linked in the minds of teachers with participation in, or performance of, particular school or classroom tasks. The term incentive is often used erroneously as a synonym for the word reward. As indicated in Chapter II, there is an important relationship between these two terms, but they are far from synonymous. Both terms refer to experiences capable of producing pleasure, satisfaction, or fulfillment. Reward is the more general term; it refers to any experience capable of producing these feelings. Rewarding experiences become incentives, however, only when they are contemplated in advance by those who receive them. This is so because the term incentive refers to the fact that this contemplation or anticipation of rewards leads people to modify their behavior in ways they believe will help secure the rewards. Thus the existence of an incentive depends upon its prior existence as a reward. Without rewards there is no reason for individuals to adjust their work behavior in order to obtain them.

It is quite possible, however, for rewards to exist without ever becoming incentives for action. If individuals cannot imagine any way of linking their own actions to the acquisition of a particular reward, it cannot serve as an incentive for action (except, perhaps, in the special sense of motivating exploratory or innovative behaviors aimed at finding ways of triggering the flow of the desired reward). This condition is most easily seen in the reaction of most ordinary workers to the rewards made available to highly talented artists or athletes. Not being able to imagine performing these roles, most people do not find that even very large rewards provide any real incentive to try.

If the reward value of an experience refers to the magnitude of the pleasure or satisfaction it produces, the incentive value of this same experience refers to the extent to which it influences behavior. Thus, the incentive value of any given reward is conceptually quite distinct from its reward value. Very large rewards have no incentive value at all for workers who believe that luck, serendipity, or capricious decisions by others completely control their distribution. By the same token, relatively small rewards can have very significant incentive values for workers who believe that they can be easily and reliably secured through modest work effort changes.

Perhaps the best way to distinguish between the concepts of reward and incentive is to note that the former belongs to *psychological* theory, while the latter properly belongs to socio-logical or *organizational* analysis. Before anticipation can turn psychologically meaningful rewards into organizationally effec-tive incentives capable of motivating social behavior, two condi-tions must be met. First, workers must concretely imagine the particular activities or tasks that are to be rewarded. For example, if workers believe that they are being rewarded for the amount of *time* they spend in the workplace, they will behave quite dif-ferently than if they believe they are being rewarded for displaying a particular *attitude*, for performing particular *tasks*, or for getting specific *results*. Second, an understandable and reliable *distribu-tion system* must be developed. Unless workers know (or at least think they know) how various rewards are structurally linked to the performance of specific work responsibilities, they will not know when or how to perform their work. Under some circum-stances, for example, reward distribution is linked exclusively to finished tasks — with no attention given to the timing or manner in which those tasks are performed. This occurs when politicians distribute the spoils of office to loyal supporters, or when farm products are purchased at an open market. In most work settings, however, workers are rewarded only if tasks are done in a prescribed manner at an appropriate time and meet specific evaluation criteria.

As Martin Rein (1973) has noted, incentives viewed in this way are to be distinguished from coercive regulations as mechanisms of social control. Workers (or citizens) who imagine a linkage between particular behavior and highly prized rewards are likely to modify their behavior voluntarily in order to reap those rewards. In the absence of an incentive scheme capable of making the linkage, however, their behavior is controlled, if at all, only by rules and regulations that are supported by a credible enforcement system. (It is possible, of course, to expand the concept of an incentive to include escape from coercive regulation, but such an extension sacrifices clarity in analysis for an artificial comprehensiveness of definition; we prefer Rein's distinction between incentive-based and regulation-based social control systems).

SCHOOL INCENTIVE SYSTEMS

The school incentive systems that link anticipated rewards to specific teaching work behavior exist at three distinct analytic levels: (a) the individual educator, (b) the group of colleagues or associates, and (c) the organizational department, school, or district. The rewards made available to teachers at each of these three levels differ quite substantially. Even more importantly, however, the incentive systems used to connect those rewards to work activities are completely different in both form and operation.

Individual incentive systems are those which provide rewarding experiences directly and separately to individual teachers. To be distributed individually, rewards must meet two conditions. First, they must be contingent entirely upon the activities of each individual: that is, teachers must believe that the rewards are garnered entirely through their own efforts — not through collaboration with others. Second, the rewards must be of a type which can become the wholly private possession of the individuals who receive them. They must not "spill over" to other teachers, who become "free riders" merely by belonging to the same group or organizational unit. By the same token, individual incentives will be destroyed if co-workers can either intentionally or inadvertently prevent other teachers from receiving or enjoying them.

If these two conditions are not met, teachers will inevitably come to see that the flow of rewards depends on the development of formal rules or informal social norms to govern cooperation with others in securing and enjoying the available rewards. This will mean, of course, that the incentive system is no longer focused on purely individual behavior and is, instead, an aspect of group or organizational life.

Perhaps a concrete example will help to clarify how this process works. When one of our instructors, Mr. D [I], articulates the very personal incentive that comes from "watching a child make a discovery," he is identifying a reward that does not have to be shared with administrators or other teachers. Except for the child, this reward is his alone. It is the archetype of an intrinsically rewarding individual incentive. But if this teacher were to be thrust into a school where exploration and discovery by children were ridiculed and rejected, where administrators or fellow teachers were able to intrude on his classroom and disrupt the discovery process he so much appreciates, this would cease to be an individual incentive — he would have to recognize the importance of developing support among his co-workers for this approach to teaching. At the very least, he would have to develop mechanisms for insulating himself and his classroom from such intrusions.

Among extrinsic rewards, personal paychecks are the most obviously individual incentives — at least when the amount of money in the paycheck is fixed by a formula and is not dependent on the actions of co-workers or the productivity of an organizational unit. But even these highly individualized rewards can be transformed into group or organization-level incentives by making teacher pay rates dependent upon some group productivity or organizational variables (such as peer evaluation judgments or student test scores).

Group incentive systems are created when (a) the rewards are distributed in such a way that teachers must cooperate to secure them or (b) the rewards themselves are of such a nature that they are necessarily shared among colleagues. The first case arises, for example, when teachers work as teams with the same group of students, or in open space schools where the ability of one teacher to work effectively depends upon others keeping their classes under control and reasonably quiet. It is explicitly created when teachers work in committees and can only gain satisfaction when the group reaches a consensus, or when they must share resources like audio-visuals or field trip transportation. The second condition is created when teachers reap the rewards of collegial camaraderie or joint recognition for collaboration in program development or implementation.

Under these conditions, sets of social rules emerge to govern interaction among individual teachers (and with other staff members). These social norms help to ensure that group members share equitably the effort required to perform the work and to reap the rewards. Needless to say, they do not always work adequately and often do more to justify feelings of hostility and alienation than to guarantee equitable work effort.

Organizational incentive systems emerge when either the collaboration required to secure desired rewards or the collective enjoyment of the rewards once received becomes formal and impersonal. This occurs when individuals come to think of their collaboration efforts as directed toward what George Herbert Mead (1934) called "generalized others": that is, the incentives are organizationally mediated whenever teachers engage in collaborative work or share in the enjoyment of specific rewards by virtue of occupying a formal role in the school organization. The use of the phrase *corporate tax incentive* to describe government support given to particular industries aptly captures the organization-level application of this term. Corporate employees may expect personal benefits from these tax incentives, but these expectations are relatively vague and indirect. The actual benefits generated are given directly to entire corporations and generate incentives for the whole organization to change behavior patterns or goals.

For teachers, a good example of how the organization-level incentive system operates can be seen in the collective bargaining process. Individual teachers expect to benefit from higher wages or improved working conditions negotiated by their union leaders, but they also recognize that those benefits are won for all members of the staff at once, and that they cannot be expected at all if the bargaining position of the union is not broadly supported. Organizational incentives are not limited to the extrinsic benefits derived from wages and working conditions, however. Teachers easily recognize the difference between working in "good" schools and "bad" schools. They derive very important psychic rewards from identification with "good" schools and are generally willing to travel further and work for lower wages in schools that have the organizational characteristics they associate with high-quality education.

TEACHERS RECEIVE BOTH INTRINSIC AND EXTRINSIC REWARDS

Both intrinsic and extrinsic rewards are distributed through each of the three incentive systems. At the organization level, extrinsic incentives operate, for example, when teachers believe that their work efforts are contributing to an expansion of resources for members of the school or district where they work.

These efforts may include working on budget or curriculum materials requests for the school, helping with tax elections, participating in union negotiations, contributing to the enhancement of the school's reputation in the community, or any of a wide variety of other activities aimed at improving the lot of the school or district organization.

At the group level, extrinsic rewards are not readily apparent in most schools. Teachers do often cooperate in arranging field trips or facilitating the maintenance of order in the school, and are publicly rewarded with expressions of appreciation from colleagues. Occasionally teachers will develop strong ties with fellow teachers and pursue mutual benefits in the form of administrative support or special funding for programs, but such group-level activity is relatively rare.

Traditionally, individual-level extrinsic rewards for teachers have been so standardized and routinized as to become essentially organization-level incentives. Salary rates and fringe benefits are so closely tied to tenure and training that most teachers see them as depending almost entirely on joining the school organization. This condition has been a major target for school reform in recent years. A wide variety of programs aimed at developing career ladders, salary bonuses, or incentive pay plans for teachers have been adopted in many states. The hope is that, by individualizing teacher access to extrinsic rewards, schools will be able to create much stronger incentives for high performance on the part of individual teachers. Actually, most attention has been focused on poor-quality teachers who, it is assumed, fail to improve because they benefit just as much as their high-performance colleagues from salary increases and other perquisites.

Our study raises serious questions about the adequacy of these recent reform efforts. Not only did our teachers rely much more on intrinsic than on extrinsic rewards, but they were also more strongly dependent on group and organization-level incentives than is recognized by most advocates of incentive or merit pay plans. It is almost certainly true that salary levels have a substantial impact on the recruitment of qualified young people into the teaching profession, but we saw no reason to suppose that differential salary expectations (at least not the relatively modest ones involved in current reform efforts) will play a significant role in motivating either the overall work effort or the development of specific skills on the part of those who are already in the system.

Intrinsic rewards, which are so important to teachers, are also distributed through each of the three different incentive systems. Intrinsic organization-level incentives — called "purposive" by

Clark and Wilson (1961) — arise when all members of a school or district are able to share in the achievements of the whole organization. Teachers who become personally identified with the purposes or goals of the school system frequently modify their work activities in substantial ways to express that identity and to gain the sense of accomplishment that it produces. The teachers whom we studied were particularly sensitive to these intrinsic organization-level incentives and adjusted their work efforts in obvious ways to pursue them. This was especially true of the program-oriented master teachers and helpers, who were able to describe in personal terms current program emphases in their schools and to take pride in the contributions their own work made to the realization of schoolwide goals.

Intrinsic group-level rewards, such as group solidarity, enjoyment of fellow teachers, and a sense of collective responsibility for educational outcomes, were also strongly felt by the teachers we studied. As noted in Chapter III, however, teachers with different work orientations held very different views of the most important source of those rewards. The master teachers and the helpers tended to view adult co-workers as the primary sources of intrinsic group-level incentives. By contrast, the instructors and coaches derived those rewards from their relationships with students.

Our data suggest that the intrinsic rewards distributed through individual-level incentive mechanisms are especially powerful in influencing teacher work performance. Teachers who take pride in the quality of their work or who enjoy watching children learn and develop are particularly responsive to these intrinsic rewards. They work long and hard to develop programs or to create lessons that will ensure the student responsiveness and success that are so important to them. More importantly, we found that the least successful teachers were also the ones who felt least rewarded in their work.

INCENTIVES AS CULTURAL EXPRESSIONS

Since the linkages between task performance and the acquisition of rewards is established by teacher belief systems, it is appropriate to say that incentive systems are an aspect of culture. Anthropologists define culture in many different ways (see, for example, Arensberg and Kimball, 1965; Boon, 1973; Gamst and Norbeck, 1976; Klapp, 1969; Kluckhohn, 1962; Markarion, 1977; and Merrill, 1961). Some definitions concentrate on the artifacts of culture — man-made tools and implements or the objects of art and religion. Many concentrate on language development or other symbolic communication processes. Still others focus on the development of values and the establishment of social mandates or taboos. Virtually all conceptions of culture agree, however, that the term *culture* includes a body of beliefs shared by the members of a cultural system and experienced as "foreign" by nonmembers. These belief systems cover at least two areas.

First, cultures define and give legitimacy to social goals or *purposes*. In other words, they are self-consciously historical — they specify the thematic links binding past, present, and future events into a sensible and purposeful continuity. In defining the dynamic character of community history, cultures also provide their members with the criteria for recognizing when their own actions contribute to (or interfere with) the realization of these legitimate historical purposes.

Second, cultural belief systems serve to *typify* (in the sense of defining and evaluating) the objects, person, and events constituting the field of social organization and action within which their members live. In other words, cultures distinguish "natives" from "foreigners" by providing the former with a frame of reference for distinguishing the important from the trivial, the good from the bad, and the meaningful from the meaningless in ordinary social relationships. By typifying objects, people, and events, cultures support the development of both cognitive knowledge and collective identity. Knowledge arises as events are linked into historical themes or processes. Collective identities emerge from the establishment of shared meanings and common purposes.

In schools and classrooms, cultural belief systems create the incentive systems for teachers by (a) establishing goals for their work, (b) giving positive and negative values to various techniques for pursuing these goals, (c) specifying social norms for collaboration with others, (d) disclosing presumed linkages between work activities and the flow of personal-, group-, or organization-level rewards, and (e) assigning values to the various types of rewards that are available. As Peters and Waterman (1982) point out, little attention has been given to the importance of these cultural systems in creating and sustaining high performance in business and industry. They argue that such cultural beliefs are far more important than either bureaucratic rules or high-powered technologies in ensuring high performance. Our research supports the general thrust of the Peters and Waterman argument: teachers with vivid cultural belief systems — ones that clearly define educational purposes and richly portray the actions needed to achieve those purposes — find it much easier to develop and implement lesson structures and classroom rules.

As detailed in Chapter III, teachers develop at least four different cultural systems for orienting themselves to their work responsibilities. The classroom cultures with which they identify result from the interaction of two contrasting views of the fundamental purpose of schooling with two equally fundamental beliefs about what activities and relationships are needed to realize those purposes. The evidence indicates that teachers find it necessary to *choose* between measurable *achievement production* and diffuse *child nurture* or development as the basic purpose of education. At the same time, they find it important to choose between adult-oriented *program implementation* and child-centered *lesson teaching* as the most appropriate technique for pursuing basic goals.

Surprisingly, we found that three of the four possible combinations of purpose and technique provided quite satisfactory incentive systems for guiding teacher work efforts. The fourth combination was inadequate and prevented weak teachers from either seeing problems in their performance or deriving satisfaction from their daily work activities. Teachers who identified their work responsibilities with the production of student achievement were motivated to appropriate work performance regardless of whether they adopted a programmatic or a lesson-structured approach to the definition of teaching techniques. Similarly, all the teachers who adopted the lesson-structured approach to technique development found their work rewarding, regardless of whether they saw the lessons as aimed at achievement production or at child nurture and development. But the five helpers in our sample — teachers who tried to combine a child nurture goal with program-structured techniques — found the school's incentive system inadequate. They not only did not enjoy their work, but they had perpetual difficulty getting oriented to their responsibilities in a way that led to successful implementation of planned activities.

It would be difficult to overestimate the importance of this finding for school improvement and reform. Teaching incentives will be weakened and performance degraded if nurture-oriented teachers are induced to shift to a program-structured view of their job without also shifting their allegiance to achievement production goals. Similarly, no matter how diligent and faithful their efforts might be, teachers who define their classroom responsibilities in terms of the implementation of formal programs must forego child nurture goals or pay a heavy price in diminished incentives. It is not just intellectually problematic; it is culturally and psychologically destructive for teachers to think that children can be nurtured and developed through adherence to externally established curricular materials structured by grade level and subject matter. The reason is simple and obvious when we look inside classrooms. For children to respond to the nurture goals of teachers, they must trust that the teachers will give absolute priority to the children's own needs and interests — never using the vulnerability created by their trust to impose external goals and demands. Conversely, if a teacher wishes to impose a school-structured program on the children, it can be justified only in terms of long-term achievement goals. What Meyer and Rowan (1978) have called the "logic of confidence" in the classroom is destroyed if teachers secure student trust and compliance on the grounds that nurture goals are being pursued and then try to use program structures and achievement measures to organize and evaluate their work.

LESSONS AND RULES: THE TECHNICAL CORE OF THE CLASSROOM

The cultural framework of classroom goals and teaching processes is given concrete expression in two universal attributes of classroom life: lesson structures and behavioral rules. These two elements constitute the *technical core* of all classroom cultures. Without these two elements, education loses its essential character and schools cease to be legitimate organizations.

Lessons are structured by *grouping* children and then engaging them in a specific *sequence of activities*. The grouping process begins long before individual teachers take charge of their classrooms. School attendance boundaries are drawn, assigning children to particular schools and substantially determining who their classmates will be. Within the school, program structures are created that generally segregate children by age group, and frequently sort them by ability, achievement, and social class as well. Additional grouping decisions are made after the teachers enter their classrooms. Individual teachers decide whether to teach large groups or small ones, occasionally bypassing group instruction entirely in order to give tutorial assistance to individual students. When grouping students, teachers determine which intellectual, attitude, emotional, ethnic, or other characteristics will form the basis of group structure. They also determine how long students will work in particular groups and what opportunities they will have to share experiences with various classmates.

A second universal characteristic of classroom lessons is the unique sequence of activities involved. Lessons involve a linear sequence of activities with a beginning, a middle, and an end. As detailed in Chapter IV, effective lessons are bounded by starting and ending rituals that separate them from other classroom events. Between these ritual demarcations, lessons unfold through (a) an opening, (b) the lesson proper (which, in turn, consists of one or more cycles of teacher elicitation, student response, and teacher evaluation), and (c) a closing which summarizes and interprets the lesson or direct students toward its application in future school work assignments or real-life situations.

Teachers give concrete structure to their lessons primarily in terms of their orientations toward the purposive and group solidary incentives which they experience. Teachers whose purposive incentive orientations emphasize achievement production tend to structure their lessons tightly, to provide more direct instruction, and to create a more "businesslike" atmosphere in the classroom. By contrast, teachers responding to a more child development incentive system tend to adopt a more open, exploratory, and venturesome lesson structure. Clearly, the first group fits more closely the teaching pattern identified as most productive by effective schools researchers. We would mark a cautionary note here, however. The role played by those teachers we identified as coaches in providing potentially alienated children with access to school programs and to their own intellectual potential appears to be absolutely essential for many children. The achievement production work style may be the most productive for children who have already acquired membership in the school and classroom culture system, but we are doubtful that this style is particularly helpful in dealing with the developmental and socialization problems that so frequently prevent students from benefiting fully from their school experiences.

Viewed from the perspective of their solidary incentive experiences, teachers who identify primarily with other adults and who therefore see schooling primarily in terms of program structures tend to concentrate on structuring lesson activities to match students' demonstrated abilities and limitations. By contrast, teachers whose solidary incentive orientations link them more closely with students than with other adults tend to see schooling in terms of specific lessons and to concentrate on structuring lessons in ways that stimulate student excitement or spontaneous engagement.

The creation and enforcement of social rules, ordinarily referred to by the phrase *classroom management*, have a different, but still important, relationship with classroom cultural systems. As shown in Chapter V, classroom rule systems are related more to the vitality of the classroom culture than to the particular teaching incentives governing overall teacher work efforts. Robust classroom cultures eliminate the need for overt rules and allow teachers to substitute "giving directions" for "enforcing rules" in their dealings with children. As cultural systems become less and less effective, teachers must rely more and more on overt rules and coercive power strategies to control student behavior. And if coercive power fails (which it often does in the context of ordinary classrooms), classroom chaos begins to destroy both the orderliness of student behavior and the vitality of the teacher's incentive to teach lessons of any sort.

PRINCIPALS' INFLUENCE ON TEACHER INCENTIVE SYSTEMS

Although principals can make direct contributions to the incentive systems available to teachers, their most potent contributions are made indirectly, by influencing the cultural system of the school and classroom. The most important incentives under direct principal control involve directing the flow of intrinsic rewards that make life more (or less) comfortable for particular teachers. Teachers are quite sensitive to social approval and disapproval, and they easily recognize signals indicating that principals do not like either their own or others' work. In rare cases, principals can successfully control such extrinsic rewards as salaries, teaching assignments, disciplinary evaluations, or (with the advent of career ladders and other differentiated staffing systems) recommendations for promotion.

When all is said and done, however, direct principal control over incentives is not very potent compared to the power at the disposal of students and co-workers to make life rewarding or miserable for the average teacher. Moreover, direct control of teacher incentives requires complex, time-consuming effort and constantly risks misinterpretation by other teachers. In the area of extrinsic rewards, such as teacher salary and other benefits, administrative control is quite limited, but there is little evidence that stronger control would enable principals to substantially affect teacher job performance. Control over intrinsic rewards is somewhat more substantial — especially the manipulation of rewards arising *outside* the classroom itself (such as attention and approval from co-workers, public recognition, and support, etc.). Even this control does not materially affect the potent incentives arising within the teaching process itself. In short, the teacher incentive system is dominated by intrinsic rewards that flow directly from teachers' success (or failure) in implementing programs and teaching lessons that reach educational goals related to student achievement or nurturance.

Clearly, the most potent influence exercised by principals operates indirectly, shaping the creation of particular incentive systems rather than triggering or inhibiting the flow of particular rewards. The data in this study clearly indicate that the most effective way for principals to alter teacher work incentives is to strengthen school and classroom cultures. By influencing teachers' orientation toward, and commitment to, particular educational goals, or by strengthening their ability to develop and implement techniques for achieving those goals, principals can substantially improve the chances that teachers will be able to reap the powerful intrinsic rewards that come from competent task performance and successful goal attainment.

In order to significantly reshape the teacher incentive system, principals must, themselves, develop an effective overall work orientation or "style" that guides their work orientation and performance. Principal work orientations define two aspects of the principals' work. First, they specify what part the principal is to play in pursuing the fundamental purposes of education. Second, they identify the proper roles for the principals to take in monitoring and facilitating teacher work efforts.

Principals almost universally recognize that they have a basic obligation to facilitate teacher work performance and to ensure that teacher efforts are directed toward the realization of appropriate educational goals. They diverge rather sharply, however, in their conceptions of how to fulfill these obligations. As described in Chapter VI, some principals adopt the view that the goals of education are best pursued by concentrating on the *organization* of school programs and activities. Others view close attention to the *execution* of particular tasks as the more critical problem, and thus concentrate on monitoring and facilitating task performance by individual teachers. In effect, principals who adopt the first view assume that educational goals are embodied in program structures — that educational outcomes are produced by assessing students and then assigning them to appropriate classes, teachers, or curricula. Principals with the second view tend to see school program structures as relatively universal, and thus believe that educational goals are best served by attending to how well teachers implement the programs rather than what programs might be inherently superior. Principals holding this latter view would be likely, for example, to favor "mainstreaming" of exceptional children and "heterogeneous grouping" of all children on the grounds that teacher performance rather than program components account for learning.

When it comes to monitoring and facilitating teacher performance, principals tend to disagree over whether the primary focus of attention should be on teacher dedication, enthusiasm, and level of effort or on their repertoire of techniques and teaching skills. Principals holding the first view see their own responsibilities in terms of inspirational leadership or supportive administration. They tend to rely on "Attaboy" memos and "pep talks" to give teachers a sense of emotional support, and they see themselves as responsible for establishing supportive relationships with the community and district-level managers. Principals who view skill and precision in task performance as the major source of educational productivity concentrate more on providing professional development support, close supervision, and managerial direction to staff. They encourage staff in-service training and frequent observations of teaching activities.

As elaborated in Chapter VI, unique principal work orientations are defined by the way principals combine their views regarding the mission of the school with their conceptions of teacher support and supervision. Principals who believe that educational goal attainment is most affected by program organization (rather than the performance of specific tasks) and that teachers' effectiveness depends more on their dedication than on their use of particular skills or techniques will adopt a work style commensurate with the label *administrator*. When this program organization orientation is combined with the view that teacher competence rather than dedication is most in need of attention, principals are more likely to adopt a *supervisor* definition of their own role. For principals who concentrate on enhancing the performance of individual teachers (rather than improving program organization), there is a similar split, between those whose primary concern is teacher dedication or level of effort and those who are more concerned with teacher skills and abilities. Those who emphasize dedication and effort cast their own role in terms of *leadership* — they try to *inspire* rather than direct high performance. Those who concentrate on skill and technique see themselves as *managers* responsible for coordinating school resources and staff training in ways that capitalize on strengths and overcome weaknesses in staff performance.

THE CULTURAL ROLES PLAYED BY PRINCIPALS

As principals develop their own particular work orientations, they develop unique strategies and techniques for supporting school and classroom culture development. As they engage in daily work activities, principals display values, enact rituals, and enforce social norms that serve to incorporate (or isolate) teachers, students, and community members into their special vision of the school. Some principals are, of course, much better at this culture development process than others. To a substantial degree, differences in their ability to create school cultures spring from variations in verbal or mental ability; to some extent, they are also the natural consequence of differences in training and experience. Our data suggest, however, that variations in principals' abilities to participate in the culture-building process are frequently created by contradictions and inadequacies in their overall orientation toward this aspect of their work rather than by limitations in their talent or training.

If the principals we studied are in any way representative of the general population of elementary school principals, there is much to be learned about how to help principals become self-conscious contributors to school and classroom cultures. Our five principals revealed little awareness of the concept of culture. They did not generally recognize that cultures exist primarily in the minds of their "natives," or that teachers and students are significantly affected by cultural systems only if they are successfully enculturated into the meanings, values, rituals, and social purposes through which incentive values are assigned to the various rewards distributed throughout the system.

Our data suggest that there are three ways in which principals routinely contribute to the enculturation of teachers and students within the school. First, principals have a powerful effect as the *interpreters* of the culture as it already exists. They spend a great deal of time "making the rounds" of the school with no specific action agenda in mind. On these rounds they interact frequently with both teachers and students. Most of these interactions have the effect of interpreting the value system of the school. The principals celebrate appropriate behavior, chastise wrongdoing, and generally use these interactions to signal the behavioral implications of basic cultural values. Perhaps the most important aspect of principals' routine interactions with teachers is their contribution to reinforcing the overall mission of the school and endorsing those activities that the principal believes help to fulfill that mission.

In a more rational and organized way, principals regularly use memoranda, staff meetings, and in-service training opportunities to interpret the cultural norms and activities expected of staff and students. Language is all important in these events. Values are intruded into the most routine communications in order to provide everyone with the orientation clues needed to become full members of the school culture system.

A second important role played by principals in the development of school cultures is *representational* rather than interpretive in character. Principals facilitate understanding and identification with the school culture by embodying values and actions appropriate to that culture in their own work style. When students are sent to the office, the principal's response — punishing or forgiving, emotional or dispassionate, supporting order or encouraging spontaneity — represents for students and teachers alike the normative character of proper social relationships in the school. When the principal deals with community members or central office administrators, teachers see in those interactions explicit indicators of the priorities and commitments deemed appropriate throughout the school.

It is important to recognize that contradictions between the interpretive and representational actions of a principal are especially damaging to the school culture. If principals articulate a belief in the importance of program structures but fail to organize effective programs, they disrupt rather than enhance the school culture. If they adopt a work style characterized by intense enthusiasm and little regard for technical precision, they will create cynicism rather than improved performance on the part of teachers if they try to enforce demands for highly skilled teaching activities.

The third important culture-building role for the principal involves *authenticating* the cultural identities of students and teachers. Since cultures exist largely in the minds of the "natives," they are easily damaged by psychological alienation or estrangement among the members. All members of a cultural group need regular feedback from individuals who hold positions of respect and authority in order to confirm their understanding of prevailing values and norms. School principals are in a uniquely powerful position to perform this culture-authenticating role. They are free to move about the building. They have obvious status and authority both within and outside the school building. They are strategically located in the communication systems of both the community and the school district and can therefore identify changes in environmental norms and values before these changes are recognized by most staff members. They have opportunities to participate in the vitally important processes of face-to-face interaction with all members of the school in order to provide this most potent form of authentication to individuals who are wondering about their worth and legitimacy in the school community. To play this authenticating role, however, principals need to understand it and self-consciously embody the language of authentication in their daily interactions.

CONCLUSION

This chapter has summarized the most salient aspects of the incentive systems operating in public elementary schools and classrooms. We have not examined the incentives responsible for initially bringing individuals into the teaching profession, nor have we examined the various incentives in their personal lives and community relationships that may encourage them to leave their chosen occupation. Incentives influencing the flow of people into and out of teaching are, to be sure, extremely important. They determine, for example, the ability levels and the initial work orientations of teachers as they first enter the schools. And, no doubt, these external incentive systems interact with those we have found operating within the schools. But we found little evidence in our study to suggest that these external incentives have any substantial impact on the day-to-day work of ordinary classroom teachers.

We have found, instead, that the cultural system of the school shapes teacher work incentives and controls the flow of rewards (and disappointments) that determine whether their lives are enjoyable and productive. The theoretical framework developed in this chapter departs in significant ways from the traditional literature on work incentives. We are persuaded, however, that school officials and public policy makers need to adopt a cultural perspective like the one presented here or risk doing irreparable harm to the already shaky level of satisfaction and joy found in the teaching profession today. In our judgment, the recent educational reforms aimed at improving teaching through the manipulation of salaries and other extrinsic rewards are doomed to failure if they are not combined with a clear understanding of the subtle and complex cultural system that sustains teachers in the midst of an emotionally intense and very demanding work environment. Manipulation of rewards which further weaken school and classroom cultures are more likely to contribute to bellicose teacher unions and high rates of teacher burnout and exiting from the profession than to substantially improved school performance.

CHAPTER VIII

Policy Implications

This final chapter explores the educational policy implications of our research. The implications described here are necessarily speculative and suggestive. Only a tiny handful of the nation's teachers and administrators have been studied. Moreover, the data were collected from a single school district, during a single academic year. Generalization is further limited by the fact that the study was designed to be exploratory in nature. Our intention was to identify and conceptualize a broad range of teacher incentives — not to formulate or test a priori hypotheses or specific policy options. Despite the tentativeness of our findings, however, the policy implications are interpreted aggressively and succinctly, foreswearing such scholarly caveats as "if supported by further research," "all other things being equal," "within the limits of our data," and other phrases underscoring the limited reliability and validity of all social science research results. Our objective here is to facilitate policy debate, not to control final decisions. We are confident that intelligent policy makers can appropriately discount what we have to say without being repeatedly told to do so.

There are actually two important reasons for examining the educational policy implications of this study. First, adopting a policy perspective helps to extend and clarify the meaning of the basic concepts developed during the course of the data analysis. In this respect, policy analysis is a natural extension of the research work and serves to test the vitality and consistency of the theoretical framework which it has produced. Second, and more importantly, tracing the policy implications of this research provides concrete guidance for both professional educators and public officials who are interested in improving the quality of public schooling. The findings of this research challenge a number of widely held presuppositions about the nature of teaching work and about how teacher trainers, school principals, district policy makers, or the public can influence it. Laying out these challenges, along with examining their implications for school policy, is an important part of our responsibility as research scholars and of the mandate of the Department of Education, whose generous support made this study possible.

Viewed from the perspective of the findings developed during this research project, it is not surprising that the virtual avalanche of education policy reforms enacted in the past three decades has produced so few significant improvements in educational quality. Most recent state and federal policy initiatives, and many well-intentioned local school district programs, are based on serious misunderstandings of both the work motivations of teachers and the nature of elementary school classroom processes. Federal policy throughout the 1960s and 1970s sought reform through add-on expansion of school services and support for curricular innovation. By 1980, it was becoming evident that reorganization of the core technology of the school was needed. Actual reform was turned over to the states following release of the report by the National Commission on Excellence, *A Nation at Risk*. The first wave of state reforms concentrated on program requirements, graduation standards, and programs for testing both teachers and students. Gradually, attention has shifted to teachers — their recruitment and retention, the development of meaningful teacher career ladders, and the nurture of professional skills and attitudes. This "second-wave" reform agenda (expressed most fully in the Carnegie Task Force report, *A Nation Prepared*, 1986) draws on insights from research on school effectiveness (see, for example, Good, 1983; Brophy, 1983; and Rosenshine and Furst, 1973) and focuses attention on the preparation, certification, and work role expectations of classroom teachers. Enhancing individual fiscal incentives for teachers is considered crucial, and the importance of intrinsic professional identity and work enjoyment rewards are finally receiving recognition.

Our study suggests, however, that major reforms are needed in three broad areas: (a) the development of culturally grounded teacher incentive systems, (b) the improvement of classroom instructional processes, and (c) a redefinition of the role of the school principal in organizing, motivating, supporting, and overseeing the work of teachers. Strategies for pursuing each of these major policy goals are elaborated below.

ESTABLISHING CULTURALLY GROUNDED TEACHER INCENTIVE SYSTEMS

Our discussion of teacher incentives policy begins with a cautionary note: beware of simplistic proposals for the reform of teacher incentive systems. It is just as easy to damage or destroy existing incentives as it is to develop new ones or to improve the effectiveness of those already available. Many recent proposals, based on oversimplified behaviorist psychologies, give far too much weight to extrinsic rewards (like salaries and working conditions) and overlook almost entirely the need to deal with the variety of subtle and powerful intrinsic rewards already found in every school and classroom. While the research reported here does not lead to specific incentive system policies, it does suggest five guidelines which all effective policies can be expected to follow.

Policy Guideline No. 1: The incentive value of most rewards can be culturally reshaped, even when the reward itself cannot be controlled at all.

As noted throughout this book, the terms reward and incentive represent particular perspectives on the various human experiences that yield satisfaction or fulfillment. Reward value is a measure of the amount of pleasure or satisfaction produced. Incentive value measures how much the reward actually modifies behavior. It is doubtless true that (all other things being equal) the greater the reward value a particular experience has for an individual, the greater incentive that individual will have to behave in ways that seem likely to produce that reward. This does not necessarily mean, however, that the most effective way for policy makers to improve teachers' incentives involve direct control over the delivery of various rewards. To the contrary, our evidence indicates that the most effective policies operate indirectly, capitalizing on the existence of important rewards delivered to teachers by students or their parents, and are not controlled by policy makers at all. Two of the most powerful rewards are (a) the teacher's ability to feel responsible for student learning outcomes and (b) the interpersonal warmth shown by students and parents who appreciate the teachers' work efforts and willingly cooperate with them in the school.

There are three ways in which education policy can enhance the capacity of these "natural" rewards to improve the quality of teaching in the schools. Policies can (a) heighten teachers' awareness of these rewards, and thus make it more likely that they will want to modify their own work habits in order to secure them, (b) help focus teachers' attention on those tasks and activities that trigger the flow of rewards already available, and (c) improve teachers' capacities to perform these rewarding tasks more effectively. These policy strategies would concentrate on school program development, instructional improvement, and teacher orientation and training — not on controlling the distribution of particular rewards. The next four policy guidelines indicate how such policies would operate.

Policy Guideline No. 2: Policies that give primary attention to strengthening organization-level, purposive incentives have the greatest chance of improving overall teacher work performance.

Teacher work efforts are strongly influenced by teachers' beliefs about the fundamental purposes of education. Teachers who see the mission of public education as the production of measurable achievement approach their work quite differently than those who see schools as child development agencies. Those holding the first view emphasize the "getting down to business" and "direct instruction" aspects of teaching identified by school effectiveness researchers as important components of schools with unusually high achievement test scores (Cohen, 1982). Teachers who hold a child development view tend to emphasize the importance of expanding learning opportunities and stimulating children's interest in school activities.

Our study indicates that the businesslike atmosphere and direct instruction techniques identified as characteristic of effective schools may not be the only route to high performance. While a child development view of the school's mission was characteristic of all five weak teachers (the helpers), it was also embraced by the four highly effective teachers (the coaches). The lower *average* performance of the nurture-oriented teachers is quite misleading if we fail to distinguish between these two subgroups. The problem of ineffective teaching by the helpers arose not so much from their desire to pursue child nurture goals as from the *contradiction* which existed between this sense of mission and their preference for program-structured approaches to instruction.

The strong performance of the four coaches was made possible by their emphasis on instructional strategies aimed at creating feelings of excitement, adventure, and creativity in the classroom. They would be unlikely to try, much less to successfully implement, instructional programs requiring the sober seriousness suggested by "direct instruction" advocates. Moreover, many children are unable to succeed in school without the support given by teachers who provide this warm, emotionally engaging personal coaching. The weak teachers were disabled because their program orientation made it impossible to "make contact" with the children they were trying to help, not because nurture is itself an unnecessary or inappropriate goal.

In addition to adopting formal policy statements and encouraging administrative attention to the clarification of educational purposes, policy makers can strengthen purposive incentives for teachers by (a) assessing and publicly reporting child growth and achievement gains directly related to clearly defined and publicly recognized purposes and (b) adopting curricular materials which emphasize the desired outcomes. They can also (c) provide staff development services for teachers to explore alternative educational goals and the techniques for reaching them and (d) base the assignment of children to school programs on their progress toward identified goals (rather than on their age, interest, or length of time spent in previous classes).

Policy Guideline No. 3: Policies that facilitate the development of appropriate group-level, solidary incentives will also significantly improve teacher work performance.

While this vision of the primary purpose of schooling provides the most powerful incentive, teachers' desires for warm, cooperative, and supportive relationships with students and co-workers create a powerful system of group-level solidary incentives. Teachers who see their work primarily in terms of "keeping school" tend to identify *other adults* in the school as their primary reference group. As a result, they tend to conceptualize classroom processes in programmatic terms, and believe children should be assigned to programs on the basis of their ability and past performance. Teachers whose primary reference group is children, however, generally see their work as "teaching lessons" rather than keeping school. They see their lessons as a sequence of short-term tasks or activities rather than global program structures. And they tend to believe that children should be assigned to tasks and activities on the basis of their needs, interests, motivation level, or potential for engagement rather than just their past performance levels.

The separation between the lesson-teaching and school-keeping motivations of teachers is the natural outgrowth of the way rewards are mediated through their primary reference groups. Students reward teachers from moment to moment. They learn (or fail to learn) the content of specific lessons, and are rewardingly cooperative (or uncooperative) by responding to specific teacher desires. By contrast, adult co-workers offer broader more global rewards — they develop continuing group identity and tend to reward overall social behavior rather than discrete actions.

Teachers motivated by school-keeping incentives tend to be much more visible and accessible to principals and other administrators. When they link the program emphasis to an achievement production system, these teachers are warmly regarded by administrators. They tend to be viewed as "master teachers" who can be trusted to follow the school curriculum guidelines and to keep the children at or near grade-level achievement norms. They are also likely to be upwardly mobile in the school system, given various administrative duties, and released from full-time classroom teaching assignments.

The weakest teachers are those who try to combine child development goals with the school-keeping, adult-centered group solidary incentives. These teachers are frustrating to administrators because their good intentions do not seem to produce adequate attention to children's educational needs. One formula for failure is for teachers who believe that schools should nurture children to become seriously concerned with pleasing their administrative superiors.

Lesson-oriented teachers, by contrast, tend to be "loners," less visible to school managers and more difficult to guide and direct. Paradoxically, the child-centered, lesson-oriented teachers also tend to be most creative and original in their teaching activities. Though viewed as difficult to manage by their principals, these teachers have the self-motivation to give careful attention to individual children's needs. Successful pursuit of child development goals appears to require that teachers be able and willing to resist pressures from school administrators, and perhaps the demands of the school's formal curriculum.

Policy makers can enhance teacher solidary incentives by facilitating the development of informal group relationships in the school. Teachers will increasingly respond to adult-centered, school-keeping incentives if they are given increased opportunities to work closely with other adults or if they find that substantial rewards are distributed directly by other adults. To the extent that school achievement depends on implementing formal programs and cooperating with administrative plans, it will be facilitated by encouraging adult-oriented group solidarity among teachers. To the extent, however, that real student learning depends on intensive work with individual children, adult solidarity will distract teachers from productive work activities. At the present time, available research does not permit us to draw unequivocal conclusions regarding which of these work orientations has the greatest value for particular children or subject areas.

Policy Guideline No. 4: Among the individual incentives available to teachers, the predominant role is played by *intrinsic rewards*.

This study supports the conclusions of earlier researchers who have found that teachers are more sensitive to intrinsic personal rewards (such as the enjoyment of their work or a sense of productiveness) than to extrinsic ones (such as salary variations or differential working conditions). The importance of this fact can hardly be overemphasized. Virtually all important intrinsic rewards are available only to those teachers who are successful in the execution of lessons and the management of classrooms. As detailed in Chapter IV, successful lessons must be properly structured. They must have adequate demarcation rituals which set them apart from each other and from other classroom activities. They must have proper openings and closings. And they must include appropriate cycles of teacher elicitation, student response, and teacher evaluation. Teachers who, for whatever reason, are unable to give proper structure to their lessons are unlikely to develop a sense of productive efficacy in their work.

In a similar vein, in order for teachers to find their classroom duties enjoyable, they must be able to create classroom rules which can be enforced through guidance and direction rather than coercion. Teachers who fail to create a sense of shared purpose and meaning in their classrooms find that children are constantly threatening to disrupt their teaching efforts. When these teachers respond by increasing normative moral pressures and coercive threats, or just repressing their awareness of student disruptions, teaching quickly becomes an onerous, tension-laden chore rather than an enjoyable social experience.

Since teacher effectiveness is so important in securing these intrinsic rewards, educational policies which succeed in improving teacher classroom performance (so long as they do not weaken teacher interest in intrinsic rewards) will be doubly effective. By stimulating better teaching, such policies will improve student learning, and by showing teachers that intrinsic satisfactions accompany improved performance, the same policies should stimulate teacher self-improvement efforts. If, however, teacher improvement policies have the effect of weakening teachers' interest in the intrinsic rewards of the work, or of directing their attention away from the classroom as the primary source of intrinsic job satisfactions, they will probably have only a temporary and limited impact on long-term teaching effectiveness.

Perhaps the most effective approach policy makers can take to individual incentive development lies in the area of staff training and development. Adequate preparation of school site administrators to assess teacher work performance and to provide corrective feedback to those whose lesson structures are weak or whose classroom management strategies are inappropriate should be a major concern for education policy makers at all levels.

> *Policy Guideline No. 5:* Although extrinsic rewards (like salaries and comfortable working conditions) play a significant role in motivating teachers — especially in their recruitment and retention — they cannot be expected to produce intense engagement or high performance.

It is doubtless true that higher salaries and more comfortable working conditions would encourage more intelligent young people to enter teaching. Policy makers would be well advised, however, to be extremely cautious in trying to stimulate day-to-day behavior changes for teachers by trying to link pay variations and other fringe benefits to their classroom performances. Not only is there little evidence to support the proposition that making compensation contingent on evaluation actually contributes to better teacher work performances, but school districts have generally found merit pay programs politically difficult to sustain. While salary variations may be symbolically important, it is almost impossible to link them to the lesson and program elements that make the greatest difference in student learning. Meanwhile, the student response rewards that are so potent as teaching incentives are already tightly linked to effective teaching practices.

The policy guidelines for improving teacher incentive systems can be summarized in terms of the four different types of teacher work orientations discussed in Chapters III and IV. The teachers whom we called "helpers" are characterized by having weak or deficient incentive systems because they try to combine child development goals with an adult-oriented group solidarity orientation. Since they identify with other adults in the school, they adopt a keeping-school approach to structuring classroom activities. Not only does this approach result in a failure to take personal responsibility for children's academic achievement, but it also robs these teachers of the sense of personal efficacy and joy which accompanies success for other teachers. The teachers whom we called "master teachers" share with the helpers an orientation toward adult solidary incentives. Since they see achievement production as the primary purpose of schooling, however, they are able to mount instructional programs based on the commitment to move children through the school's formal curriculum and to "get down to business" — that is, to give the students needed academic skills. These teachers know that they work for the school district and larger community which it serves. Consequently, they are able to aggressively pursue the children who are having learning problems and to entice, cajole, pressure, or otherwise encourage them to work on important achievement goals. As a result, these teachers do develop personally satisfying, intrinsically rewarding experiences of efficacy and joy in the classroom. Unfortunately, they also tend to be drawn away from the classroom to perform schoolwide administrative and organizational tasks which yield direct contact with the adults who provide them with group solidary incentives.

The teachers whom we called "coaches" and "instructors" are divided on the question of whether schooling is intended primarily for child development or achievement production. They agree, however, in seeing relationships with children as the primary source of solidary incentives. Thus it is likely that the coaches will sacrifice test score gains for the development of broader, more idiosyncratic learning goals for children. They take pride in social development among children and find great joy in the unique performances by individual children rather than high averages among groups. The instructors take the opposite view of their teaching responsibilities. They find their greatest joy in seeing intellectual mastery among children and try to get all children equally involved in their lessons. They can comfortably concentrate on improving the performance of a whole group or class without feeling that it restricts the learning of individual children. Both groups of teachers tend to be unresponsive to administrative priorities and demands and thus appear to be hard to manage.

ENHANCING SCHOOL ACHIEVEMENT

Beyond its implications for teacher incentive systems, our research calls for rethinking policies aimed at improving school achievement. Most recent state and federal policy initiatives aimed at improving educational quality have focused on what Spady (1982) calls the "elusive technical core" of the educational process. Policies attempting to improve school performance through "mastery learning," "competency testing," "staff development," "school accreditation," "school improvement planning," "effective schools management," and other recent state and district initiatives are virtually all based on some set of assumptions regarding the incorporation of improved teaching techniques, rational planning processes, or sophisticated student assessment procedures into the schools. These state and federal reform efforts have tried to encourage development of the schools' technical core by raising output expectations — increasing course requirements, establishing test score requirements for graduation and promotion, and specifying in greater detail the content of various courses. Many have also tried to improve the quality of various inputs into the system — raising standards for teachers, giving good teachers broader responsibility and influence, funding textbooks, and other technical core elements. Little attention has been given, however, to the possibility that the technical core of the school is created and sustained by its social organization. The research reported here indicates that schools have a "cultural core" which defines and structures its "technical core," thus controlling overall school performance. This cultural core supports and directs teacher work efforts — and it limits the effectiveness of efforts to employ any techniques not compatible with it. The importance of the cultural core as a prerequisite to the development of the schools' technical core suggests three guidelines for policy makers seeking the development of both.

Policy Guideline No. 6: Cultural and technical elements of school organizations need to be carefully distinguished — policies aimed at improving one can easily damage the other.

Cultures work by being shared and embraced as valued social norms and traditions. Technologies work by being explicitly interpreted — the relationship between behaviors and outcomes must be accurately specified. Cultures are affective, holistic, and not altogether conscious to those who are influenced by them. Technologies are rational, linear, and self-consciously employed to produce desired results. Cultural failures are attributed to alienation, misunderstanding, or inauthenticity. Technical failures are attributed to ignorance, error, or negligence on the part of those who seek to employ them. Individuals who are confronted by a culture in which they cannot participate feel alienated, worthless, and disoriented. Those who are confronted by a technology they cannot master feel confused, incompetent, and fearful of taking action. Access to a cultural system requires the incorporation of its values and presuppositions regarding social purposes and symbolic meanings. Acquisition of a technology requires comprehension of its component elements and an understanding of how to apply them. Cultures work by producing shared perceptions and common goals among the members. Technologies work by making future events predictable and contingent upon specifiable actions. For the technologist, "seeing is believing." For members of a cultural group, "believing is seeing."

Early in the twentieth century, "scientific management" became both a slogan for reform and a description of the central ingredient in the way many executives defined their work responsibilities. In Frederick Taylor's (1911) classic formulation of this conception of management, technology was seen as the essence of the productive process. A quarter of a century later, Elton Mayo and his colleagues stimulated a second revolution in American corporate management by highlighting the importance of group processes and social relationships in controlling the productivity of industrial workers (Roethlisberger and Dickson, 1939). This work gave rise to the so-called human relations school of management and directed executive attention to the importance of individual motivation and group psychological processes in the shaping of work behavior.

Recent scholarship on corporate management has changed directions once again. Challenged by puzzling differences between work norms and processes in different corporations (and in different countries), some scholars have begun to emphasize the important roles played by executives in shaping cultural norms, establishing social rituals, and interpreting organizational purposes (see especially Ouchi, 1981; Deal and Kennedy, 1982; Peters and Waterman, 1982; and Schein, 1985). "Culture management" differs from both scientific management and human relations management. Cultural managers may continue to be concerned with the technical processes of production and with the social relationships among workers, but they give particular attention to the development of a clear sense of organizational purpose or mission and a vivid set of values, rituals, and social norms which serve to incorporate individual workers into the productive enterprise, conferring an identity upon them and giving them a sense that their own worth and value will be enhanced by the success of the corporation.

The research reported here indicates just how vital culture

management is in the school. High-performing teachers need a cultural base from which to begin their work. Technical sophistication is important, but it is no substitute for cultural identity.

Policy Guideline No. 7: There are two key elements in the school's cultural core: common purposes and shared typifications of the processes to be used in pursuing them. Policies should be developed in ways which support these two cultural elements.

Regardless of their specific approach to teaching, strong teachers universally display strong commitments to a particular conception of the basic mission of the school, which they readily link to specific ideas about how that mission can be realized. The greatest failing of most recent educational policies and programs lies in the failure to recognize that teachers can successfully incorporate these programs into classroom activities only if they *believe in* their purposes and *comprehend* their procedures. Teachers who attempt to incorporate program and procedural requirements which they cannot grasp or do not believe in are doomed to the sort of performance which results when one tries to operate a piece of machinery while trying to read the manual at the same time.

Weak teachers are not necessarily those who cannot execute lessons competently. Many individuals who can explain how to work a problem, give a good lecture, or lead an effective discussion are rendered inadequate as teachers because they do not know how to incorporate these activities into an overall cultural system in the classroom. As a result, they are perpetually trying, as one student put it, to "do someone else's program." Operationally, policies support or erode the schools' cultural base to the extent that they form a coherent, understandable framework for teaching work. By "coherent," we mean that explicit job responsibilities do not conflict with each other, that they consistently focus attention on an appropriate mix of child development and achievement production goals, and that they encourage teachers to develop appropriate relationships with both students and co-workers. By "understandable," we mean providing adequate staff development and socialization processes, and giving teachers time to incorporate new expectations into daily work routines.

Policy Guideline No. 8: Once the cultural core of the school is established, a technical core consisting of (a) appropriate lesson structures and (b) effective rule systems must be embedded within that culture.

The technical core of the classroom consists of its lesson

structures and its rule system. The lesson has two dimensions. The first is its group structure, and the second is its time structure. Group structures range from single individuals to whole classes. Most elementary schoolteachers operate with some sort of inter- mediate group structure. Grouping patterns usually vary from time to time and from subject to subject; most teachers do at least some whole-class instruction, but few do completely individualized work. The time structure of a lesson, as described in Chapter IV, consists of five basic elements: (a) the starting demarcation, (b) the opening, (c) the lesson proper, (d) the closing, and (e) the ending demarcation. The lesson proper is, in turn, divided into cycles of teacher elicitation, student response, and teacher evaluation, punc- tuated by teacher elaborations of the opening and various disrup- tions or distractions. Every teacher who succeeds in getting students fully engaged in the learning process incorporates the basic elements of this lesson structure into his or her classroom activities.

Rule formation is the essential ingredient in the technology of classroom management. To be successful in structuring classroom activities, teachers must formulate rules which students can understand, can rely on for controlling each other's behavior, and can accept as fair and judiciously applied. If teachers formulate such rules, communicate them to children in understandable ways, and enforce them when challenged, they quickly find that they are able to "give directions" rather than "issue commands" or "make threats" when controlling children's behavior.

Supporting this technical core may be much simpler than the limited success of recent reforms would seem to suggest. We found few teachers who could clearly articulate either the lesson struc- tures or the rule systems which they themselves used, much less provide an overview of options they were not using. For many teachers, lessons are seen as a network of subject matter elements rather than a dynamic social process, and rules are seen only as vehicles for routinizing classroom behavior rather than as expres- sions of cultural values as the integrity of the classroom social group. Raising the cultural aspects of the classroom technical core to full consciousness for teachers would, we suspect, go far in helping them develop effective lessons and broadly accepted rules.

To summarize: the three policy guidelines for improving school achievement require that students become willing and knowledgeable participants in the classroom culture. That culture must be so structured that students understand how they are expected to behave. Moreover, the expected behavior must have the form of responses to teachers elicitations during the conduct of a lesson. During the teaching of lessons, children must learn to "disappear" as individuals and then "reappear" as students. They must measure their own actions in relation to the expected form and content of proper responses to a teacher's elicitations. And the teacher must communicate the criteria which will be used to assess the adequacy of each student's responses. Neither willful nor unintentional violations of those criteria must be allowed to persist or the lesson structure will disintegrate.

IMPROVING SCHOOL ADMINISTRATION

The role of the school principal in the development of an effective school has recently become a matter of intense concern among educators and policy makers alike. Two policy guidelines can be drawn from the analysis of elementary school principal work orientations and activities presented in Chapter VI of this report.

> *Policy Guideline No. 9:* Role flexibility (not ambiguity) is critical to an effective principalship. Principals must know how and when to act the part of "manager," "leader," "administrator," or "supervisor" in working with teachers.

Much of the literature on school principals identifies the "ambiguity" of their work roles as a serious problem (see Greenfield, 1982, for an excellent review). Using the term *ambiguity* to describe the fact that principals must deal with a wide variety of expectations and can choose among a number of alternative basic work styles seems to make their work seem ill-defined and unclear. This lack of specificity in principal role definitions should be viewed much more positively, however. *Flexibility* rather than *ambiguity* is the term which best captures the work orientations of effective elementary school principals. As is described in Chapter VI, principals who adopt a single, consistent role definition for themselves display substantial contradictions in their work behavior. To be effective, principals must be willing and able to alter their role definitions and resulting work styles to accommodate two factors: (a) their own unique strengths and limitations and (b) the circumstances and needs of their work setting.

Four basic functions were emphasized in the work styles of the principals we studied. Each of these functions tended to be the central concern in one of the four work role definitions adopted by our principals. The principal whom we called a "manager" emphasized the importance of organizing and coordinating school programs and teacher activities. The "leader" principal concentrated on trying to stimulate and motivate high-quality performances from teachers and students. The "administrator" saw his role in terms of providing support to teachers by ensuring that routine services run smoothly and adequate opportunities and resources are provided to enable teachers to pursue their work responsibilities effectively. The "supervisor" principal saw oversight of teacher and student performance as the primary function of her job and concentrated on seeing to it that minimally satisfactory work performances were given by all school employees. After examining the work efforts of these principals and comparing them with a fifth principal whose work style was more flexible, we conclude that it is counterproductive for principals to try to concentrate on one rather than another of these basic functions. All need to be performed if schools are to operate effectively, and principals need to be able to move comfortably from one function to another — even though these functions call for rather different work orientations and this flexibility may seem a bit inconsistent to casual observers. The inconsistencies of role flexibility are to be preferred to the behavioral contradictions that arise when a principal adopts a rigidly consistent role which fails to accommodate the diverse needs and operational complexities of typical elementary schools. For policy makers, this means resisting the temptation to specify narrow job requirements for principals and to concentrate instead on expanding their repertoire of skills and increasing their ability to shift quickly from one functional area to another while maintaining consistent commitment to educational goals and strong cultural norms.

> *Policy Guidline No. 10:* Policies that support cultural meanings in the school must reinforce three culture management roles for school principals: (a) *interpretive* roles aimed at defining and articulating cultural purposes and norms, (b) *representational* roles aimed at revealing and modeling appropriate activities and behaviors, and (c) *authenticating* roles aimed at recognizing and confirming the participation and membership of children, teachers, and citizens.

The legacy of "scientific management" and "human relations" approaches to the management of productive organizations has deprived most managers of an understanding of the processes of culture management and has blunted their sense of responsibility for establishing a cultural core within the workplace. There is a growing body of scholarly literature on the development of organizational cultures, but little attention is yet being given by education policy makers to the role played by cultural rather than technical elements in effective school management. At a minimum, three culturally guided managerial roles make important contributions to the vitality and effectiveness of any organization.

First, it is important for executives to articulate and interpret the purposes toward which their organizations are directed and the social norms and values which govern pursuit of those purposes. Political and religious leaders understand this function more adequately than most school managers. Political leaders recognize the importance of holidays and other national celebrations in defining national goals and social norms. Religious leaders regularly reinterpret the mission of their institutions and articulate the proper behavior of group members in pursuit of those purposes. School principals need to be encouraged to incorporate this sense of symbolic, figurehead leadership into their work.

A second culture management role springs from the fact that the concrete behaviors needed to realize particular cultural purposes must be identified and made explicit. Principals can serve an important function for teachers and students by identifying and modeling the activities and behavioral norms expected of them. In this regard, political and religious leaders are not noticeably more effective than school administrators. Much of the erosion of public support for major political and religious institutions in contemporary American society stems from the widespread belief that these leaders do not "practice what they preach." One factor contributing to this situation is the failure in most institutions to appreciate the importance of giving authentic expression (as well as lip service) to basic cultural norms.

A third culture management role which principals should be encouraged to develop focuses on recognition and authentication of individuals or activities which represent basic cultural values. Art critics and connoisseurs play this sort of role quite effectively in helping contemporary society distinguish fine art from popular, but in most segments of society very little attention is paid to this vital cultural process. Ceremonial functions (such as student or teacher recognition assemblies, honor rolls, awards and prizes, etc.) constitute a major mechanism for this cultural authenticating function. Behavioristic psychologies have weakened the effectiveness of these ceremonial functions in recent years, however, by focusing attention on the reward value of the honors and prizes for the recipients rather than the culture authenticating value for those who observe and support these ceremonial recognitions. Such a psychological interpretation cheapens the currency of honor among the recipients and encourages managers to cynically use ceremonial functions in an effort to manipulate subordinates and to turn toward extrinsic (usually monetary) rewards rather than to rely on intrinsically meaningful, symbolic ones.

To summarize: the research reported here indicates that school administration can be substantially strengthened if school principals are encouraged to use their role flexibility to attend appropriately to organization, motivation, support, and oversight functions without trying to be overly consistent in adhering to a single preferred management style. The principalship can also be substantially strengthened by identifying and supporting three uniquely cultural management roles: interpretation, representation, and authentication.

CONCLUSION

The ten policy guidelines discussed in this chapter fall far short of the detail needed to help policy makers formulate specific policies for educator training and certification, school program accreditation, student assessment, curriculum materials, school governance, or school finance. They do, however, consistently point to an overall strategy of school policy development which challenges the narrow and overly technical presuppositions of many policies derived from traditional scientific management and human relations approaches to school organization and control. By highlighting the importance of cultural processes in the conduct of education, these guidelines could go far in helping policy makers avoid the mistakes of the last three decades and in encouraging an overall improvement in the quality of education as well as in the commitment of teachers and school administrators to serving the needs of the nation's children.

Bibliography

Adams, D.M. (1963) *Simulation Games: An Approach to Learning.* Worthington, Ohio: C.A. Jones Pub. Co.

Arensberg, Conrad M., and S.T. Kimball (1965) *Culture and Community.* New York: Harcourt, Brace and World, Inc.

Argyris, C. (1957) *Personality and Organization.* New York: Harper.

———, (1973) "Personality and organization theory revisited." *Administrative Science Quarterly*, 18, pp. 141-167.

Association for Educational Communications and Technology (AECT) (1980) "Managing People, Demystifying the Communication Gap: An Interview with Morris Mossey," *Instructional Innovator*, 25, No. 7, pp. 14-16.

Atkinson, J.W. (1964) *An Introduction to Motivation.* Princeton, N.J.: Van Nostrand.

Averch, H.A. (1975) "Federal role in science education: What's inside NSF's proposed budget?" *Science Teacher*, 43, pp. 40-43.

Axelrod, R. (1981) "The emergence of cooperation among egoists." *The American Political Science Review*, 75 (June), pp. 306-318.

Baird, L.L. (1973) "Teaching styles: An exploratory study of dimensions and effects." *Journal of Educational Psychology*, 64, (Fall), pp. 15-21.

Bandura, A. (1977a) "Self-efficacy: Toward a unifying theory of behavior change." *Psychological Review*, 84, pp. 191-215.

———, (1977b) *Social Learning Theory.* Englewood Cliffs, N.Y.: Prentice-Hall.

Bandura, A., N.E. Adams, and J. Beyer (1977) "Cognitive processes mediating behavioral change." *Journal of Personality and Social Psychology*, 35, pp. 125-139.

Barnard, C. (1938) *Functions of the Executive.* Cambridge: Harvard University Press.

Baron, A. (1983) "Suddenly, education is a hot issue: But politicians are confused on how to deal with it." *Los Angeles Times*, Part VI, (Sunday, June) pp. 1, 3.

Bates, J. (1979) "Extrinsic reward and intrinsic motivation: A review with implications for the classroom." *Review of Educational Research*, 49, No. 4 (Fall), pp. 557-576.

Becker, H.S. (1952) "The career of the Chicago public school teacher." *American Journal of Sociology*, 57 (March), pp. 470-477.

——, (1968) "The teacher in the authority system of the public school." In Robert R. Bell and H.R. Stud, eds., *The Sociology of Education*. Homewood, Ill.: Dorsey Press, pp. 1-53.

——, (1970) *Sociological Work: Method and Substance*. Chicago: Aldine Pub. Co.

Benn, S.I., and R.M. Peters (1959) *The Principles of Political Thought*. New York: The Free Press.

Bennett, S. (1976) "Teaching styles and pupil progress." *Times Educational Supplement*, 3178, pp. 19-20.

Berman, P., and M.W. McLaughlin (1976) "Implementation of educational innovation." *Education Forum*, 40 (March), pp. 344-370.

Bhaerman, R.D. (1973) "Merit pay? No!" *National Elementary Principal*, 52, No. 5, pp. 63-68.

Blau, P.M., and W.R. Scott (1962) *Formal Organizations*. San Francisco: Chandler Pub. Co.

Bloland, P.A., and T.J. Selby (1980) "Factors associated with career change among secondary school teachers: A review of the literature." *Educational Research Quarterly*, 5, No. 3 (Fall), pp. 14-24.

Blumberg, A., and W. Greenfield (1980) *The Effective Principal: Perspectives on School Leadership*. Boston: Allyn and Bacon.

Bogie, C.E., and D.W. Bogie (1978) "Teachers' preferences toward alternate systems of salary increment." *Education*, 99, No. 2 (Winter) pp. 215-220.

Boon, J.A. (1973) "Further operations of 'culture' in anthropology: A synthesis of and for debate." In L. Schneider and C.M. Bonyeau, *The Idea of Culture in the Social Sciences*. London: Cambridge University Press.

Broedling, L.A. (1977) "The uses of the intrinsic-extrinsic distinction in explaining motivation and organizational behavior." *Academy of Management Review*, 2, pp. 267-276.

Brookover, W.B., et al. (1978) "Elementary school social climate and school achievement." *American Educational Researcher Journal*, 15, (Spring), pp. 301-318.

Brophy, J.E. (1983) "How teachers influence what is taught and learned in classrooms." *Educational and Psychological Measurement*, 43, No. 1 (Spring), pp. 177-180.

Brophy, J., and C. Evertson (1976) *Learning from Teaching: A Developmental Perspective*. Boston: Allyn and Bacon.

Calder, B.J., and B.M. Staw (1975) "Self-Perception of intrinsic and extrinsic motivation." *Journal of Personality and Social Psychology*, 31, no. 4, pp. 599-605.

California Commission on the Teaching Profession. (1985) *Who Will Teach Our Children? A Strategy for Improving California's Schools: The Report of the California Commission on the Teaching Profession*. Dorman L. Commons, Chair. Sacramento, Calif.: The California Commission on the Teaching Profession.

Callahan, Raymond E. (1962) Education and the Cult of Efficiency. Chicago: University of Chicago Press.

Cammann, C., and E.D. Lawler (1973) "Employee reactions to a pay incentive plan." *Journal of Applied Psychology*, 58, no. 2, pp. 163-172.

Carlson, R.K. (1965) "Divergent thinking processes for motivation," *Education*, 85, no. 9, pp. 551-555.

Carnegie Forum on Education and the Economy. Task Force on Teaching as a Profession (1986) *A Nation Prepared: Teachers for the 21st Century: The Report Task Force on Teaching as a Profession*. Washington, D.C.: The Forum.

Charters, W.W. Jr. (1964) "An approach in the formal organization of the school," in D.E. Griffiths, ed., *Behavioral Science and Educational Administration, the Sixty-third Yearbook of the National Society for the Study of Education* (NSSE). Chicago: University of Chicago Press, pp. 243-261.

Cherrington, D.L., H.L. Reitz, and W.E. Scott, Jr. (1973) "Effects of reward and contingent reinforcement on satisfaction and task performance." In W.E. Scott and L.L. Cummings, eds., *Readings in Organizational Behavior and Human Performance*. Rev. ed. Homewood, Ill.: Richard D. Irwin, Inc., pp. 153-160.

Clark, C.M., and R.J. Yinger (1980) "The hidden world of teaching: Implications of research on teacher planning." *Research Series No. 77*. East Lansing, Mich.: The Institute for Research on Teaching.

Clark, P.B., and J.Q. Wilson (1961) "Incentive systems: A theory of organizations." *Administrative Science Quarterly*, 6, (September), pp. 129-166.

Clarke, G.E. (1973) "Merit rating: myth or possibility?" *National Elementary Principal*, 52, no. 5, pp. 101-103.

Cohen, M. (1982) "Effective schools: Accumulating research findings." *American Education* (January-February), pp. 13-16.

Coleman, J.S. (1966) *Equality of Educational Opportunity.* Washington, D.C.: U.S. Office of Education.

————, (1969) *Incentives in American Education.* Baltimore, Md.: Johns Hopkins University, Report No. 40 (under DHEW Grant: OEG 2-7-061610-0207). ERIC Document ED 030 191.

Creighton, D.L. (1974) "Philosophies, incentives and education." Unpublished paper prepared under contract to the National Institute of Education (DHEW Contract No. NIE-P-74-0125).

Daniel, T.L., and J.K. Esser (1980) "Intrinsic motivation as influenced by rewards, task interest, and task structure." *Journal of Applied Psychology,* 65, no. 5, pp. 566-573.

Dawis, R.V., G.E. England, and L.H. Lafquist (n.d.) "A theory of work adjustment: A revision." Minneapolis: University of Minnesota, Industrial Relations Center, Bulletin 47.

Deal, T.E., and A.A. Kennedy (1982) *Corporate Cultures: The Rites and Rituals of Corporate Life.* Menlo Park, Calif.: Addison-Wesley Pub. Co.

Deci, E.L. (1972) "The effects of contingent and noncontingent rewards and controls on intrinsic motivation." *Organizational Behavior and Human Performance,* 8, no. 2 (October), pp. 217-229.

————, (1975) *Intrinsic Motivation.* New York: Plenum.

————, (1976) "The hidden costs of rewards." *Organizational Dynamics,* 4, no. 3, pp. 67-72.

Deutsch, M. (1949a) "A theory of cooperation and competition." *Human Relations,* 2, pp. 129-152.

————, (1949b) "The effects of cooperation and competition upon group processes: An experimental study." *American Psychologist,* 4, pp. 263-264.

Dewey, John. (1920) *Reconstruction in Philosophy.* New York: Holt.

Diaz, Frank E. (1974) *A Conceptual Framework for the Study of Incentives in American Public Education.* McLean, Va.: Frank Diaz Associates (under DHEW Contract No. NIE P-74-0086).

Dreeben, R. (1970) *The Nature of Teaching: Schools and the Work of Teachers.* Glenview, Ill.: Scott, Foresman and Co.

Drucker, P.F. (1954) *The Practice of Management.* New York: Harper and Row.

Dubin, R. (1968) *Human Relations in Administration.* Englewood Cliffs, N.J.: Prentice-Hall.

Dunnette, M.D., J.P. Campbell, and M.D. Hakel (1967) "Factors contributing to job satisfaction and job dissatisfaction in six occupational groups." *Organizational Behavior and Human Performance,* 2, pp. 143-174.

Dyer, L., and R. Theriault (1976) "The determinants of pay satisfaction." *Journal of Applied Psychology,* 61, no. 5, pp. 596-604.

Ebmeir, H., and T.L. Good (1979) "Effects of instructing teachers about good teaching on the mathematics achievement of fourth grade students." *American Educational Research Journal,* 16 (Winter), pp. 1-16.

Edmonds, R.R. (1979) "Effective schools for the urban poor." *Educational Leader,* 37 (October), pp. 15-18.

————, (1982) "Programs of school improvement: An overview." *Educational Leader,* 40 (December), pp. 4-11.

Educational Research Service (1979) "Merit pay for teachers." *E.R.S. REPORT.* Arlington, Va.: Educational Research Service.

ERIC Clearinghouse on Educational Management (1980) "Teacher motivation. Research Action Brief Number 13." Eugene, Oreg.: University of Oregon, ERIC Document ED 196 116.

ERIC Clearinghouse on Educational Management (1981a) "Merit pay. Research Action Brief Number 15." Eugene, Oreg.: University of Oregon, ERIC Document EA 013 259.

ERIC Clearinghouse on Educational Management (1981b) "Motivating teachers." *The Best of ERIC on Educational Management.* Eugene, Oreg.: University of Oregon, ERIC Document EA 013 983.

Erikson, E.H. (1950) *Childhood and Society.* New York: W.W. Norton.

Erlandson, D.A., and M.C. Pastor (1981) "Teacher motivation, job satisfaction, and alternatives — directions for principals." *NASSP Bulletin,* 65, no. 442 (February), pp. 5-9.

Evans, W.A. (1970) "Pay for performance: Fact or fable." *Personnel Journal,* 23, no. 3 (September), pp. 726-731.

Farr, J.L., R.J. Vance, and R.M. Mcintyre (1977) "Further examinations of the relationship between reward contingency and intrinsic motivation." *Organizational Behavior and Human Performance,* 20, pp. 31-53.

Festinger, L. (1957) *A Theory of Cognitive Dissonance.* Evanston, Ill.: Row, Peterson.

Fey, J. (1969) "Classroom teaching of mathematics." *Review of Educational Research*, 39 (October), pp. 535-551.

Finn, R.H., and S.M. Lee (1972) "Salary equity: Its determination, analysis and correlates." *Journal of Applied Psychology*, 56, no. 4, pp. 283-292.

Flanders, N.A. (1965) "Note on the use of Flanders interaction analysis." *Journal of Educational Research*, 58 (January), pp. 222-224.

———, (1970) *Analyzing Teaching Behavior*. Reading, Mass.: Addison-Wesley Pub. Co.

Floden, R.E. (1981) "The logic of information-processing psychology in education." In David C. Berliner, ed., *Review of Research in Education*, vol. 9. Washington, D.C.: American Educational Research Assoc.

Fuller, B., et al. (1982) "The organizational context of individual efficacy." *Review of Educational Research*, 52, no. 1 (Spring), pp. 7-30.

Gamst, F.C., and E. Norbeck, eds. (1976) *Ideas of Culture Sources and Uses*. New York: Holt, Rinehart and Winston.

Geertz, C. (1973) *The Interpretation of Cultures*. New York: Basic Books.

Georgopoulos, B.S., Mahoney, G.M., and Jones, N.W. Jr. (1957) "A psychological approach to productivity." *Journal of Applied Psychology*, 41, pp. 345-353.

Glassman, N.S. (1974) "Merit pay: A case study in a California school district." *Instructional Science*, 3, pp. 89-110.

Goldthorpe, J.H., et al. (1968) *The Affluent Worker: Industrial Attitudes and Behavior*. London: Cambridge University Press.

Good, T.L. (1983) "Classroom research: A decade of progress." *Educational Psychology*, 18, pp. 127-144.

Good, T.L., B.J. Biddle, and J.E. Brophy (1975) *Teachers Make a Difference*. New York: Holt, Rinehart and Winston.

Goodman, P.S., and A. Friedman (1971) "An examination of Adam's theory of inequity." *Administrative Science Quarterly*, 16, no. 3, pp. 271-288.

Greene, C.N. (1973) "Causal connections among managers' merit pay, job satisfaction, and performance." *Journal of Applied Psychology*, 58, no. 1 (August), pp. 95-100.

Greenfield, W.D., Jr. (1982) "Research on public school principals: A review and recommendations." Final Report to the National Institute of Education, Contract No. 81-02-08, June 1, 1982 (xeroxed).

Hackman, J.R. (1977) "Work design." In J. Richard Hackman and J.L. Suttle, ed., *Improving Life at Work*. Santa Monica, Calif.: Goodyear Pub. Co., Chapter 3, pp. 96-162.

Hackman, J.R., and R.G. Oldham (1980) *Work Redesign.* Menlo Park, Calif.: Addison-Wesley Pub. Co.

Harmon, P. (1980) "Holistic performance analysis: It's time for an updated technology of instruction." *Educational Technology,* 20, no. 11 (November), pp. 5-13.

Heidegger, M. (1972) *On Time and Being.* Translated by J. Stumbaugh. New York: Harper and Row, Inc.

Heider, F. (1958) *The Psychology of Interpersonal Relations.* New York: John Wiley and Sons.

Herzberg, F. (1966) *Work and the Nature of Man.* Cleveland: World Pub. Co.

Herzberg, F., B. Mausner, and B.B. Snyderman (1959) *The Motivation to Work.* 2nd ed. New York: John Wiley and Sons.

Hinton, B.L. (1968) "An empirical investigation of the Herzberg methodology and two-factor theory." *Organizational Behavior and Human Performance,* 3, pp. 217-238.

————, (1972) "The experimental extension of equity theory to interpersonal and group interaction situations."

Organizational Behavior and Human Performance, 8, pp. 434-439.

Holmes Group (1986) *Tomorrow's Teachers: A Report of the Holmes Group.* East Lansing, Mich.: The Holmes Group, Inc.

Homans, G.C. (1961) *Social Behavior: Its Elementary Forms.* New York: Harcourt, Brace and World.

Hook, C.M., and B.V. Rosenshine (1979) "Accuracy of teacher reports of their classroom behavior." *Review of Educational Research,* 49, (Winter), pp. 1-12.

Hough, M., and R.I. Harrold (1979) "Incentive systems for the further education of N.S.W. high school teachers: An initial analysis." *Journal of Educational Administration,* 17, no. 1 (May), pp. 106-109.

House, R.J., and L.A. Wagdon (1967) "Herzberg's dual-factor theory of job satisfaction and motivation: A review of the evidence and criticism." *Personnel Psychology,* 20, pp. 369-389.

Hoy, W.K., and C.G. Miskel (1978) *Educational Administration: Theory, Research, and Practice.* New York: Random House, Inc.
————, (1982) *Educational Administration: Theory, Research and Practice.* 2nd ed. New York: Random House.

Husserl, E. (1962) *Ideas.* Translated by Boyce Gibson. New York: Collier Books.

Isherwood, G.B., and R.W. Tallboy (1979) "Reward systems of elementary school principals: An exploratory study." *The Journal of Educational Administration,* 17, no. 2 (October), pp. 160-170.

Jablonsky, S.F., and D.L. DeVries (1972) "Operant conditioning principles extrapolated to the theory of management." *Organizational Behavior and Human Performance,* 7, no. 2, pp. 340-358.

Jackson, P. (1968) *Life in Classrooms.* New York: Holt, Rinehart and Winston.

Jacques, E. (1966) "The science of society, *Human Relations,* 19, no. 2, pp. 125-137.

James, W. (1890) *Principles of Psychology.* 2 Volumes. New York: Holt, Rinehart and Winston.

Jenkins, G.D., Jr., and E.E. Lawler, III (1981) "Impact of employee participation in pay plan development." *Organizational Behavior and Human Performance,* 28, no. 1 (August), pp. 11-128.

Kaiser, J.S. (1981) "Motivation deprivation: No reason to stay." *Journal of Teacher Education,* 32, no. 1 (September-October), pp. 41-43.

Katz, D. (1973) "The motivational basis of organizational behavior." IN W.E. Scott and L.L. Cummings, eds., *Readings in Organizational Behavior and Human Performance.* Rev. ed. Homewood, Ill.: Richard D. Irwin, Inc., pp. 127-129.

Katz, D., and R.L. Kahn (1966) *The Social Psychology of Organizations.* New York: John Wiley and Sons.

Katz, R. (1978) "Job longevity as a situational factor in job satisfaction." *Administrative Science Quarterly,* 23, (June), pp. 204-221.

Kaufman, D., and M.L. Fetter (1980) "Work motivation and job values among professional men and women: A new accounting." *Journal of Vocational Behavior,* 17, no. 3, pp. 251-262.

Keller, R.T., and A.D. Szilagyi (1978) "A longitudinal study of leader reward behavior, subordinate expectancies, and satisfaction." *Personnel Psychology,* 31, no. 1, pp. 119-129.

Kessleman, G.A., M.T. Wood, and E.L. Hagen (1974) "Relationships between performance and satisfaction under contingent and noncontingent reward systems." *Journal of Applied Psychology,* 59, no. 3, pp. 374-376.

Kimball, R.B. (1975) "The effectiveness of rewards and incentives for teachers." ERIC Document No. ED 115 599. Washington, D.C.: U.S. Dept. of Health, Education and Welfare, National Institute of Education.

King, N. (1973) "Clarification and evaluation of the two-factor theory of job satisfaction." In W.E. Scott and L.L. Cummings, eds., *Readings in Organizational Behavior and Human Performance* Rev. ed. Homewood, Ill.: Richard D. Irwin, Inc., pp. 141-153.

Klapp, O.E. (1969) *Collective Search for Identity.* New York: Holt, Rinehart and Winston.

Kluckhohn, R., ed. (1962) *Culture and Behavior.* New York: Free Press of Glencoe.

Kopelman, R.E. (1976) "Organizational control system responsiveness, expectancy theory constructs, and work motivation: Some interrelations and causal connections." *Personnel Psychology*, 29, no. 2, pp. 205-220.

Korman, A.K. (1970) "Toward an hypothesis of work behavior." *Journal of Applied Psychology*, 54, no. 1, pp. 31-41.

Korman, A.K., J.H. Greenhaus, and I.J. Badin (1977) "Personnel attitudes and motivation." *Annual Review of Psychology*, 28, pp. 175-196.

Krajewski, R.J., Martin, J. and Walden, J. (1980) "Tips for the elementary principal: Combining leadership and management." *Education Canada: The National Magazine for Adult Education*, 20, no. 3, (Fall) pp. 38-43.

Kukla, A. (1972) "Foundations of an attributional theory of performance." *Psychological Review*, 79, no. 6, pp. 454-470.

Landy, F.J., and D.A. Trumbo (1976) *Psychology of Work Behavior.* Homewood, Ill.: Dorsey Press.

Larson, E. (1982) "High-performers are 'different folks.'" Interview with Charles A. Garfield. Originally printed in the Wall Street Journal, reprinted in *Press-Enterprise*, January 24, D-3.

Latham, G.P., and D.L. Dossett (1978) "Designing incentive plans for unionized employees: A comparison of continuous and variable ratio reinforcement schedules." *Personnel Psychology*, 31, no. 1, pp. 47-61.

Lawler, E.E., III (1970) "Job attitudes and employee motivation: Theory, research, and practice." *Personnel Psychology*, 23, pp. 223-237.

——, (1977) "Reward systems." In J. Richard Hackman and J.L. Suttle, eds., *Improving Life at Work.* Santa Monica, Calif.: Goodyear Pub. Co., Inc., Chapter 4, pp. 163-226.

Lawler, E.E., III, and J.R. Hackman (1969) "Impact of employee participation in the development of pay incentive plans: A field experiment." *Journal of Applied Psychology*, 53, no. 6, pp. 467-471.

Lawler, E.E., III, and L.W. Porter (1967) "The effect of performance on job satisfaction." *Industrial Relations*, 7, no. 23 (October).

Lewin, K. (1935) *A Dynamic Theory of Personality*. New York: McGraw-Hill.

——— , (1938) *The Conceptual Representation and the Measurement of Psychological Forces*. Durham, N.C.: Duke University Press.

Locke, E.A. (1969) "What is job satisfaction?" *Organizational Behavior and Human Performance*, 4, pp. 309-336.

London, M., and G.R. Oldham (1977) "A comparison of group and individual incentive plans." *Academy of Management Journal*, 1, pp. 34-41.

Lortie, D.C. (1969) "The balance of control and autonomy in elementary school teaching." In A. Etzioni, ed. *The Semi-Professions and Their Organization*. New York: Free Press, Chapter 1, pp. 1-53.

——— , (1975) *School Teacher: A Sociological Study*. Chicago: University of Chicago Press.

Lunetta, V.N., and A. Hofstein (1981) "Simulations in science education," *Science Education*, 65 (January), pp. 243-252.

McClelland, D.C. (1961) *The Achieving Society*. Princeton, N.J.: Van Nostrand.

McDowell, S. (1973) "Merit salaries (and other devices)." *Education Canada*, 13, no. 1, pp. 14-19.

McGregor, D. (1960) *The Human Side of Enterprise*. New York: McGraw-Hill.

MacMillan, D.L. (1973) *Behavior Modification in Education*. New York: Macmillan Co.

Madaus, G.F., et al. (1979) "Sensitivity of measures of school effectiveness." *Harvard Educational Review*, 49 (May), pp. 207-230.

Magoon, A.J. (1977) "Constructivist approaches in educational research." *Review of Educational Research*, 47, no. 4 (Fall), pp. 651-695.

March, J.G., and J.P. Olsen (1976) *Ambiguity and Choice in Organizations*. Oslo, Norway: Universitetsforlaget.

March, J.G., and H. Simon (1958) *Organizations*. New York: John Wiley and Sons.

Markarian, E.S. (1977) "The concept of culture in the system of modern sciences." In B. Bernardi, ed., *The Concept and Dynamics of Culture*. The Hague: Mouton Pub.

Marozas, D.S., and D.C. May (1980) "Factors which motivate job acceptance among teachers of severely and profoundly mentally retarded children." *Education and Training of the Mentally Retarded*, 15, no. 4, pp. 293-297.

Martin, E. (1978) "Can society pay for altruism? Or, why virtue must be its own reward." Occasional paper. Chapel Hill, N.C.: Institute for Research in Social Science, University of North Carolina.

Maslow, A.H. (1954) *Motivation and Personality*. New York: Harper and Row, Publishers.

Mead, G.H. (1934) *Mind, Self, and Society*. Chicago: University of Chicago Press.

Mehan, H. (1979) *Learning Lessons*. Cambridge, Mass.: Harvard University Press.

Merleau-Ponty, M. (1964) *The Primacy of Perception and Other Essays*, James Edie, ed. Evanston, Ill.: Northwestern University Press.

Merrill, F.E. (1961) *Society and Culture*. 2nd ed. Englewood Cliffs, N.J.: Prentice-Hall.

Meyer, H.H. (1975) "The pay-for-performance dilemma." *Organizational Dynamics*, 3, no. 3, pp. 39-50.

Meyer, H., E. Kay, and J.P.R. French, Jr. (1973) "Split roles in performance appraisal." *Harvard Business Review*. (January-February), pp. 123-129.

Meyer, J.W., and B. Rowan (1978) "The structure of educational organizations." In M.W. Meyer and Associates, eds., *Environments and Organizations*. San Francisco: Jossey-Bass, pp. 78-109.

Miller, H.G., and K.J. Swick (1976) "Community incentives for teacher excellence." *Education*, 96, no. 3 (Spring), pp. 235-237.

Miller, L.K., and R.L. Hamblin (1963) "Interdependence, differential rewarding and productivity." *American Sociological Review*, 23, pp. 768-788.

Mintzberg, H. (1973) *The Nature of Managerial Work*. New York: Harper and Row Publishers.

Miskel, C. (1974) "Intrinsic, extrinsic, and risk propensity factors in the work attitudes of teachers, educational administrators, and business managers." *Journal of Applied Psychology*, 59, no. 3, pp. 339-343.

——— , (1982) "Motivation in educational organizations." *Educational Administration Quarterly*, 18, no. 3 (Summer), pp. 65-88.

Miskel, C., J.A. DeFrain, and K. Wilcox (1980) "A test of expectancy: Work motivation theory in educational organizations." *Educational Administration Quarterly*, 16, no. 1 (Winter), pp. 70-92.

Mitchell, D.E. (1974) "The Nature of the Work in the Organization of Schools: Toward a Phenomenology of the Teaching Task." A paper presented at the American Education Research Association annual meeting, April 15-19, 1974, Chicago, Illinois.

Mitchell, D.E., and C.T. Kerchner (1982) "Labor relations and teacher policy." In Lee Shulman, ed., Handbook on Teaching and Policy. New York: Longman

Mitchell, T.R., and A. Biglan (1971) "Instrumentality theories: Current uses in psychology." Psychological Bulletin, 76, no. 6, pp. 432-454.

Mount, M.K., and P.M. Muchinsky (1978) "Person-environment congruence and employee job satisfaction: A test of Holland's theory." Journal of Vocational Behavior, 13, pp. 84-100.

Murnane, R.J. and D.K. Cohen (1986) "Merit pay and the evaluation problem: Why most merit pay plans fail and a few survive." Harvard Educational Review, 56 (Fall), pp. 1-17.

National Commission on Excellence in Education (1983) A Nation at Risk: The Imperative for Educational Reform. Washington, D.C.: U.S. Government Printing Office.

Natriello, G., and S.M. Dornbush (1983) "Bringing behavior back in: The effects of student characteristics and behavior on the classroom behavior of teachers." American Educational Research Journal, 20 (Spring), pp. 29-43.

Nord, W.R. (1969) "College companions for patients in mental institutions." Todays Education, 58 (December), pp. 28-29.

Notz, W.W. (1975) "Work motivation and the negative effects of extrinsic rewards: A review with implications for theory and practice." American Psychologist (September), pp. 884-891.

Oliver, P. (1980) "Rewards and punishments as selective incentives for collective action: Theoretical investigations." American Journal of Sociology, 85, no. 6, pp. 1356-1375.

O'Reilly, C.A. III (1977) "Personality-job fit: Implications for individual attitudes and performance." Organizational Behavior and Human Performance, 18, pp. 36-46.

O'Reilly, C.A., III, and D.F. Caldwell (1980) "Job choice: The impact of intrinsic and extrinsic factors on subsequent satisfaction and commitment." Journal of Applied Psychology, 65, no. 5, pp. 559-565.

Ornstein, A.C. (1982) "What are we teaching in the 1980's?" Young Child, 38 (November), pp. 12-17.

Ouchi, W. (1981) Theory Z: How American Business Can Meet the Japanese Challenge. Reading, Mass.: Addison-Wesley Pub. Co.

Owens, R.G. (1970) Organizational Behavior in Schools. Englewood Cliffs, N.J.: Prentice-Hall.

Parsons, T. (1959) "The school class as a social system: Some of its functions in American society." *Harvard Educational Review*, 29, no. 4, pp. 69-90.

Patchen, M. (1962) "Supervisory methods and group performance norms." *Administrative Science Quarterly*, 7, no. 3, pp. 275-294.

Peters, L.H. (1977) "Cognitive models of motivation, expectancy theory and effort: An analysis and empirical test." *Organizational Behavior and Human Performance*, 20, pp. 129-148.

Peters, T.J., and R.H. Waterman, Jr. (1982) *In Search of Excellence: Lessons from America's Best-Run Companies*. New York: Harper and Row.

Peterson, D. and K. Peterson (1984) "A research-based approach to teacher evaluation," *NASSP Bulletin*, 68 (Fall) pp. 39-46.

Pfeffer, J., and Salancik, G.R. (1977) "Organizational context and the characteristics and tenure of hospital administrators." *Academy of Management Journal*, 20, pp. 74-88.

Phillips, J.S., and R.G. Lord (1980) "Determinants of intrinsic motivation: Locus of control and competence information as components of Deci's cognitive evaluation theory." *Journal of Applied Psychology*, 65, no. 2, pp. 211-218.

Pierce, C.S. (1963) *The Pragmatic Philosophy of C.S. Pierce*, Manley Thompson, ed. Chicago: University of Chicago Press, Phoenix Books.

Pincus, J. (1974) "Incentives for innovation in the public schools." *Review of Educational Research*, 44 (Winter), pp. 113-144.

Pinder, C.C. (1976) "Additivity versus nonadditivity of intrinsic and extrinsic incentives: Implications for work motivation, performance, and attitudes." *Journal of Applied Psychology*, 61, no. 6, pp. 693-700.

Porter, D.O., and D.C. Warner (1973) *The Politics of Budgeting Federal Aid: Resource Mobilization by Local School Districts*. Beverly Hills, Calif.: Sage.

Porter, L.W., and E.E. Lawler III (1965) "Properties of organization structure in relation to job attitudes and job behavior." *Psychological Bulletin*, 64, no. 1, pp. 23-51.

Porter-Gehrie, C., and P. Brieschke (1981) "Understanding classroom intrusions in a complex school organization." *The Elementary School Journal*, 81, no. 4, pp. 239-243.

Pritchard, R.D. (1969) "Equity theory: A review and critique." *Organizational Behavior and Human Performance*, 4, pp. 176-211.

Purkey, S.C., and M.S. Smith (1982) "Too soon to cheer? Synthesis of research on effective schools." *Educational Leadership*, 40 (December), pp. 64-69.

Reiff, J.C., Cannella, G.S. and B.L. and Perry (1979) "Relating readiness for reading with perception and visual seriation skills." *Reading Improvement*, 16, no. 3 (Fall), pp. 236-41.

Rein, M. (1973) "Work incentives and welfare reform in Britain and the United States." In B. Stein and S.M. Miller, eds., *Incentives and Planning in Social Policy*. Chicago: Aldine Pub. Co.

Roethlisberger, F.J., and W.J. Dickson (1939) *Management and the Worker: An Account of a Research Program Conducted by the Western Electric Company, Hawthorne Works*. Cambridge, Mass.: Harvard University Press.

Rosenshine, B., and N. Furst (1973) "The use of direct observation to study teaching." In R. Travers, ed., *Second Handbook of Research on Teaching*. New York: Rand McNally.

Rowan, W.W., G.P. Latham, and S.B. Kinne III (1973) "Effects of Goal Setting and Supervision on Worker Behavior in an Industrial Situation." *Journal of Applied Psychology*, 58, no. 3, pp. 302-307.

Rutter, M., B. Maughan, P. Mortimer, J. Ouston with A. Smith (1979) *Fifteen Chores and Hours: Secondary Schools and Their Effects on Children*. Cambridge, Mass.: Harvard University Press.

Salancik, G.R., and J. Pfeffer (1978) "A social information processing approach to job attitudes and task design." *Administrative Science Quarterly*, 23, no. 2 (June), pp. 224-251.

Sarason, S.B. (1972) *The Culture of the School and the Problem of Change*. Boston: Allyn and Bacon.

Savage, D.G. (1983) "Teaching incentive merit pay: Politics or good policy," *Los Angeles Times* Part I (August, 23), pp. 11, 16-17.

Schein, E.H. (1985) *Organizational Culture and Leadership*. San Francisco: Jossey-Bass.

Scheflen, K.C., EE. Lawler III, and J.R. Hackman (1971) "Long term impact of employee participation in the development of pay incentive plans: a field study revisited." *Journal of Applied Psychology*, 55, no. 2, pp. 182-186.

Schutz, A. (1967) *The Phenomenology of the Social World*. Evanston, Ill.: Northwestern University Press.

Schwab, D.P., and L.L. Cummings (1973) "Theories of performance and satisfaction: A review." In W.E. Scott and L.L. Cummings, eds., *Readings in Organizational Behavior and Human Performance*. Rev. ed. Homewood, Ill.: Richard D. Irwin, Inc., pp. 130-141.

Scott, W.E., and P.J. Cherrington (1974) "Effects of competitive, cooperative, and individualistic reinforcement contingencies." *Journal of Personality and Social Psychology*, 30, pp. 748-758.

Sergiovanni, T.J. (1967) "Factors which affect satisfaction and dissatisfaction of teachers." *The Journal of Educational Administration*, 5, pp. 66-82.

Sergiovanni, T.J., and F.D. Carver (1980) *The New School Executive: A Theory of Administration*. 2nd ed. New York: Harper and Row.

Sergiovanni, T.J., et al. (1980) *Educational Governance and Administration*. Englewood Cliffs, N.J.: Prentice-Hall.

Shavelson, R.J. (1983) "Review of research on teachers' pedagogical judgments, plans and decisions." *Elementary School Journal*, 83 (March), pp. 392-413.

Shulman, L.S., and G. Sykes (1983) *Handbook of Teaching and Policy*. New York: Longman.

Simon, A., and E.G. Boyer, eds. (1967) *Mirrors for Behavior: An Anthology of Classroom Observation Instruments*, 1-6. Philadelphia: Humanizing Learning Program, Research for Better Schools, Inc.

———, (1970) *Mirrors for Behavior: An Anthology of Classroom Observation Instruments*, 7-12. Philadelphia: Humanizing Learning Program, Research for Better Schools, Inc.

Simon, Herbert (1979) "Information processing models of cognition." *Annual Review of Psychology*, 30, pp. 363-396.

Skinner, B.F. (1953) *Science and Human Behavior*. New York: The Free Press.

———, (1971) *Beyond Freedom and Dignity*. New York: Knopf.

Slavin, R.E. (1977) "Classroom reward structure: An analytical and practical review." *Review of Educational Research*, 47 (Fall), pp. 633-650.

———, (1980) "Cooperative learning." *Review of Educational Research*, 50, no. 2 (Summer), pp. 315-342.

Smith, J.V. (1972) "Merit compensation: The idea and the reality." *Personnel Journal* (May), pp. 313-316, 326.

Smith, L.M., and W. Geoffrey (1968) *The Complexities of an Urban Classroom*. New York: Holt, Rinehart and Winston.

Smith, P.C., L.M. Kendall, and C.L. Hulin (1969) *The Measurement of Satisfaction in Work and Retirement*. Chicago: Rand McNally.

Soar, R.S. (1972) "Teacher behavior related to pupil growth." *International Review of Education*, 18, no. 4, pp. 508-528.

Spady, W.G. (1982) "Outcome-based instructional management: A sociological perspective." *Australian Journal of Education*, 26, no. 2, pp. 123-143.

Spradley, J.P., and D.W. McCurdy (1972) *The Cultural Experience: Ethnography in a Complex Society.* Chicago: Science Research Associates, Inc.

Spuck, D.W. (1974) "Reward structures in the public high school." *Educational Administration Quarterly,* 10, pp. 18-34.

Steffensen, J.P. (1963) "Merit salary programs in six selected school districts." United States Department of Health, Education, and Welfare, Bulletin no. 22.

Stumpf, S.A., and S. Rabinowitz (1981) "Career stage as a moderator of performance relationships with facets of job satisfaction and role perceptions." *Journal of Vocational Behavior,* 18, pp. 202-218.

Sykes, G. (1983) "Teacher preparation and the teacher workforce: Problems and prospects for the 80's." *American Education,* 19 (March), pp. 23-30.

Taylor, F. (1911) *The Principles of Scientific Management.* New York: Harper and Row.

Terborg, J., P. Richardson, and R.D. Pritchard (1980) "Person-situation effects in the prediction of performance: An investigation of ability, self-esteem, and reward contingencies." *Journal of Applied Psychology,* 65, no. 5, pp. 574-583.

Tharenou, P. (1979) "Employee self-esteem: A review of the literature." *Journal of Vocational Behavior,* 15, pp. 316-346.

Thompson, S. (1979) "Motivation of teachers." *ACSA School Management Digest,* Series 1, No. 18. ERIC/CEM Research Analysis Series, No. 46. Burlinghame, Calif., and Eugene, Oreg.: Association of California School Administrators and ERIC Clearinghouse on Educational Management, University of Oregon. ERIC Document ED 178 998.

Thurow, L. (1983) "Merit pay alone is no answer to America's educational failing." *Los Angeles Times,* Part IV (Sunday, June 26), p. 3.

Tikunoff, W.J., D.C. Berliner, and R.C. Rist (1975) *Special Study A: An Ethnographic Study of the Forty Classrooms of the Beginning Teacher Evaluation Study Known Sample.* San Francisco: Far West Laboratory for Educational Research Development.

Training/HRD (1979) "Is giving incentives a good idea?" 16, no. 7, (July), pp. a4-a5.

————, (1980) "Incentives provide the winning edge." 17, no. 7 (July), pp. a1-a4.

United States Department of Education (1984) *The Nation Responds,* Washington, D.C.: U.S. Department of Education.

Vaughan, I. (1980) "Motivation — the reward and the undermining of children's interest." *Cambridge Journal of Education*, 10, no. 2, pp. 43-54.

Voeglin, E. (1952) *The New Science of Politics: An Introduction.* Chicago: University of Chicago Press.

Vroom, V. (1964) *Work and Motivation.* New York: Wiley.

Waller, W. (1932) *Sociology of Teaching.* New York: Wiley.

Watson, J.B. (1924) *Behaviorism.* New York: W.W. Norton and Co. Inc.

Weber, G., and W.H. Marmion (1969) *Merit Pay and Alternatives: Descriptions of Some Current Programs.* Washington, D.C.: Council for Basic Education.

Weick, K.E. (1966) "The concept of equity in the perception of pay." *Administrative Science Quarterly*, 11, pp. 413-439.

———, (1976) "Educational organizations as loosely coupled systems." *Administrative Science Quarterly*, 21, pp. 1-19.

Weissman, R. (1969) "Merit pay — What merit?" *Education Digest*, 39, no. 9, pp. 16-19.

Whiddon, S. (1978) "Performance incentives in personnel administration." ERIC Document ED 166 855. Washington, D.C.: U.S. Dept. of Health, Education, and Welfare, National Institute of Education.

Williams, R.T. (1978) "Teacher motivation and satisfaction." *NASSP Bulletin*, 62 (December), pp. 89-94.

Winter, G. (1966) *Elements for a Social Ethic.* New York: Macmillan Company.

Workman, E.A., and R.L. Williams (1980) "Effects of extrinsic rewards on intrinsic motivation in the classroom." *Journal of School Psychology*, 18, no. 2, pp. 141-147.

Yinger, R.J. (1978) "A study of teacher planning: Description and a model of preactive decision making." Research Series No. 18. East Lansing, Mich.: The Institute for Research on Teaching.

Yukl, G.A., and G.P. Latham (1975) "Consequences of reinforcement schedules and incentive magnitudes for employee performance: Problems encountered in an industrial setting." *Journal of Applied Psychology*, 60, no. 3, pp. 294-298.

Yukl, G.A., G.P. Latham, and E.D. Purcell (1976) "The effectiveness of performance incentives under continuous and variable ratio schedules of reinforcement." *Personnel Psychology*, 29, no. 2, pp. 221-231.

Yukl, G.A., K.N. Wexley, and J.D. Seymour (1972) "Effectiveness of pay incentives under variable ratio and continuous reinforcement schedules." *Journal of Applied Psychology*, 56, no. 1, pp. 19-23.

Zaleznick, A. (1977) "Managers and leaders: Are they different?" *Harvard Business Review*, 55, no. 3, p. 71.

Index